NC

ISSUES IN WETLANDS PROTECTION

The Conservation Foundation is a nonprofit research and communications organization dedicated to encouraging human conduct to sustain and enrich life on earth. Since its founding in 1948, it has attempted to provide intellectual leadership in the cause of wise management of the earth's resources. The Conservation Foundation is affiliated with World Wildlife Fund.

ISSUES IN WETLANDS PROTECTION:

BACKGROUND PAPERS PREPARED FOR THE

NATIONAL WETLANDS POLICY FORUM

edited by
Gail Bingham, Edwin H. Clark II,
Leah V. Haygood, and Michele Leslie

The Conservation Foundation
Washington, D.C.

Issues in Wetlands Protection:
Background Papers Prepared for the National Wetlands Policy Forum

Printed by Thomson-Shore, Inc., Dexter, Michigan

Book orders should be directed to The Conservation Foundation, P.O. Box 4866, Hampden Post Office, Baltimore, Maryland 21211. Telephone: (301) 338-6951.

Library of Congress Cataloging-in-Publication Data

Issues in wetlands protection : background papers prepared for
  the National Wetlands Policy Forum / edited by Gail Bingham ...
  [et al.]
        p.   cm.
   ISBN 0-89164-119-X
    1. Wetland conservation--United States. 2. Wetlands--
United States--Management. I. Bingham, Gail. II. National
Wetlands Policy Forum (U.S.).
   QH76.I76   1990   90-1631
   333.91'8'0973--dc20   CIP

⊛   Cover and text printed on recycled paper.

TABLE OF CONTENTS

WETLANDS ISSUES

In the summer of 1987, at the request of the U.S. Environmental Protection Agency, The Conservation Foundation convened the National Wetlands Policy Forum, chaired by Governor Thomas H. Kean of New Jersey, to address major policy concerns about how the nation should protect and manage its valuable wetlands resources.

The Forum attempted to draw into the process as many perspectives about wetlands protection and management as possible. It has been independent of established institutions and has attempted to step back from the fray of ongoing policy conflicts to take a broad view of how this nation can better protect and manage its wetlands resources. The 20 members of the Forum included three governors, a state legislator, and heads of state agencies; a town supervisor; chief executive officers of environmental groups and businesses; farmers and ranchers; and academic experts. In addition, senior officials from the five principal federal agencies involved in wetlands protection and management participated as ex-officio members. These officials supplied valuable information and insights but were not asked to endorse the Forum's recommendations.

In November 1988, the Forum released its final report, "Protecting America's Wetlands: An Action Agenda."[1] The consensus report contains over 100 recommendations on ways to improve wetlands conservation, involving federal, state, and local governments, as well as private interests.

---

[1] Copies of the Forum's final report can be obtained for $5.00 each by writing or calling: P.O. Box 4866, Hampden Post Office, Baltimore, MD, 21211, attn: The Conservation Foundation; (301) 338-6951. In 1989, the Forum released three concept papers that build on the report's recommendations in the areas of federal legislation, federal executive action, and state wetlands programs. Copies of these papers can be obtained by writing or calling: The Conservation Foundation, 1250 24th Street, NW, Washington, DC 20037; (202) 293-4800.

Some of the Forum's recommendations can and should be adopted administratively by the agencies responsible for implementing existing wetlands programs. Other recommendations will require legislative action, mostly in the form of amendments to existing federal statutes. Although they may be enacted independently, the Forum considered its entire set of statutory recommendations, at all levels of government and in the private sector, to comprise an integrated package.

Everyone involved -- conservationists, industrialists, government officials, developers, farmers -- will have to cooperate in implementing the Forum's recommendations to make what is necessarily a complicated and difficult protection system work in a coordinated and comprehensive fashion, with less frustration and cost to all concerned.

As it undertook its deliberations about what policies the nation should follow to protect its remaining wetlands resources, the National Wetlands Policy Forum requested its staff to prepare a series of background papers on several of the issues it was addressing to provide a better information base for the Forum members to make their decisions. This volume is the collection of those papers, with only minor editing.

The process of preparing and discussing these papers and the issues they address resulted in several insights into the problems of wetlands protection and management in the United States.

One of the most bothersome was that very little is known about this resource: the rate at which wetlands currently are being altered, the causes of these losses, how to measure the functions wetlands provide, and even how many types of wetland ecosystems exist. We are confident that loss of wetlands acreage and function continues, and that substantially greater efforts must be made if we are to protect and manage these resources effectively. But a truly focused and efficient protection and management system will require significantly more information than is available now.

A second, related insight is that the current statistics on wetlands alterations provide a very incomplete picture of what is happening to the resource. They are likely to miss some types of alterations completely-- particularly those that involve chemical or biological changes in the absence of physical loss. Some evidence suggests that these uncounted alterations may be quite significant. On the other hand, for some of the alterations that are counted, the functional losses may not be as large as the statistics would indicate.

A third insight relates to the importance of the hydrology of these systems. It should not be surprising that water is as important as land to an effective wetland system. But most of the nation's wetlands management and protection programs focus almost exclusively on the land alone. In many parts of the country, however, changes in the hydrologic regime are probably a more important cause of wetlands alterations than direct land use changes. Thus, an effective wetlands program needs to look closely at water as well as the land.

A fourth insight is that the implementation of the federal wetlands regulatory program, Section 404 of the Clean Water Act, has addressed only a small portion of the total conversions -- perhaps 10 to 15 percent. Again, a major reason is that it focuses primarily on land use changes and pays very little attention to the water. Thus, focusing only on possible modifications to the Section 404 program may leave many of the causes of wetlands alterations inadequately addressed. A more comprehensive approach is required. Comprehensive planning for land and water resources is one way to improve protection for wetlands while providing better information and more predictable land use decisions for landowners.

A fifth insight is that, outside of Alaska, the majority of the nation's wetlands are privately owned. As a result, effective wetlands programs must encourage private landowners to exercise aggressively their stewardship responsibilities to manage and protect the valuable wetlands resource. However, the burden for wetlands stewardship should not be placed solely on private landowners. The public and private sectors must share the burdens of wetlands conservation. In addition, recognizing that private landowners have an economic stake in their wetlands, strong programs of economic incentives are needed to encourage and assist the private sector to exercise its management responsibilities to protect the public values wetlands provide. Incentives, such as subsidies and tax breaks, together with improved public education about wetlands values, will supplement regulatory programs.

A sixth realization is that even if all activities that result in the loss of wetlands -- those that affect the hydrologic regime as well as those that focus on land uses -- were suddenly stopped, we would still continue to experience substantial and unacceptable losses in many parts of the country. As set forth in the first paper in this volume, there is a "base rate" of conversion that results from both past activities and natural events.

A preeminent example is the continued loss of 30 to 60 square miles of Louisiana coastal wetlands annually. These losses predominately result from the flood control systems built along the Mississippi River over the past four decades or more. Even if no new activities were undertaken along the Louisiana coast, most of these losses would continue. Thus, any effective wetlands management policy cannot concern itself only with controlling new activities that cause losses. It will have to take positive steps to attempt to address some of the past activities that cause continued losses, as well as including a strong wetlands restoration and creation component.

This conclusion is particularly true in view of the threat of global warming, which has recently gained widespread attention. The Forum did not address this issue, but it only serves to emphasize the importance of quickly implementing many of the Forum's recommendations. Global warming could well drown many of our coastal wetlands and dry out many of those in the interior. Positive steps will have to be taken to offset these problems if the nation is to achieve a no-overall-net-loss goal.

These are some of the insights that emerged from the background papers prepared for the National Wetlands Policy Forum. We hope that they, and others, will be apparent to the reader as he or she peruses the papers in this volume. The papers are being reproduced here in order to make them available to a wider audience. The Forum hopes that its analyses and the recommendations contained in its final report will stimulate a nationwide discussion about what policies and actions will best promote the improved protection and management of these precious resources among all levels of government as well as the private and non-profit sectors. We hope that these papers will help inform that discussion.

The papers were prepared by The Conservation Foundation staff and the National Wetlands Policy Forum's technical consultants. Although the primary authors for each paper are indicated, each benefitted substantially, not only from review by the other staff and technical advisors, but more significantly, from review and comments by Governor Kean's staff and the individuals staffing the Forum members. In an exercise such as the National Wetlands Policy Forum, the individuals providing staff support to the individual members often receive much less credit than they deserve. Without them, the entire effort would have been much more difficult and much less productive.

We also want to give particular thanks to Marsha White who was not only responsible for typing these and all the other documents prepared for the Forum, but for much of the general logistical support for all the Forum's activities as well.

Finally, we again would like to express our sincere appreciation to the Environmental Protection Agency, The Pew Charitable Trusts, The Mary Flagler Cary Trust, the H.J.Heintz Company Foundation, and the ARCO Foundation for their generous support of all the Forum's activities; to the John D. and Catherine T. MacArthur Foundation and the William and Flora Hewlett Foundation for their support of The Conservation Foundation's dispute resolution program; and to the Ford Foundation for its support of The Conservation Foundation's work in water policy.

Edwin H. Clark, II   Gail Bingham

Project Directors
National Wetlands Policy Forum

THE NATIONAL WETLANDS POLICY FORUM MEMBERSHIP

The Honorable Thomas H. Kean, Chairman
  Governor, State of New Jersey

The Honorable Carroll Campbell, Vice Chair
  Governor, State of South Carolina

The Honorable Booth Gardner, Vice Chair
  Governor, State of Washington

Peter A.A. Berle
  President, National Audubon Society

William D. Blair, Jr.
  Past President, The Nature Conservancy

Willard T. Chamberlain
  Senior Vice-President for Corporate Affairs, ARCO

John DeGrove
  Florida Atlantic University

Nancy R. Elliott
  Supervisor, Town of Yorktown Heights, New York

James G. Gosselink
  Louisiana State University

Peter Grenell
  Executive Director, California State Coastal Conservancy

Jay D. Hair
  President, National Wildlife Federation

Dick Hollier
  Hollier Farms, Inc.

Dennis Kelso
  Commissioner, Alaska Department of Environmental Conservation

Frederic D. Krupp
  Executive Director, Environmental Defense Fund

Jack Larsen
  Vice-President, the Weyerhaeuser Company

Melvin Simon
  Chairman, Melvin Simon and Associates, Inc.

F. John Taylor
   Taylor Grain and Livestock

John Turner
   President, Wyoming Senate

Robert Wetherbee
   Vice-President, National Association of Conservation Districts

Shirley McVay Wiseman
   Shirley Wiseman and Associates

Ex-Officio Participants

William P. Horn (succeeded by Susan Recce)
   Assistant Secretary, U.S. Department of the Interior

J. Curtis Mack II (succeeded by B. Kent Burton)
   Assistant Secretary, U.S. Department of Commerce

Peter C. Myers
   Deputy Secretary, U.S. Department of Agriculture

Robert Page (preceded by John Doyle)
   Assistant Secretary, Department of the Army

Lee M. Thomas
   Administrator, U.S. Environmental Protection Agency

Representatives

Brenda S. Davis, Robin O'Malley, George G. McCann, and Richard
   Schwabacher, representing Governor Kean

John N. McMillan, Sr., and William D. Marshall,
   representing Governor Campbell

Andrea Riniker and William Alkire,
   representing Governor Gardner

Hope Babcock, representing Mr. Berle

Nathaniel Williams, representing Mr. Blair

Robert J. Jirsa, Judith L. Baird, and Mike Joyce, representing Mr. Chamberlain

Barbara Brumback, representing Mr. DeGrove

Bonnie O'Brien, representing Ms. Elliott

Elizabeth Riddle, representing Mr. Grenell

J. Scott Feierabend and Jan Goldman-Carter, representing Mr. Hair

Fran Hunt, representing Mr. Hollier

Douglas R. Redburn, representing Mr. Kelso

James T.B. Tripp, representing Mr. Krupp

David Mumper, Patricia Hill, and Scott Berg,
    representing Mr. Larsen

Fred Worstell, representing Mr. Simon

Mark Maslyn, representing Mr. Taylor

Rich Olson, representing Mr. Turner

Steven N. Meyer, representing Mr. Wetherbee

J. Michael Luzier, representing Ms. Wiseman

Susan E. Recce and Martin L. Smith, representing Mr. Horn

J. Roy Spradley, Jr., representing Mr. Mack

Mack Gray, representing Mr. Myers

David Barrows, representing Mr. Page

John Meagher and Dianne Fish, representing Mr. Thomas

Science and Policy Advisors

Malcolm Baldwin, Baldwin Associates

Jon Kusler, Assoc. of State Wetland Managers

Joseph S. Larson, University of Massachusetts

Daniel E. Willard, Indiana University

GLOSSARY of ABBREVIATIONS and ACRONYMS

ADIDs (Advanced Identification Programs)

BLM (Bureau of Land Management)

BOR (Bureau of Outdoor Recreation)

BuRec (Bureau of Reclamation)

CERCLA (Comprehensive Environmental Response, Compensation and Liability Act (better known as Superfund))

CEQ (Council on Environmental Quality)

CF (The Conservation Foundation)

Corps (U.S. Army Corps of Engineers)

CREST (Columbia River Estuary Task Force)

CRP (Conservation Reserve Program)

CVP (Central Valley Project, California)

CZMA (Coastal Zone Management Act)

DOD (U.S. Department of Defense)

DOE (U.S. Department of Energy)

DOT (U.S. Department of Transportation)

EIS (Environmental Impact Statement)

EPA (U.S. Environmental Protection Agency)

EWRA (Emergency Wetlands Resources Act of 1986)

FAHP (Federal Aid Highway Program)

FERC (Federal Energy Regulatory Commission)

FHwA (Federal Highway Administration)

FmHA (Farmer's Home Loan Administration)

Forum (National Wetlands Policy Forum)

FWCA (Fish and Wildlife Coordination Act)

FWS (U.S. Fish and Wildlife Service)

GAO (General Accounting Office)

GPO (U.S. Government Printing Office)

HEP (Habitat Evaluation Procedure)

HMDC (Hackensack Meadowlands Development Commission of New Jersey)

LWCF (Land and Water Conservation Fund)

MOA (Memorandum of Agreement)

MOU (Memorandum of Understanding)

NEPA (National Environmental Policy Act)

NMFS (National Marine Fisheries Service)

NOAA (National Oceanic and Atmospheric Administration)

NPDES (National Pollutant Discharge Elimination System)

NRI (National Resources Inventory)

NWI (National Wetland Inventory)

OTA (Office of Technology Assessment)

RCRA (Resource Conservation and Recovery Act)

RPMCs (Resource Planning and Management Committees)

SAMPs (Special Area Management Plans)

§ (Section)

SCS (Soil Conservation Service)

SCORPS (State Comprehensive Outdoor Recreation Plans)

Superfund (Comprehensive Environmental Response, Compensation and Liability Act (also known as (CERCLA))

Swampbuster (provision of the Food Security Act of 1985)

TDCs (Transfer of Development Credits)

TPL (Trust for Public Land)

TVA (Tennessee Valley Authority)

TNC (The Nature Conservancy)

USDA (U.S. Department of Agriculture)

USFS (U.S. Forest Service)

WEP (Watershed Enhancement Program)

WET (Wetland Evaluation Technique, also known as "Adamus Method")

PERSPECTIVES ON WETLANDS LOSS AND ALTERATIONS

Michele Leslie and Edwin H. Clark II

Policy discussions on wetlands frequently focus on the number of acres of wetlands that have been lost, the number that remain, and the current rate at which wetlands are being converted to other types of environments. Disagreements on all these factors often generate substantial controversy about how serious the problem of wetlands loss is, how well the existing programs are working to stem these losses, and whether additional programs are needed.

Although some of these would seem to be relatively straight forward questions, upon further consideration they are not. For instance, even the definition of "loss" is ambiguous. What exactly is being lost? The land itself usually remains, although there has been a change in the complex nature of the functions and benefits the wetland in its original state provided. But what functions have been lost, and to what extent?

Thinking about different types of functions and how they are lost suggests that, although the existing "loss" estimates may provide important indications of general trends, they fail to present a comprehensive picture of the condition of our nation's wetlands or the causes of their alteration. Such a comprehensive assessment would require much more consideration be given to the concept of wetlands functions, the different types of wetlands alteration (including physical, chemical, and biological alterations) that can occur, and what activities cause these alterations.

LOSS OF WETLAND FUNCTIONS

Wetlands provide a wide range of different functions and benefits (see Table 1-1), such as flood and sediment control, water quality improvement, fish

---

The authors are former associate and former vice-president, respectively, The Conservation Foundation, Washington, D.C.

Table 1

WETLAND FUNCTIONS

A. Flood Conveyance--Riverine wetlands and adjacent floodplain lands often form natural floodways that convey flood waters from upstream to downstream points.

B. Barriers to Waves and Erosion--Coastal wetlands and those inland wetlands adjoining larger lakes and rivers reduce the impact of storm tides and waves before they reach upland areas.

C. Flood Storage--Inland wetlands may store water during floods and slowly release it to downstream areas, lowering flood peaks.

D. Sediment Control--Wetlands reduce flood flows and the velocity of flood waters, reducing erosion and causing flood waters to release their sediment.

E. Fish and Shellfish--Coastal wetlands are important sources of nutrients for commercial fin and shellfish industries.

F. Habitat for Waterfowl and Other Wildlife--Both coastal and inland wetlands provide essential breeding, nesting, feeding, and predator escape habitats for many forms of waterfowl, mammals, and reptiles.

G. Habitat for Rare and Endangered Species--Almost 35% of all rare and endangered animal species are either located in wetland areas or are dependent upon them, although wetlands constitute only about 5% of the nation's lands.

H. Recreation--Wetlands serve as recreation sites for fishing, hunting, and observing wildlife.

I. Water Supply--Wetlands are increasingly important as a source of ground and surface water with the growth of urban centers and dwindling ground and surface water supplies.

J. Food Production--Because of their high natural productivity, both tidal and inland wetlands have unrealized food production potential for harvesting of marsh vegetation and aquaculture.

K. Timber Production--Under proper management forested wetlands are an important source of timber, despite the physical problems of timber removal.

L. Historic, Archaelogical Values--Some wetlands are of archaelogical interest. Indian settlements were located in coastal and inland wetlands which served as sources of fish and shellfish.

M. Education and Research--Tidal, coastal, and inland wetlands provide educational opportunities for nature observation and scientific study.

N. Open Space and Aesthetic Values--Both tidal and inland wetlands are areas of great diversity and beauty and provide open space for recreational and visual enjoyment.

O. Water Quality--Wetlands contribute to improving water quality by removing excess nutrients and many chemical contaminants. They are sometimes used in tertiary treatment of wastewater.

Source: Adapted from Kusler.[3]

and wildlife production, and provision of diverse recreational and educational opportunities.[1]   Loss of these benefits is the principal motivation of concern about--and thus, the estimates of--the extent of wetlands loss.

Because the degree to which specific wetland areas serve these various functions has proved to be highly variable, overall estimates of areal losses can fail to communicate important information about changes in specific functional capabilities.   Thus, it would be more meaningful to measure loss of the functions themselves than the amount of areal loss.   As discussed later in this paper, some functional losses may be incurred without an apparent areal loss, while some detectable areal losses may not represent a total loss of wetland functions or benefits.   This same variability in the degree to which wetlands serve certain functions also makes it difficult to measure losses of wetlands functions, however.

Site-Specific Variability

The U.S. Fish and Wildlife Service (FWS) has identified 55 different classes of wetland and deepwater habitats, which were further defined by subclass.[2]   These systems vary widely in terms of structure, function, and effectiveness in providing specific benefits.   The type and magnitude of benefits also depend upon the context or geographic setting for a particular wetland.   Thus, a relatively small wetland area located near a flood-prone residential or farm community may offer greater flood-protection benefits than a larger wetland of the same type not located near developed or cultivated land.   Similarly, the actual benefits provided by a wetland area with high waterfowl habitat potential depend in part upon the location of the area and scarcity of that type of environment within the region.   Finally, the realization of benefits can depend in part upon the social significance of wetland environments within a community or region.   Thus, for example, a community which values local wildlife may benefit from its local wetlands, in a way that a community with less interest in wildlife resources does not.

Problems Quantifying Lost Benefits

Numerous efforts have been made to quantify the services provided by wetlands. The Wetlands Value Data Base, maintained by the FWS, contains more than 7,000 abstracts of reports of benefits provided by specific wetland areas.[3] As an example of a detailed valuation study, the Office of Technology Assessment[4] referenced a case where the U.S. Army Corps of Engineers (Corps) calculated that the loss of all 8,422 acres of wetlands within the Charles River Basin, Massachusetts, would produce average annual flood damage of over $17 million.

Despite the extensive efforts in this area, it remains difficult both conceptually and technically, to quantify accurately the full range of benefits provided by the nation's wetlands, or even by specific wetland areas. Mitsch and Gosselink[5] identified a number of generic problems including difficulties raised by the multiple-value nature of wetlands and by the dynamics of marginal value (generally, as the amount of wetland decreases, the value of the remaining wetland increases; although there may be threshold levels required for certain functions, such as meeting habitat requirements for certain wildlife populations). The dynamic nature of wetlands, technical difficulties, and cost also are barriers to the accurate measurement of many ecological services. Other types of benefits, such as the "existence" or "intrinsic" values of wetlands are even more intangible, and thus less scientifically and economically demonstrable.

TYPES OF WETLANDS ALTERATION

As wetlands can provide a wide range of functions, so they can be altered, and thereby lose their ability to provide these functions, in diverse ways (Table 1-2). They may be changed physically by filling, draining, excavating, or clearing. Such alterations may affect some functions but not others. For instance, they may eliminate a wetland's utility in providing habitat for some species, but increase it for others. Alterations may have

Table 1-2

TYPES OF WETLAND ALTERATION

Physical

1. Filling: adding any material to change the bottom level of a wetland or to replace the wetland with dry land;

2. Draining: removing the water from a wetland by ditching, tiling, pumping, etc.;

3. Excavating: dredging and removing soil and vegetation from a wetland;

4. Diverting Water Away: preventing the flow of water into a wetland by removing water upstream, lowering lake levels, or lowering groundwater tables;

5. Clearing: removing vegetation by burning, digging, application of herbicide, scraping, discing, mowing or otherwise cutting;

6. Flooding: raising water levels, either behind dams or by pumping or otherwise channeling water into a wetland;

7. Diverting or Withholding Sediment: trapping sediment, through construction of dams, channelization or other types of projects; thereby inhibiting the regeneration of wetlands in natural areas of deposition, such as deltas;

8. Shading: placing pile-supported platforms or bridges over wetlands, causing vegetation to die;

9. Conducting Activities in Adjacent Areas: disrupting the interactions between wetlands and adjacent land areas, or incidentally impacting wetlands through activities at adjoining sites;

Chemical

1. Changing Nutrient Levels: increasing or decreasing levels of nutrients within the local water and/or soil system, forcing changes in wetland plant community;

2. Introducing Toxics: adding toxic compounds to a wetland either intentionally (e.g. herbicide treatment to reduce vegetation) or unintentionally, adversely affecting wetland plants and animals;

Biological

1. Grazing: consumption and compaction of vegetation by either domestic or wild animals;

2. Disrupting Natural Populations: reducing populations of existing species, introducing exotic species or otherwise disturbing resident organisms.

little effect on the wetland's ability to provide flood control, and excavation may even increase its ability to recharge groundwater.

Even if there are no physical changes, a wetland may be altered by chemical contamination or biological changes. Such alterations may have little effect on a wetland's physical appearance, but can seriously interfere with its ability to perform certain beneficial functions. This was dramatically exemplified recently, in the case of the Kesterson National Wildlife Refuge in the San Joaquin Valley of California, where widespread waterfowl mortalities and deformities have been caused by the concentration of selenium in the local irrigation return flows entering the refuge. A recent literature review indicated that the potential for agricultural chemicals, particularly aerially-applied insecticides, to enter prairie potholes and reduce the quality of these wetlands for wildlife is great.[6]

Further, while many alterations of wetlands are localized, the cumulative effects of relatively small-scale wetland alterations can have regional or national implications. For example, the cumulative reduction of certain types of wetland habitat can have broad-scale implications for populations of migratory birds. Or, taken collectively, the alteration of relatively small areas of riparian wetland could increase a region's risk of flood damage.

Thus, any comprehensive assessment of the condition of the nation's wetlands would have to consider multiple types of alteration, the degree to which wetland functions are actually being lost as a result of these alterations, and the cumulative effects of certain trends in functional losses.

AREAL LOSS: A MEASURABLE INDICATOR OF ALTERATION

Past efforts to identify the status and trends of the nation's wetlands have ignored many of these considerations, focusing mainly on changes in certain physical attributes. Even this is not a trivial task, for the seemingly straightforward problem of identifying what is a wetland and where its boundaries lie is a task requiring substantial professional judgement.

Nevertheless, the availability of aerial photographs and satellite imagery from various time periods has permitted comparative analyses of what readily observable changes have occurred within sample areas within the United States. Such analyses, at the national and regional level, do provide valid indicators of the condition of the nation's wetlands. However, as projections based upon sampled-area analyses, they are associated with some statistical error. Also, since available trend studies are based upon readily available alterations, they do not fully reflect changes in specific functional capacities, or even all types of alteration.

National Estimates

The FWS has completed the most extensive and rigorous statistical survey of the condition of the nation's wetlands. The initial results of this survey, published in 1983,[7] indicated that 99 million acres of wetlands remained within the coterminous U.S., with an additional 200 million acres thought to be located in Alaska. This National Wetlands Trends Study, initiated by the FWS in 1979, documented wetland and deepwater habitat gains and losses in the lower 48 states between the 1950s and the 1970s.

The study indicated that about 9 million acres of wetlands had been converted to other types of environments during the 20-year period, representing an average annual net loss of 458,000 acres.[8] The FWS will present detailed information on wetlands losses between 1974 and 1984 in a second National Wetlands Trends Study, scheduled for completion in 1990.

The Office of Technology Assessment[9] (OTA) reviewed the 1983 survey results, along with other information, and came to two conclusions that are widely quoted. One is that the U.S. has lost between 30 and 50 percent of the wetlands that existed within the lower 48 states at the time of European colonization.

7

The second was that, by the early 1980s, the rate of wetlands loss in the U.S. probably had declined by half, representing an average annual rate of 275,000 acres. This adjustment, however, was highly speculative.

FWS National Wetlands Trends Study

The original wetlands status and trends study involved developing a national overview by examining aerial photographs taken in the 1950s and the 1970s of selected sample areas in the coterminous U.S. In total, 3,635 four-square-mile areas, representing a stratified random sample, were selected for examination.[10] The presence and extent of wetlands within the sample areas were determined by reviewing aerial photographs at scales of 1:20,000 for 1950s images and 1:40,000 for 1970s images.

The survey was designed to produce national estimates that, on average, have a probability of 90 percent of being within 10 percent of true totals. However, statistical error varied widely among the specific habitat categories examined, and estimates were not considered useful at the state level.

Tiner[11] noted that limited gains had been found in wetlands associated with reservoir and pond construction, beaver activity, and marsh creation projects. However, it was reported that these gains were far exceeded by losses of forested, emergent, and scrub-shrub wetlands in palustrine environments (96 percent of total losses); and losses within estuarine environments (4 percent of total losses). The most extensive wetland losses were reported for Louisiana, Mississippi, Arkansas, North Carolina, North Dakota, South Dakota, Nebraska, Florida, and Texas. Greatest losses of forested wetlands were reported for the Lower Mississippi Valley; greatest losses of shrub wetlands in North Carolina; and inland marsh drainage was found to be most prevalent in the Prairie Pothole Region of the Dakotas and Minnesota, Nebraska's Sandhills and Rainwater Basin, and Florida's Everglades. Estuarine wetland losses were found to be greatest in the Gulf States (for example, Louisiana, Texas, and Florida).

OTA Study of Wetlands Use and Regulation

In response to a request by the Senate Committee on Environment and Public Works, OTA carried out a detailed review of available information on the nation's wetlands and their management. In the course of this study, OTA estimated that the rate of wetlands loss within the coterminous U.S. had declined to about 275,000 acres per year between 1975 and 1980.[12] The downward adjustment was based on reported reductions in the rates of some types of agricultural drainage. The Office of Technology Assessment noted that U.S. Department of Agriculture (USDA) estimates of federally-assisted surface and subsurface drainage of farmland showed that the rate of drainage between 1975 and 1980 had declined to 426,000 acres per year, compared to 850,000 acres per year reported for the 1955-to-1975 period. The National Wetlands Trends Study had indicated that about 80 percent of freshwater wetland losses between the mid-1950s and the mid-1970s could be attributed to agricultural conversions.

The Office of Technology Assessment also noted that the effects of federal wetlands protection programs were taken into account in developing a revised loss rate estimate. However, the nature of this analysis and its contribution to the estimate are not clear.

SCS National Resources Inventory

Every five years, the USDA Soil Conservation Service (SCS) prepares a National Resources Inventory (NRI), which is a multiple resource survey addressing parameters such as land use, land capability, and erosion potential on privately-owned land. Results of the 1982 NRI, based on an on-the-ground survey of 300,000 randomly selected points (in contrast to the four-square-mile sample areas used in the National Wetlands Trends Study), will be summarized in an upcoming SCS bulletin.[13] The SCS only recently has used NRI data to develop estimates of the extent of wetlands. Based on 1982 NRI data, 76 million acres of wetland were identified on non-federal land in the coterminous U.S.

NOAA Coastal Wetlands Inventory

The National Oceanic and Atmospheric Administration (NOAA) carries out strategic assessments of the nation's coastal and oceanic regions and evaluations of the status and trends of coastal fisheries habitat. As part of these efforts, NOAA is in the process of developing a national coastal wetland data base. An initial step in this process was to inventory the information available from federal and state governmental agencies, and public and private research organizations. This information indicated the presence of over 11 million acres of wetlands along the Atlantic, Gulf of Mexico, and Pacific coastlines.[14]

In addition to this initial effort, NOAA is working to develop a comprehensive and consistently derived data base describing the areal extent and distribution of wetlands in the coterminous U.S. This project involves the use of a systematic grid sampling procedure on wetland maps produced for the National Wetland Inventory (NWI) of the FWS.[15] A summary of NWI data for the New England coast is being completed, and work is progressing for the Gulf of Mexico and the San Francisco Bay area.[16]

USFS Surveys

Using data from the U.S. Forest Service (USFS) periodic field surveys, Abernathy and Turner[17] estimated that in 1980 there were 22.9 million hectares (56.6 million acres) of forested wetlands in the U.S. (excluding Alaska, Arizona, California, Hawaii, and New Mexico). This represents a loss of 2.74 million hectares (6.77 million acres) over the last 40 years or an average annual rate of 0.3 percent since 1940. Most losses have occurred within the Mississippi River valley floodplain, where the majority of forested wetlands are found. These researchers concluded that forested wetlands have been lost at a rate up to five times higher than non-wetland forests.

Regional Estimates

Numerous regional and state wetlands surveys and trend studies have been carried out. These include a study of wetlands in five mid-Atlantic states, which constitutes the first regional intensification of the National Wetlands Trends Study. Results of this study indicated that about 7.1 million acres of wetlands were present in the 5-state region in the late 1970s, with more than 132.6 thousand acres of palustrine (inland) vegetated wetlands being lost since the 1950s.[18] Other efforts have focused on Louisiana's coastal wetlands, where land loss is thought to be occurring at a rate of about 35,200 acres per year (100 acres per day),[19] and the Mississippi River alluvial floodplain forests which have experienced rapid decline.[20]

CAUSES OF WETLANDS ALTERATION: RECENT TRENDS

Although The National Wetlands Trends Survey identified agricultural drainage activities as the primary cause of wetlands alteration, a number of other factors may be important as well--particularly in terms of chemical or biological alteration (Table 1-3).

Some of these factors relate directly to discrete events or individually distinct actions within specific areas. For example, fill or excavation activities, drainage, spills, fires, and clearing can be considered discrete events, since they tend to alter wetlands within relatively confined time and space.

In contrast, some of the factors relate to gradual, subtle, on-going processes. These include long-term changes in water level or sediment loads, concentrations of chemical constituents (for example, nutrients, contaminants), or the composition of the biological community (for example, diversity, natural succession).

Table 1-3

TYPES AND CAUSES OF WETLANDS ALTERATION

PHYSICAL

Changes in topography or elevation

 Gradual processes:

  Long-term decreases in waterborne sediment load. Example Causes: Flood Control Levees, Reservoirs

  Long-term increases in sediment loads. Example Cause: Denuding watershed

  Natural changes in land or water levels. Example Causes: Crustal rebound, Subsidence, Sea-level rise

 Discrete events:

  Fill or excavation activities. Example Causes: Commercial or residential development, Mining, Dredged material disposal

  Natural deposition or erosion causes. Example Causes: Deposition during flood, Flood erosion

Changes in local or regional hydrology

 Gradual processes:

  Reductions in available groundwater or surface water. Example Causes: Increased upstream withdrawals, Groundwater overdraft

  Increases in water availability. Example Cause: Low flow augmentation from reservoirs

 Discrete events:

  Reductions in available water. Example Causes: Drainage of agricultural lands, Filling upstream reservoirs, Diverting water

  Increases in water. Example Cause: Flooding from reservoir filling

CHEMICAL

Changes in nutrient levels

 Gradual processes:

  Increases in nutrient loadings. Example Causes: Runoff from agricultural lands, Runoff from suburban lawns,
  Use of wetland for waste water disposal

  Decreases in nutrient loadings. Example Cause: Removal of uplands from agriculture

 Discrete events:

  Increases in nutrient loadings. Example Causes: Fertilizer spill, Sewer overflow

  Decreases in nutrient loadings. Example Causes: Addition of phosphate removal procedures at sewage treatment plant,
  Phosphate ban, Adoption of animal waste BMPs

Changes in toxic substances or contaminants

 Gradual processes:

  Increased loadings. Example Causes: Hazardous waste disposal, Industrial waste water discharges, Deposition from air

  Decreased loadings. Example Cause: Clean up of industrial discharges

 Discrete events:

  Increased loadings. Example Causes: Pesticide applications, Spills of oil or toxic substances

  Decreased loadings. Example Cause: Superfund clean up

Table 1-3 (continued)

CHEMICAL (cont'd)

Changes in salt levels
    Gradual processes:
        Increased levels.   Example Causes: Reduced freshwater inflow, Cutting navigation channels
        Decreased levels.   Example Cause: Reduction in irrigation return flows

Changes in pH
    Gradual processes:
        Increased acidity.   Example Causes: Acid precipitation, Acid mine drainage, Reduced industrial alkaline discharges
        Decreased acidity.   Example Causes: Increased irrigation return flow, Reduced industrial acid discharges

BIOLOGICAL

Changes in biomass levels
    Gradual processes:
        Biomass decreases.   Example Cause: Grazing
        Biomass increases.   Example Cause: Vegetation growth after clearing
    Discrete events:
        Biomass decreases.   Example Causes: Fire, Clearing, including timbering
        Biomass increases.   Example Cause: Planting

Changes in community composition
    Gradual processes:
        Example Causes: Natural successional changes, Harvesting of commercially or recreationally important species,
        Changes in noise or other disturbance levels
    Discrete events:
        Example Causes: Elimination of species (e.g., pests), Introduction of exotic species

OTHER

Changes in temperature
    Gradual processes:
        Example Cause: Climate change
    Discrete events:
        Example Cause: Discharge of heated effluents

13

One special type of factor, which is not clearly accounted for in the simple classification system described in Table 1-3, relates to the indirect or regional effects of certain types of discrete events or actions. For example, in addition to the direct discrete alteration--such as drowning wetlands located in a reservoir area--these actions would be likely to affect wetlands located downstream indirectly by reducing the amount of water available or otherwise modifying the wetland's hydrologic regime. These types of factors could be excluded from the "discrete event" category, if consideration were limited to actions within wetland boundaries. Similarly, these factors could be missed within the "gradual processes" category, since attendant effects may be relatively rapid, not gradual or long term.

<u>Updating Past Trends Studies</u>

For certain types of wetland alteration, some indication of changes in the rate of wetlands alteration over time might be gleaned from data indicating changes in the annual rate of activities causing these alterations. For example, fill or excavation, two types of discrete events that alter wetlands, can be related to numerous types of activities, including commercial or residential development and mining. Thus, general annual statistics on the level of activity within these sectors should suggest changes in the annual rate of associated wetlands alteration. However, this approach is subject to important limitations. For many general activity categories (for example, commercial or residential development, agriculture, mining) only a small percentage of actions within each category may be associated with wetlands alteration, and this percentage may not be stable over time or geographically. Consequently, the relationship between national activity levels and alteration rates may not be linear, and the relative importance of different activities in causing wetland alterations may change over time.

Still, it is likely that agricultural development, because of the large amount of land involved, has remained the most significant sector involved in direct wetlands losses. Tiner[21] found that drainage to create additional arable land was responsible for 87 percent of total losses between 1955 and 1975, with urban development and other development causing 8 percent and 5 percent of losses, respectively. As noted previously, the OTA[22] examined USDA farmland drainage statistics for 1955 through 1980 and reasoned that reduced rates in drainage probably resulted in a substantial reduction in the rate of wetlands loss. OTA referenced a decline in total cropland planted nationwide between 1954 and 1972 from 355 million to 295 million acres, but anticipated an increase in the demand for cropland over the following 20 years. Recent agricultural statistics show that total cropland did, in fact, increase to 383 million acres in 1982.[23] In an unpublished study by EPA, it was noted that, more recently (1982-1985), acres of harvested cropland have decreased at the national level (by 33 million acres) as crop prices have declined and production costs have increased.[24] These declines are projected to continue, through 1990/91 for some crops, such as wheat, corn and soybeans. However, it also was noted that a number of wetland regions continue to show increases in harvested cropping activity. For example, North and South Carolina, North and South Dakota, and Nebraska all show increases in harvested cropland acres between 1982 and 1985.

The Swampbuster provision of the 1985 Food Security Act, which specifies that farmers who drain wetland on their property will be ineligible to receive any federal farm subsidies, would be expected to reduce the rate of wetlands alteration attributable to agricultural drainage. However, farmers do not rely equally on federal subsidies. For example, farmers in North Dakota, as of 1984, received more than 50 percent of their income from subsidies.[25] In contrast, subsidies only represented 10 percent of farm income in Alabama. These subsidy rates are closely linked to the type of crops grown in these regions: North Dakota farms grow a predominance of wheat, a heavily subsidized crop, and Alabama farmers grow a predominance of soybeans, a largely unsubsidized crop.

The OTA reported that other major causes of wetlands losses between 1955 and 1975 were filling for urban development (925,000 acres), construction of impoundments (621,000 acres) and drainage, excavation, and filling as part of forest management, mining, and other activities.[26] Recent statistics

15

indicate that urban development has increased between 1975 and 1985, exemplified by a 44 percent increase in total new floor space.[27] The regions experiencing the greatest rates of urbanization are among the less populated areas, such as the Southeast and Pacific regions. Questions remain over the extent to which the Section 404 program has slowed the impact of this as well as other development on wetlands.

The rate at which new reservoir capacity has been added in the U.S., however, has decreased sharply.[28] This would suggest attendant decreases both in wetlands losses due to impoundment construction and in wetland gains in areas adjacent to new impoundments.

Mining activities have actually intensified between 1975 and 1985, with increases in coal mining more than off-setting decreases in the metals industry. The net change was about a 10 percent increase in the mining production index.[29] No information is available about the extent to which the Surface Mining Control and Reclamation Act or the Section 404 program may have prevented this increased activity from altering wetlands.

Forestry production, as indicated by industrial roundwood levels, has varied from year to year, but has not changed substantially between 1975 and 1985. As noted by EPA, the acreage of commercial forestland in the U.S. has declined since the 1950s, with a total of about 30 million acres likely to have been converted primarily to cropland and residential development between 1952 and 1990.[30] However, several states have adopted forest management acts which may limit clearing of wetlands within forested areas.

These data are, at best, indicative. They suggest that the rate of activity in some of the economic sectors linked most strongly to wetlands alterations has not dropped significantly between 1975 and 1985, and in some cases has increased significantly during that period. Since 1985, there have been declines in some sectors, including agriculture. Overall, the data do not demonstrate that the rate of wetlands alteration has increased since 1975. Wetlands protection efforts have increased over this period. And the costs of wetlands alteration may have increased as well, making it less economically attractive. For example, draining wetlands may no longer be economical in certain farming areas because of increased drainage costs, decreased crop prices, and reductions in USDA subsidies.

Other Causes of Alteration

As indicated earlier, however, not all wetlands alteration results from such discrete events. In some cases, gradual on-going processes have well-documented effects. Perhaps the best example in the U.S. is the progressive loss and alteration of Louisiana's coastal wetlands as a result of a number of human activities and natural factors. Here, past flood control and channelization projects are among many activities that continue to reduce the level of sediment and nutrients transported by the Mississippi River. Natural sea-level rise and land subsidence also has contributed to dramatic changes in this region. In these cases, even if there were no new human activity at all--for instance, no new flood levees or channels--the rate of loss would continue. Such long-term gradual changes create a base rate of alteration which continues despite a reduction in discrete altering activities.

This base rate can be significant. Investigators have concluded that the rate of wetlands loss in coastal Louisiana, for instance, has actually been increasing rapidly in recent years. The Louisiana Wetland Protection Panel[31] noted average annual losses of 39 square miles of deltaic plain wetland between 1955 and 1978, increasing to 45 square miles in 1985.

Some trends in gradual processes that can alter wetlands functions can be difficult to identify. Water quality trends vary widely regionally and locally, with some areas showing net improvements and others showing deterioration. As noted in a recent study by the GAO,[32] state and federal surveys indicate that surface water quality probably is improving nationwide, although the sparseness of empirical data and methodological shortcomings make national assessments uncertain. The extent of groundwater contamination and the incidence of a wide range of trace constituents and toxic metals are not well known. However, localized water quality problems are well documented, and these would be likely to affect some wetland systems.

These impacts may also be occurring gradually, and be part of the base rate. The effects of the contaminants build up slowly over time even if the rate of contamination does not change. Thus a hazardous waste dump will continue to leak and contaminate an ever-widening area long after new dumping has stopped. And the effects may be equally slow in appearing. The problems being found in some western wildlife refuges do not usually result from sudden changes in agricultural activities, but rather from our slow recognition of the problem combined with the slow accumulation of contaminants in the refuges to seriously detrimental levels.

CONCLUSIONS

Although past measures of wetlands alteration differ, narrowing the gaps in estimates of total wetlands loss would still be imprecise, since such estimates focus on visible changes in areal extent, not on functional losses. Consequently, some of the acreage reported as a loss to the national wetlands inventory may continue to provide some portion of benefits (for example, wetlands converted to farmland or farm ponds that still provide some wildlife habitat benefit). Conversely, some wetlands that are reported as remaining within the inventory may be functioning at a lesser level due to more gradual or less visible changes in the system (for example, reductions in capability to support wildlife due to localized contamination).

A reduction in the rate of some types of agricultural development and the effects of government regulation may have reduced the rate of wetlands conversion between 1975 and 1980, as concluded by OTA.[33] However, a review of more recent statistical indicators suggests a complex picture, with stability or growth through the early 1980s in some activities associated with wetlands alteration. Subsequently, some sectors, including agriculture, have experienced declines.

There are indications that some regional changes in environmental conditions (for instance, hydrologic and water quality parameters) may be resulting in an increasing amount of wetlands loss and modification. These regional changes can reflect a gradual on-going response to multiple human activities and natural events. Accordingly, in the future, it may become increasingly difficult to identify specific causes of wetlands alteration.

There is substantial variability among wetlands in terms of functional characteristics and capability to provide a wide range of benefits. The benefits provided by a specific area depend on the type of wetland and the context or geographic setting.

REFERENCES

1. Kusler, J.A., Our National Wetland Heritage: A Protection Guidebook (New York: Environmental Law Institute, 1983); and Sather, J.H. and R.D. Smith, An Overview of Major Wetland Functions and Values, FWS/OBS-84/18 (Fort Collins, Colo.: Western Energy and Land Use Team, U.S. Fish and Wildlife Service, 1984).

2. Cowardin, L.M., V. Carter, F.C. Golet, and E.T. LaRoe, Classification of Wetlands and Deepwater Habitats of the United States, FWS/OBS-79/31 (Washington, D.C.: Office of Biological Services, U.S. Fish and Wildlife Service, 1979).

3. Bill Wilen, U.S. Fish and Wildlife Service, personal communication, 1987.

4. Office of Technology Assessment, Wetlands: Their Use and Regulation, OTA-O-206 (Washington, D.C.: U.S. Congress, Office of Technology Assessment, 1984).

5. Mitsch, W.J. and J.G. Gosselink, Wetlands (New York: Van Nostrand Reinhold Company, 1986).

6. Grue, C.E., M.W. Tome, G.A. Swanson, S.M. Borthwick, and L.R. DeWeese, Agricultural Chemicals and the Quality of Prairie-Pothole Wetlands for Adult and Juvenile Waterfowl - What are the Concerns? Proceedings of the National Symposium on Protection of Wetlands from Agricultural Impacts, U.S. Fish and Wildlife Service (Washington, D.C.: U.S. Department of the Interior, 1988).

7. Frayer, W.E., T.J. Monahan, D.C. Bowden, and F.A. Graybill, Status and Trends of Wetlands and Deepwater Habitats in the Coterminous United States, 1950's to 1970's (Fort Collins: Colorado State University, 1983).

8. Ibid.; and Tiner, R.W., Wetlands of the United States: Current Status and Recent Trends (Newton Corner, Mass.: U.S. Fish and Wildlife Service, 1984).

9.   Office of Technology Assessment, <u>Wetlands: Their Use and Regulation</u>.

10.   Frayer, et al., <u>Status and Trends of Wetlands</u>.

11.   Tiner, <u>Wetlands of the United States</u>.

12.   Office of Technology Assessment, <u>Wetlands: Their Use and Regulation</u>.

13.   Keith Schmude, Soil Conservation Service, personal communication 1987.

14.   Alexander, C.E., M.A. Broutman, and D.W. Field, <u>An Inventory of Coastal Wetlands of the USA</u> (Rockville, Md.:   National Oceanic and Atmospheric Administration, U.S. Department of Commerce, 1986).

15.   Charles Alexander, National Oceanic and Atmospheric Administration, personal communication, 1987.

16.   Ibid.

17.   Abernethy, Y. and R.E. Turner, "U.S. Forested Wetlands: 1940-1980," <u>BioScience</u> 37(10):721-727, 1987.

18.   Tiner, R.W. and J.T. Finn, <u>Status and Recent Trends of Wetlands in Five Mid-Atlantic States: Delaware, Maryland, Pennsylvania, Virginia, and West Virginia</u> (Newton Corner, Mass.: U.S. Fish and Wildlife Service, 1986).

19.   Louisiana Wetland Protection Panel, <u>Saving Louisiana's Coastal Wetlands: The Need for a Long-Term Plan of Action</u>, EPA-230-02-87-026 (Washington, D.C.: U.S. Environmental Protection Agency, 1987).

20.   Gosselink, J.G. and L.C. Lee, <u>Cumulative Impact Assessment in Bottomland Hardwood Forests</u> (Baton Rouge: Center for Wetland Resources, Louisiana State University, 1987).

21.   Tiner, <u>Wetlands of the United States</u>.

22.   Office of Technology Assessment, <u>Wetlands: Their Use and Regulation</u>.

23.   U.S. Department of Agriculture, <u>Agricultural Statistics: 1986</u> (Washington, D.C.: U.S. Government Printing Office, 1986).

24.   Kenneth Adler, U.S. Environmental Protection Agency, personal communication, 1987.

25.   Ibid.

26.   Office of Technology Assessment, <u>Wetlands: Their Use and Regulation</u>.

27.   U.S. Department of Commerce, <u>Statistical Abstract of the United States: National Data Book and Guide to Sources</u> (Washington, D.C.:   U.S. Department of Commerce, 1987).

28. U.S. Geological Survey, <u>National Water Summary 1983--Hydrologic Events and Issues</u>, USGS Water Supply Paper 2250 (Washington, D.C.: U.S. Geological Survey, 1984), p. 34.

29. U.S. Department of Commerce, <u>Statistical Abstract</u>.

30. Kenneth Adler, U.S. Environmental Protection Agency, personal communication, 1987.

31. Louisiana Wetland Protection Panel, <u>Saving Louisiana's Coastal Wetlands</u>.

32. General Accounting Office, <u>Wetlands: The Corps of Engineers Administration of the Section 404 Program</u>, GAO-RCED-88-110 (Washington, D.C.: U.S. Congress, General Accounting Office, 1988).

33. Office of Technology Assessment, <u>Wetlands: Their Use and Regulation</u>.

GOALS FOR WETLANDS PROGRAMS

Leah V. Haygood

Goals for wetlands management are found in a wide variety of documents. Local, state, and federal governments set goals in legislation and executive orders, and in regulations, comprehensive plans, and other administrative documents. Goals have also been developed by private and not-for-profit organizations and through multiparty dialogues. Examples in most of these categories are given below.

Federal goals

No single piece of legislation expresses federal goals for wetlands protection and management. However, qualitative and quantitative goals that relate directly or indirectly to wetlands management are embedded in several pieces of federal legislation. The most recent example of a federal goal statement is the **Emergency Wetlands Resources Act of 1986**,[1] which states that:

> ...the existing Federal, State, and private cooperation in wetlands conservation should be strengthened in order to minimize further losses of these valuable areas and to assure their management in the public interest for this and future generations... It is the purpose of this chapter to promote, in concert with other Federal and State statutes and programs, the conservation of the wetlands of the nation in order to maintain the public benefits they provide and to help fulfill international obligations.

The **Coastal Zone Management Act**[2], passed in 1972 and amended in 1980, does not refer specifically to wetlands in stating its purpose, but coastal wetlands are included among the resources covered by the statement that:

Ms. Haygood is associate, The Conservation Foundation, Washington, D.C.

...it is the national policy to preserve, protect, develop, and where possible, to restore or enhance, the resources of the Nation's coastal zone for this and succeeding generations...

The **Clean Water Act**[3] sets quantitative goals that apply to wetlands which are waters of the United States:

> The objective of this chapter is to restore and maintain the chemical, physical, and biological integrity of the Nation's waters...
>
> 1. it is the national goal that the discharge of pollutants into the navigable waters be eliminated by 1985;
>
> 2. it is the national goal that wherever attainable, an interim goal of water quality which provides for the protection of fish, shellfish and wildlife and provides for recreation in and on the water be achieved by July 1, 1983;
>
> 3. it is the national policy that the discharge of toxic pollutants in toxic amounts be prohibited...

Section 404 of the Clean Water Act establishes the major federal regulatory program covering wetlands, but sets no explicit goals for their management.

In addition to legislative goals, in May 1977, President Carter issued **Executive Order 11990, "Protection of Wetlands,"** which sets goals for the resource and for federal agency action:

> ...in order to avoid to the extent possible the long and short term adverse impacts associated with the destruction or modification of wetlands and to avoid direct or indirect support of new construction in wetlands wherever there is a practicable alternative, it is hereby ordered...

Executive Order 11988, "Flood Plain Management," also issued in 1977, indirectly addresses wetlands by requiring federal agencies to avoid direct or indirect support for floodplain development wherever there is a practical alternative.

Goals for wetlands management are also found in federal regulations and agency policies. The Army Corps of Engineers (Corps) published final regulations on November 13, 1986 which include in Section 320.4 **"general policies for evaluating permit applications."** The policy states that the decision-making criterion to be used in permit evaluation is "that the benefits of the proposed alteration outweigh the damage to the wetlands resource," and provides guidance in evaluating the balance:

> ...That decision should reflect the national concern for both protection and utilization of important resources. All factors which may be relevant to the proposal must be considered including the cumulative effects thereof: among those are conservation, economics, aesthetics...

Though now somewhat dated, in 1973 the U.S. Environmental Protection Agency (EPA) adopted a **"Statement of Policy on Protection of Nation's Wetlands,"** which lists values of wetland resources and affirms that:

> ...in its decision processes, it shall be the Agency's policy to give particular cognizance and consideration to any proposal that has the potential to damage wetlands, to recognize the irreplaceable value and man's dependence on them to maintain an environment acceptable to society, and to preserve and protect them from damaging misuses.

More recently, through its **Wetlands Strategic Planning Initiative**[4] process, EPA developed an "implementation plan" which states five goals for wetlands management including:

> ...improve protection of all wetlands to minimize losses; identify, protect, and restore the most valuable and vulnerable geographic wetland areas; reduce information gaps...reduce inconsistencies in federal policies and laws to enhance wetland protection; and increase the understanding and use of ecological values in public and private decisions on wetlands.

<u>State goals</u>[5]

In contrast to the federal government, many states have legislation specifically establishing regulatory and non-regulatory programs for wetlands and stating policies or goals for those programs. Almost all of the "coastal" states (including those with Great Lakes coastline) have enacted coastal zone legislation pursuant to the Coastal Zone Management Act. At least 14 states have legislation covering inland wetlands.[6]

The **Connecticut Inland Wetlands Act**[7] might be considered representative of goals established in state legislation:

> To protect, preserve and maintain inland wetlands; minimize their disturbance and pollution; maintain water quality; prevent damage from erosion, turbidity or siltation; prevent loss of fish and other beneficial aquatic organisms, wildlife and vegetation and the destruction of natural habitats thereof; deter and inhibit danger of flood and pollution; protect wetland values; protect water supplies; provide a balancing of need for growth and use of land.

Some state legislation provides sets of policies which are considerably more specific. The **California Coastal Act,**[8] for example, includes dozens of policies of relevance to wetlands, for example:

> ...diking, filling, or dredging in existing estuaries and wetlands shall maintain or enhance the functional capacity of the wetland or estuary. Any alteration of coastal wetlands...shall be limited to very minor incidental public facilities, restorative measures, nature study, commercial fishing facilities in Bodega Bay, and development in already developed parts of south San Diego Bay...

Goals for wetlands management may also be found in state program planning documents and regulations. The 1986-87 **Program Plan of the Wetlands Section of the Washington State Department of Ecology,** for example, sets out six goals for agency action:

o   Protect the resources and ecology of wetland areas in the State of Washington.

o   Promote better administration of the Shoreline Management Act as it relates to wetlands.

o   Promote informed planning and decision-making related to wetland resources at all levels of government.

o   Assist local governments in the development of programs to protect sensitive areas including wetlands.

o   Increase public awareness of wetland values.

o   Protect the public interest associated with wetlands, while recognizing and protecting private property rights consistent with the public interest.

Local goals

Local governments may have ordinances specifically addressing wetlands management, particularly in regions of the country such as the Northeast or Upper Midwest where states delegate some wetlands regulatory responsibilities to local governments. These ordinances may state goals or purposes. For example, a Lexington, Massachusetts ordinance states:

> The purposes of the Wetland Protection District are to preserve and maintain the groundwater table; to protect the public health and safety by protecting persons and property against the hazards of flood water inundation; and to protect the community against the costs which may be incurred when unsuitable development occurs in swamps, marshes, along water courses, or areas subject to floods.

Goals for wetlands management may also be found in planning documents of local governments and regional planning bodies. Such planning agencies, responsible for translating general policies to specific land-use decisions, may set relatively specific goals. For example, the Regional Plan for South Florida provides a quantitative goal relating to wetlands loss:

Beginning in 1987, eliminate the net loss of functional wetlands systems in the Region and protect remaining wetland systems.

The Plan specifies three measures of its success in implementing the goal:

1.   Quality and quantity of the wetlands in the Region.

2.   Percent of restored/enhanced wetlands.

3.   Reduction in the loss of wetlands.

International goals

The **Convention on Wetlands of International Importance Especially as Waterfowl Habitat,** signed at Ramsar, Iran in 1971, and often referred to as the "Ramsar Convention," includes a statement of finding of the importance of wetlands and states:

...Each contracting Party shall designate at least one wetland to be included in the List (of wetlands of international importance) when signing this Convention...

...The Contracting Parties shall formulate and implement their planning so as to promote the conservation of the wetlands included in the List, and as far as possible the wise use of wetlands in their territory.

Some 45 countries, including the United States, are signatories to the Convention.   In the past couple of years, attention has focused on further defining "wise use" so that it can better serve as a measure of management of wetlands which are not officially designated for protection.

A May 1986 agreement between the Canadian Minister of the Environment and the U.S. Secretary of the Interior sets goals to restore, protect, and improve over six million acres of waterfowl habitat by the year 2000.   It also sets specific spending goals for both countries.

Goals of various consensual processes

The National Wildlife Federation Corporate Conservation Council, formed in 1982, developed as its first project **"A Statement of Policy and Practices for the Conservation of Wetlands."** The statement lists values of wetlands and states:

> Because many of the natural resources of wetlands are renewable they should be protected. However, they also should be managed to allow compatible development of other economic uses. Associated with such development should be efforts to enhance the productivity of adjoining wetlands to offset any productivity that may be lost.

> The National Wildlife Federation's Corporate Conservation Council affirms that protection of renewable wetlands values is of vital importance to the nation and such values should be maintained. The Council believes that proceeding with the careful development of wetlands for their non-renewable resource values may well be compatible with the desired goal of minimizing lasting disturbance of wetlands.

In April 1987, Environment Canada, the federal environmental agency, and the Federation of Ontario Naturalists, a non-profit conservation group, published **"Wetlands Conservation Policy in Canada: Recommendations by Non-Government Organizations,"** a document resulting from a workshop held in February of that year. The workshop developed a "Recommended Policy Framework" that set out as objectives:

> To ensure that a national wetlands conservation policy as well as any programs formulated under it are linked to other land, soil, water, air and wildlife conservation policies in order to secure the wise use of Canada's wetland ecosystems and meet Canada's international wetlands conservation responsibilities.

> To arrest the loss and to encourage the rehabilitation of Canada's wetlands by:

> a. maintaining the integrity of wetland ecosystems;

> b. preserving the genetic diversity of wetlands ecosystems;

> c. ensuring the enjoyment and economic use of wetland ecosystems is sustainable.

REFERENCES

1.   16 U.S.C.A. Section 3901.

2.   16 U.S.C.A. Section 1452.

3.   33 U.S.C.A. Section 2151.

4.   U.S. Environmental Protection Agency Wetlands Strategic Planning Process "Implementation Plan."

5.   The April 1986 sections on state and local goals are intended to provide a representative rather than complete catalogue of state and local level goals. The selection of state goals submitted to Wetlands Forum staff is not comprehensive. In addition, as many state laws are modeled on approaches in other states, a complete catalogue would be quite repetitive.

6.   State Wetland Protection Programs--Status and Recommendations, prepared by C. Deming Cowles et al., for EPA (December 1986) identifies 13 states as having specific inland wetland laws. The passage of New Jersey's Freshwater Wetlands Protection Act in 1987 brings the total to at least 14.

7.   Connecticut General Statute 22a-36.

8.   Ann. Cal. Pub. Res. Code, Section 30121.

ADVANCE PLANNING FOR WETLANDS PROTECTION AND MANAGEMENT

Leah V. Haygood and Robert S. Reed

INTRODUCTION

Wetlands exist as integral elements of ecological and economic landscapes, but are rarely managed as such. Wetlands are inseparable from local and regional hydrology and may perform a range of functions or provide benefits, the effects of which extend regionally, nationally, or internationally. These can include natural and economic benefits such as flood storage, provision of habitat to migratory waterfowl, oil exploration, and timber harvest, all of which may extend beyond the immediate area.

Yet, regulatory decisions about activities in or affecting wetlands are often made on a case-by-case basis on fairly narrow grounds. A bewildering range of programs exist which address particular functions associated with wetlands. Some of these programs, particularly at state and national levels, may offer the potential to manage certain functions of wetlands in an integrated regional framework, but may not provide for consideration of the full range of wetland values. Local land use planning and zoning may offer the opportunity to consider wetland values comprehensively, but political jurisdictions do not necessarily correspond to ecologically significant boundaries.

Over the past several decades, government agencies and private interests have responded to these shortcomings in existing decision-making processes by experimenting with an inventive array of approaches to advance planning for wetlands management--"special area management planning," "advance designation," "negotiated land development," "focal point planning," and "advance identification"--often in the context of larger planning objectives.

The authors are associate and former research fellow, respectively, The Conservation Foundation.

These processes show considerable promise as a vehicle for arriving at more sensible policies and decision making and for ensuring consistency between government programs and between shared community goals and private action. They also can provide much-needed predictability in government regulatory and land-use decisions.

In this paper, the term "planning processes" or "negotiated planning processes" is used as the generic description of this array of area-wide, multi-project planning approaches. Generally, these are processes which engage more than one agency or organization (and often many including environmental, development, and citizen interests) in an exercise of jointly setting goals or priorities for a particular location and its land or water resources. Often, the plans are intended to have regulatory results. Wetlands may be the focus of the planning process or just one of several resources in a "multi-objective" effort. Many of these processes have been initiated in response to controversy. Some differ from traditional planning processes in the way public involvement is structured and in the range of issues addressed; others are similar to various intergovernmental coordination efforts. Elements of plans developed through these processes may include maps, policies, general permits, classification or ranking of wetlands and uplands, demonstration projects, acquisition and other management options for particular wetlands, formation of new regional planning entities, or memoranda of agreement for interagency coordination.

Yet, at this point, the promise of these processes remains largely undocumented, if not untested. The relatively small number of cases, their wide diversity (planning areas range from hundreds of acres to thousands of square miles), and the prevailing lack of information about implementation of the plans means that it is both difficult to generalize about the cases (although this may never be either possible or useful), and difficult to provide definitive answers about how to conduct advance planning processes successfully. It may, however, be useful to address several questions that a sponsor or participant in a process would need to ask.

Thus, the first section of this paper briefly summarizes the development of advance planning approaches, outlines several types of planning processes that have been used for wetlands protection and management, and briefly discusses the advantages and disadvantages of such processes. The second section explores several issues related to the initiation and design of advance planning processes for wetlands management, drawing on a variety of case examples, ten of which are summarized in Appendix 3-A.

BACKGROUND

Development of Planning Approaches to Wetlands Protection and Management

Many early efforts at planning for wetlands management arose to deal with conflicting views about resource use in coastal zones. In these cases, wetlands were recognized as ecologically important but also attractive sites for development. These efforts also recognized that existing planning units (generally a political jurisdiction) were not necessarily appropriate for valuable and threatened natural resources. Thus, planners began to address "special areas" through regional processes. One of the first such efforts, The first San Francisco Bay Plan, for example, was developed in the 1960s in response to a 1959 study by the U.S. Army Corps of Engineers (Corps) that showed a rate of wetlands loss to development around the Bay of two to three square miles each year.

Public concern over pollution in the Bay and the loss of wildlife habitat led to a cooperative effort of federal, state, and local agencies to identify areas for preservation and establish permitting procedures for proposed development.[1] In 1969, the California legislature created the San Francisco Bay Conservation and Development Commission as a permanent body charged with ongoing planning and permitting responsibilities.

In 1975, at Grays Harbor, Washington, federal, state, and local government agencies came together to develop a detailed, site-specific, long-range plan for development and conservation of the Harbor and its wetlands. Although problems subsequently emerged in completing the process and adopting the plan, the initial success of the project was an impetus to Congress to include a provision in the 1980 amendments to the Coastal Zone Management Act (CZMA) specifically encouraging Special Area Management Planning (SAMP), as the process came to be known.

Dozens of other planning processes with significant wetlands components have been carried out under state and local zoning authority, under the federal Endangered Species Act habitat conservation planning process, through the "advance identification" process of EPA and the Corps, and through a range of *ad hoc* authorities and processes.

The variety of planning processes that have been developed and used reflects differences in their purposes, the authorities under which they are conducted, the resources and issues addressed by the process, and the agencies and interests involved, among other factors. Some processes have been used to implement regulatory programs by designating in advance areas where no permits would be issued, and those where development might occur. Others have focused on nonregulatory actions, including enhancement and acquisition. Inventory and classification projects have been used for educational purposes to alert landowners to the presence and type of wetlands on their property and likely responses of government agencies. Other processes simply attempt to coordinate multiple regulatory and nonregulatory programs or to develop new programs.

Types of Planning Processes

Special Area Management Plans

The 1980 amendments to the Coastal Zone Management Act[2] define a SAMP process as:

> "a comprehensive plan providing for natural resource protection and reasonable economic growth containing a detailed and comprehensive statement of policies, standards, and criteria to guide public and

private uses of lands and waters; and mechanisms for timely implementation in the specific geographic areas within the coastal zone."

The CZMA program has an established system for providing grants to states and communities. These grants can be used to fund SAMP processes. The CZMA does not, however, outline a procedure for conducting such processes, and grants are only available to localities within the coastal zone. Many planning processes have been carried out using CZMA funds. Several have led to the designation of estuaries as National Estuarine Sanctuaries.

The Corps of Engineers has adopted the SAMP concept and incorporated it into the Corps' own policies. The Corps can undertake SAMP processes in either coastal or inland areas. The Corps funds its program through a "special studies" segment of its overall regulatory budget.

Corps SAMP efforts are usually initiated at the district level. Local or regional regulators may identify a trend in permit applications or recognize threats to an especially valuable resource and feel both the resource and the review budget would be better served by planning than by regulating.

A Regulatory Guidance Letter issued October 2, 1986 by the Office or the Chief of Engineers outlines four criteria that must be met before the Corps will begin a SAMP process:

o   the area should be environmentally sensitive and under strong development pressure;

o   ideally, there should be strong public involvement throughout the process;

o   there should be a sponsoring local agency to ensure that the plan fully reflects local needs and interests; and

o   all parties must be willing at the outset to conclude the process with definitive regulatory products.

The last two criteria set the SAMP process apart from the ADID process (see below), which may benefit from local interest and involvement, but does not necessarily require it. The ADID process also does not necessarily yield concrete regulatory products.

SAMPs can be conducted at a variety of levels, as evidenced by the difference in two SAMPs: a planning effort within the City of Anchorage, Alaska (see Appendix 3-A), and the Grays Harbor estuary planning effort mentioned in the introduction.

Advance Identification

EPA and the relevant Section 404 permitting agency (generally the Corps) have joint authority under the Section 404(b)(1) guidelines of the Clean Water Act[3] to identify wetlands that are suitable or unsuitable for discharge permits. This "advance identification" authority may be used to facilitate the federal regulatory process or for appropriate state or local action. Unless tied to general permitting or other regulatory authority, designation of sites as suitable or unsuitable for disposal is a guide to but not a guarantee of permit issuance or denial.

As initiated by EPA, ADID generally involves a cooperative effort between state, federal, and sometimes local agencies to inventory, characterize, and map wetland resources. Public participation during the process is not required, but is encouraged by EPA guidance and is generally practiced. Following inventory, characterization, and mapping, EPA and the Corps jointly issue a public notice of the suitable/unsuitable designations for public review. The maps and suitable/unsuitable designations are intended to guide regulatory decisions and private actions and lend predictability to the Section 404 permitting program.

At the close of 1988, 13 ADID processes had been completed throughout the country, 19 were underway, and 8 were in the planning stage. Sites have ranged from a 2.7 million acre area in the Rainwater Basins region of Nebraska, to a program in 18 towns in southern Maine, in which EPA and the Corps (in consultation with state, regional, and other federal agencies) identified activities (as opposed to specific locations) that would be generally suitable and unsuitable in the region.

In addition to EPA's authority to undertake ADID studies, under Section 404(c), EPA can prohibit or restrict any discharges at specific sites. EPA may only take such action if it believes such a discharge would cause unacceptable adverse impacts on water supplies, fish and wildlife, and recreation. EPA has exercised this authority in response to particular permit requests and after an unpermitted fill has occurred, but has not used it to designate in advance areas where discharge is prohibited.

Land Use Plans

Land use planning and zoning authorities are powerful tools for managing resource use and can be appropriately applied to conserve wetlands. Planning or zoning authorities exist at the state, local, and regional (multi-municipality or multi-state) levels and through special districts. Where local or state planning and zoning programs exist, wetlands management plans must be coordinated with them to be implemented successfully.

At the state level, the Coastal Zone Management Act provides for grants to coastal states to develop and implement management programs for the coastal zone. NOAA reviews and approves state Coastal Zone Management Programs (CZMP), which may include implementation of wetland protection provisions or acquisition of wetlands. However, federal program requirements allow considerable flexibility in the emphasis and elements of a state program. In addition, wetlands are only one of many resources addressed in state programs. Thus, the extent to which CZMPs are an effective vehicle for wetlands protection and advance planning varies from state to state.

State CZMPs may require that local government plans be consistent with the state plan. In Alaska, for example, some 25 local coastal zone management plans have been approved that are consistent with state and federal requirements.

Some states have consistency requirements that apply to inland as well as coastal areas. In Oregon, local land use plans must conform to a set of state "goals" or policies for land use.[4]   Florida has a number of innovative programs for coordinating state, regional, and local planning and assigning planning authority to the most appropriate level of government. It grants authority for regional planning to a system of regional planning commissions which provide guidelines with which local jurisdictions must comply.[5]   The regional commissions may take a more direct planning role in response to proposals for projects that could have regional impact.

Under Chapter 380 of the Florida State and Regional Planning Act, Florida also practices intergovernmental coordination through Resource Planning and Management Committees (RPMCs) and, where necessary, designation of Areas of Critical State Concern. The purpose of the RPMCs, which have been used about 12 times to date, is to involve interested parties and managers in cooperative processes that identify resource issues and resolve conflicts in advance. RPMC processes result in management plans for incorporation into local comprehensive plans and land use regulations, thus giving local governments the opportunity to address problems locally. Since such issues are of regional concern, if local agencies fail to adequately address them, the area may be designated an Area of Critical State Concern, which allows for state review and appeal of all local development orders. The RPMC process, thus, promotes advance planning and provides a vehicle for introducing state goals and policies to the local level.[6]

Where state planning programs exist, whether statewide or in coastal areas, state policies on wetlands management must be considered in advance planning, and state agencies may become important players in the development of plans for wetlands resources.

At the regional or local level, planning and zoning can be powerful tools to protect wetlands in advance of proposals to alter them. Through comprehensive planning processes, local governments develop policies and objectives based on an inventory and analysis of factors, including natural resources, existing land uses, population and economic activity and projections of trends in those areas. Planners then develop a comprehensive or master plan which shows, often on overlay maps, the result expected after a specified time from application of the policies to the planning region. Depending on the state and locality, such a plan may or may not be binding in itself. Local jurisdictions use zoning and other ordinances to control what kinds of development or activities can occur where. The validity of zoning ordinances often depends upon the existence of a comprehensive plan.

Local ordinances can be used to protect wetlands and other natural features of the landscape. For example, Maryland's Natural Resource District overlay zone in the Zoning Code of Harford County, applies to stream corridors, wetlands over 40,000 square feet in area, and steep slopes. The ordinance states: "tidal and non-tidal wetlands shall not be disturbed by development. A buffer of at least seventy-five feet shall be maintained in areas adjacent to wetlands."[7] Exceptions include agricultural activities, existing mining and excavation operations, and road and utility crossings.

Thus, the local zoning ordinances protect both wetlands and adjacent areas. However, as is the case with almost all zoning ordinances, the Zoning Board may grant a variance from the requirements under specified circumstances. In addition, although developers may be aware of restrictions on development in wetlands, unless the local jurisdiction maps its wetlands, builders may not know in advance that wetlands occur on a particular piece of property.

In some areas of the country, planning and zoning is coordinated by regional planning authorities which encompass several towns or unincorporated areas. In addition, state legislatures sometimes create special regional planning bodies based on boundaries of natural features and endowed with certain powers of state and local governments. Examples include the New York's Adirondack Park Agency and the Hackensack Meadowlands Development Corporation (HMDC).

The concept of National Reserves, which involves regional planning, has been applied only in the New Jersey Pinelands, an area rich in natural resources, particularly wetlands and groundwater. The Pinelands National Reserve was established by Congress in 1978 to protect the unique resources of the region.

Even land use plans addressing regional jurisdictions, however, may fail to account for the full range of effects on wetlands resources. Land use plans are typically drawn to fit political boundaries. Federally-initiated programs, such as SAMPs and EPA ADID, may more easily address areas defined by resource characteristics.

Greenways and River Corridor Plans

Greenway planning is a broad term describing a variety of processes used to conserve natural, cultural, historical, and recreational resource values through numerous techniques, applied in a variety of geographic areas.[8] Many greenways have been sited in river or stream corridors and thus are of significance to wetlands management. Wetlands resources, however, are not necessarily the focus nor the sole beneficiaries of greenways. The recent report of President Reagan's Commission on Americans Outdoors recommended creation of a national "network of greenways" for recreation and open space conservation.[9]

Planning for greenways along river and stream corridors should involve, among a range of possible participants, the administrators of outdoor recreation, floodplain, and wetlands programs. Wetlands and floodplain managers share the common objective of minimizing construction in low-lying, frequently flooded areas, and the resulting low density development contributes to maintenance of open space for recreation. This common interest makes coordination not only desirable, but essential to avoid duplication in the use of government resources for acquisition, regulation and management of stream corridors. The city of Tulsa, Oklahoma, conducted planning for a greenway following a 1984 flood which caused significant damage to the city.

Greenway planning poses several challenges. The greenway planning concept is not established in legislation or regulation, and the multi-jurisdictional nature of many greenways may complicate planning. While greenway planners may utilize local land use or other traditional planning tools, they are likely to depend heavily on private efforts, such as voluntary land conservation, actions of nonprofit land trusts, and private fund raising. Thus, although development of greenways can support the goals of federal programs, direct participation of federal officials can be constrained by the many objectives and players involved.

Habitat Conservation Plans

The Endangered Species Act[10] authorizes the Fish and Wildlife Service to prepare and implement Habitat Conservation plans in certain situations to protect endangered species. Because critical habitats for endangered species often cut across various jurisdictions and encompass private as well as public lands, development of such plans may involve a number of parties and a wide range of environmental and economic considerations.

Habitat Conservation Plans provide a balancing mechanism. While the Act prohibits actions that "harass, harm, or kill" endangered species, "incidental" impacts may be allowed where a plan exists. Planning is intended to ensure that such harm occurs incidental to lawful activities, and that impacts to the species are minimized, mitigated, and will not appreciably threaten its survival.[11]

Where endangered species depend on wetlands for critical habitat, conservation plans can be the vehicle for coordinated planning and management. Federal, state, and local governments and environmental and development interests have negotiated a few Habitat Conservation Plans, including one in North Key Largo, Florida, which included a significant wetlands component.

<u>Other Wetlands-Related Planning Initiatives</u>

<u>Estuary Conservation and Management</u>:   Over   the   next   five   years,
"Comprehensive   Conservation   and   Management   Plans"   are   expected   to   be
developed   for   11   estuaries   under   the   auspices   of   EPA's   National   Estuary
Program.   Based   on   the   experience   with   programs   to   address   water   quality
issues   in   the   Great   Lakes   and   Chesapeake   Bay,   in   1985,   Congress   appropriated
funds   for   EPA   to   study   and   assess   four   estuaries: Narragansett   Bay   in   Rhode
Island,   Buzzards   Bay   in   Massachusetts,   Long   Island   Sound   in   New   York   and
Connecticut,   and   Puget   Sound   in   Washington.   Albemarle-Pamlico   Sounds   in
North   Carolina   and   the   San   Francisco   Bay/Sacramento-San   Joaquin   Delta
system   in   California   were   added   in   1986.   The   1987   Water   Quality   Act
formally   established   the   National   Estuary   Program   and   added   the   Delaware
Inland   Bays,   the   New   York-New   Jersey   Harbor,   Sarasota   Bay   in   Florida,   and
Galveston   Bay   in   Texas.

Under   the   National   Estuary   Program,   the   EPA   Administrator   convenes   a
Management   Conference   to   oversee   development   of   the   management   plan.   The
Conference   consists   of   representatives   of   EPA,   state   and   local   governments,
interstate   and   regional   agencies,   industries,   public   interest   groups,   universities,
and   the   general   public.   The   Conference   is   responsible   for   identifying   several
issues   important   to   the   estuary   which   have   implications   for   the   maintenance   or
improvement   of   water   quality.   The   issues   selected   then   become   the   focus   of
the   management   plan.   Thus,   where   wetlands   are   identified   as   a   critical   focus
of   attention,   the   Conference   and   management   plan   can   be   vehicles   for
coordinated   planning.

<u>Cumulative Impact Assessment and Management</u>:   EPA   has   engaged   in   a
pilot   program   in   the   Tensas   Basin   of   Louisiana   to   test   an   experimental
technique   for   assessing   cumulative   wetlands   impacts.   Researchers,   in   an
attempt   to   completely   characterize   the   environmental   condition   of   the   Basin,
conducted   detailed   surveys   and   analyses   of   the   hydrology,   water   quality,   and
biota   of   the   area.   In   addition,   the   researchers   conducted   a   goal-setting
exercise   to   evaluate   the   feasibility   of   using   cumulative   impact   assessment   in

resource management. The assessment represents the first step in determining goals and plans for managing the area and for containing impacts through the EPA ADID process.[12] If successful, the assessment technique will be applied elsewhere and the management program will be expanded to other areas.

State Comprehensive Outdoor Recreation Plans (SCORPs): Each state is required to produce a SCORP every five years to be eligible for federal assistance from the Land and Water Conservation Fund (LWCF). SCORPs are intended to review state recreation opportunities and outline priorities for future land acquisition and recreational facilities development. The LWCF Act[13] was amended in 1986 by the Emergency Wetlands Resources Act.[14] The Wetlands Act recognizes the contribution of wetlands in providing fish and wildlife habitat and offering significant recreational and commercial benefits. In amending the LWCF Act, it requires states to consider wetlands in SCORPs. More specifically, states are expected to identify the agencies and organizations involved in wetlands management, evaluate existing and proposed wetlands protection mechanisms, assess wetlands resources, identify wetlands loss and degradation factors, and establish priorities for protection.

In revising SCORPs to reflect wetlands needs, states may request assistance from a variety of sources, including both public agencies and private organizations. In many cases the effort may represent the first attempt to assess statewide wetlands resources. The documents reflecting these efforts should greatly enhance the information available to local, state, and regional planners.

Negotiated General Permits: The Corps of Engineers has begun using negotiation as a means to reach agreement on development proposals in advance of permit issuance. Through negotiation, the participants (which may include developers, local interests, and environmental groups) attempt to resolve differences through direct discussion, often with the assistance of a facilitator. The Corps retains final authority over permit decisions, but if consensus among the participants is reached, their recommendation has a strong influence on the permit decision.

Because of the resources it absorbs, the process is not used in individual permit decisions. It is more likely to result in regional general permits with negotiated modifications or restrictions.

Advantages and Disadvantages of Planning for Wetlands Management

The planning processes undertaken to date have not been systematically documented and have varied enough in purpose, geographic scope, range of participants, and products, that it is difficult to generalize about their successes and weaknesses. However, because these processes attempt to take a more comprehensive look at the resource and public and private policies for its management, they appear to show promise for achieving several goals that are difficult to accomplish when agencies must react on a case-by-case basis.

A planning process, if it results in a consensus among the public agencies and private organizations concerned about a particular resource, can be the vehicle for setting consistent goals and priorities across a variety of government and private programs such as local planning and zoning, floodplain management, river corridor planning, open space preservation, and Section 404 regulation. This can allow consideration not only of the wetlands themselves but also those uplands on which the wetland may be functionally dependent, within an overall picture of development and preservation, assuming that the boundaries of the planning area are set appropriately. In the Southeast Wisconsin example (see Appendix 3-A), the planning process identified both wetlands and remnant prairie uplands for acquisition and preservation by the state and The Nature Conservancy. Where planning processes incorporate regulatory authority, they can provide a measure of predictability and uniformity to decisionmaking.

While planning processes can be used to coordinate existing policies and programs, they can also be used to develop new policies and address issues outside of the scope of established authorities and procedures. The Timber, Fish and Wildlife agreement, for example (see Appendix 3-A), incorporates provisions which allow interested parties including environmental and tribal interests to participate directly in the review of proposed forestry operations in Washington state prior to permitting by the state.

Several other planning efforts have been able creatively to address questions of equity in the effects of the plan on public and private interests. As part of its plan of conservation and development, the Hackensack Meadowlands Development Commission created a tax-sharing formula which allows increases in tax revenues to towns that experience development to be apportioned to towns with large wetland open spaces where development is restricted.[15] The Key Largo Habitat Conservation Plan and the Pinelands plan have incorporated provisions for transfer of development rights (see Appendix 3-A).

Engaging in planning processes for wetlands management is not without drawbacks, however. Such processes can be very time and resource-intensive for the individuals and agencies involved. The expense may be justified if it is viewed as the cost of making many future decisions at the present time; however, this only holds true if the plan is binding and is successfully implemented.

In all instances, a truly comprehensive plan which addresses land and water resources and their functional interdependencies is likely to require that relevant authorities and programs at all levels of government and the private sector be coordinated and brought to bear on the plan for a particular area. If all relevant agencies are not involved, or if federal agencies in particular are not willing or able to commit to exercise their regulatory authority consistent with the plan, the development of a plan could in effect add a layer of bureaucracy and confusion, rather than reducing it.

Coordinating diverse agencies has proven a challenge in some instances, particularly when the agencies perceive differences in their mandates or authorities. In the Hackensack Meadowlands, for example, EPA has undertaken an advance identification effort which was intended to be integrated into the revisions to the HMDC master plan, thus providing integrated guidance on local/state and federal regulatory decisions. However, EPA has proposed actions in the Meadowlands which run counter to HMDC's existing plan. At the same time, HMDC maintains that it does not have authority to consider alternative sites for development if they lie outside the Meadowlands district.

As noted above, federal agencies have several kinds of authority to engage in advance planning activities. At the state level, the picture is varied. Some states (for instance, New York, Massachusetts, and New Jersey) have programs specifically aimed at planning for wetlands protection. Others (such as Florida) have mechanisms for reviewing local plans, ensuring consistency with state goals, and initiating planning processes. In other states, while agencies may participate in planning processes as representatives of state interests and regulatory authorities, they lack mechanisms for initiating planning efforts or encouraging local agencies to undertake them. Locally, many communities have land use planning and zoning authority which is a powerful tool, but which may not be sufficient to coordinate the variety of public and private programs of relevance to wetlands in their jurisdiction.

While adequate authority often exists to support multi-interest planning efforts, institutional mechanisms and rewards to support such processes are largely lacking. Most of the processes conducted to date have occurred on an *ad hoc* basis. In some cases, important parties have not been involved in a timely fashion because it was not recognized that they needed to be involved or, simply, due to lack of travel funds or staff time necessary for effective participation. For federal agency staff, in particular, participation in local land use decisions may be unfamiliar or may seem inappropriate. To assure that these processes are applied where they would be helpful, institutional mechanisms--to trigger initiation of a process, assure adequate technical information and funding, structure participation, and oversee implementation--are needed, but at this point are not provided in a systematic way.

Finally, while development of a plan may appear to be the endpoint of the process, it is really just the beginning of on-the-ground implementation. Some planning processes have reached agreement on a plan and commenced

46

implementation. Others, including the pioneering Grays Harbor SAMP, have been underway for years and still are not fully adopted.[16] Given that there is no single "cookbook" approach to planning for wetlands management, the following section explores several questions relating to designing or initiating a planning process.

ISSUES IN INITIATING AND DESIGNING A WETLANDS MANAGEMENT PLANNING PROCESS

People often initiate advanced planning processes in areas where conflict has emerged over the use of natural resources. Most such planning processes take place within existing institutional and environmental contexts. However, some situations are likely to offer more flexibility than others. The questions that follow should be addressed in designing a planning process. They assume an *ad hoc* process rather than one that is prescribed by law or regulation, because most of the planning processes examined had some elements of an *ad hoc*, one-time-only process, even if they took place within an institutional framework. Therefore, the following sections examine questions assuming some flexibility in the design of the process. It may be helpful, however, to create a more "institutionalized" type of process, which in effect provides answers up front to some of the questions one would ask in designing a process, such as which agencies should be involved and under what authority the planning process would take place.

Defining the Planning and Management Area

There are two basic alternatives in defining a planning area. It can be selected based on functional dependency--a watershed or an ecosystem, for example, depending on the functions planned for--or based on political boundaries. In practice, the selection of a management area may involve consideration of both factors.

From a natural resource management point of view, selection of an area for development of a negotiated land use plan should ideally be based on functional criteria. Inclusion of entire ecosystems allows planners to take into account the widest possible range of influences on the protected resource. Delineating regional ecosystem boundaries, however, can be difficult. Ecosystems are defined by environmental conditions, including climate and landscape. Isolated wetlands, such as the potholes of the Northern Plains, might be thought of as independent systems. Yet every system is to some degree influenced by those adjacent or nearby. The mobility of waterfowl, an important feature of pothole wetlands, increases the interaction and interdependence of these systems. Determining where complete and separate ecosystems exist is, therefore, difficult and often subjective.

Another option for defining the planning area based on functional considerations is to use watershed boundaries. This approach has several advantages, including: relative ease of locating the boundaries of a watershed; the match, to the extent it exists, between size of a drainage basin and non-ecological factors, such as political boundaries; and the significance of watersheds as units for the many wetlands functions which are related to hydrology. Other wetland functions, however, such as wildlife habitat, may not always correspond to watershed boundaries.

Based on an understanding of the resource and areas on which it is functionally dependent, the selection of a planning area can also be tailored to particular situations. For example, some planning processes concentrate on areas in which activities occur that threaten the resource, such as areas adjacent to water bodies.

In practice, efforts to manage wetlands based on their functionally dependent areas are often circumscribed by a number of factors, including existing land use patterns and political boundaries. In addition, the geographic scope of many planning projects is strongly influenced by the initiator of the process. Planning projects initiated by a town planning department, for example, are likely to include all or part of the town, and may not account for watershed or other natural boundaries. However, the use of existing jurisdictions has some distinct advantages. For example, political boundaries conform better to existing institutional structures which may make the plan easier to implement.

Even for processes initiated by existing institutions, however, there may be flexibility in the choice of planning area. The plan may address only specially threatened areas or resources (which may be based on functional characteristics), thus streamlining the planning and focusing implementation efforts.

The boundaries of a planning area may also be determined by proponents of a particular project, based primarily on land ownership. In Florida, for example, developers, local, regional, and state planning officials, and others may engage in negotiations over changes to major development proposals determined to be "developments of regional impact." In one such development, wetlands were incorporated into the site's surface water management plan and the elimination of some wetlands of minimal size was mitigated through the creation of wetlands that were connected to existing, larger wetland systems.

Who Should Be Involved in a Planning Process, and How Should Their Involvement Be Structured?

The direct involvement of a variety of government agencies and, in many cases, public and private interests, is one of the key characteristics that distinguishes negotiated planning processes from more traditional processes of agency planning in the context of a particular mandate. It is generally agreed that in order to reach an agreement that holds up over time and can be successfully implemented, all affected interests should be involved in some way. However, determining who needs to be involved and how they should participate is challenging.

Although most negotiated planning processes for wetlands management currently include all government agencies that have legal authority over elements of the plan, this has not always been the case. The Columbia River Estuary Task Force (CREST) for example, was organized in 1974 by local government agencies in Oregon and Washington to develop a long-range plan for the estuary and its shore lands (see Appendix 3-A). The Task Force consulted with a local citizen advisory committee and state and federal agencies, but did not give them a direct decision-making role. Following extensive studies in the estuary, CREST adopted a regional management plan in 1979 which allocated most anticipated development to the Oregon portion of the estuary. The Oregon Land Conservation and Development Commission, a state agency responsible for ensuring that local plans are consistent with statewide planning policies, reviewed the plan and rejected portions of it. In early 1981 the CREST Council requested the assistance of neutral mediators to conduct a negotiation over changes to the plan which would include state and federal officials. The negotiators reached agreement in June of 1981.[17]

The experience in this case and others suggests that it is important to secure effective participation by all agencies that have authority over implementation of the plan. The more difficult questions arise over whether and how to involve constituencies who lack legal authority but who might nonetheless have the ability to block implementation of a plan. Several observers have attributed problems in securing agreement on the Grays Harbor plan to the lack of direct business and environmental interest representation in the negotiations, though these interests were included on an advisory committee.[18] Some processes have succeeded including only representatives of government agencies as full members of the negotiating group. The CREST negotiations are one example of this, though it should be noted that the mediators in that case did extensive interviews of all interested parties, including landowners and environmental leaders and discussed with them who should be represented in the negotiations.

Planning processes can involve stakeholders in a variety of ways. The most direct representation is by including all interests in face-to-face negotiations, perhaps with the assistance of a mediator. The CREST negotiations, the Timber, Fish and Wildlife agreement, and the Key Largo habitat conservation plan development were handled this way. Somewhat less direct is formation of an advisory committee made up of representatives of all affected interests, as in the Southeast Wisconsin regional plan. Finally, responsible agencies can organize public meetings as a means of obtaining broad public review. Public meetings, however, do not provide for effective dialogue and do not entail shared decision-making. Public meetings are also often used as supplements to negotiated processes. No single model of representation of interest groups is appropriate to every planning project. However, it is important that initiators of planning processes carefully consider the question of who should be represented and how.

Should Wetlands Be Classified and/or Ranked as Part of a Planning Process?

Most planning processes which address wetland resources include an inventory of all wetlands within the planning area. Some inventories use analytical techniques such as the HEP or WET to characterize wetlands.[19]

Based on inventories and descriptions or characterizations, wetlands can be categorized in several different ways. They might simply be classified by type, or they might be classified by the degree of stress on the wetland (in other words, the likelihood that it would be a target of development or subject to degradation). Wetlands might also be categorized by their condition. For example, wetlands might be divided into three categories: undisturbed natural wetlands, wetlands which are degraded but restorable, and irreversibly damaged wetlands. Such systems of categories can be the basis on which planners prescribe qualitatively different management strategies or set priorities for the timing of actions.

Some planning processes take the further step of grouping wetlands based on their relative value or importance. This latter step, which will be referred to as "ranking," has generated controversy both in concept and in practice because of its presumed implication that some wetlands may be sacrosanct and some expendable. The concept of wetland ranking involves placing inventoried wetlands into three to five broad categories based on the combined importance of their ecological services and intrinsic values.[20] While systems such as HEP and WET exist to identify or predict the functions of a particular wetland (and provide a basis for comparison to functions performed by other wetlands), ranking inherently requires judgments about the value to society of the functions performed. Thus, ranking goes beyond science and into the realm of policy.

Federal, state, or local policies and programs may be applied based on the ranking system. Depending on those policies and regulatory authorities, the wetlands ranking might set priorities for acquisition, might prescribe in advance the outcome of permit applications, might outline a permit process or criteria to apply, or might be simply advisory. Wetlands ranking has been carried out in the context of planning processes and state regulatory programs. Several examples of different approaches are outlined below.

Some SAMPs have used an approach which prescribes permit decisions based on wetlands ranking. In the city of Anchorage, Alaska, for example (see Appendix 3-A), urban development was rapidly occupying all available upland development sites. Rather than react to Section 404 applications on a case-by-case basis, the Corps, EPA, FWS, the National Marine Fisheries Service, the City of Anchorage, the Real Estate Association, Trustees of Alaska (an environmental group), and the Alaska Departments of Fish and Game, Environmental Conservation, Transportation and Public Facilities, and Natural Resources, worked together to inventory and rank the city's wetlands for preservation (which would allow only very limited development such as recreational use), conservation (allowing limited conversions with mitigation), development (which would be carried out under a general permit), and special study, which would require a case-by-case investigation. Similar wetland planning projects have occurred in Sitka and Juneau.

EPA and the Corps have also used the advanced identification process described in the previous section to rank wetlands in several parts of the country.

The state of Massachusetts employs a system which in effect assigns wetlands to two broad classes. Under the Inland Wetlands Restriction Act and the Coastal Wetlands Restriction Act, wetlands are mapped on a town-by-town basis. Those wetlands identified as particularly valuable are designated for restriction. Following a public hearing, a Restriction Order is enacted which prohibits certain activities which would harm the wetlands. The Order is recorded on the deed of the property to give notice of the restriction to future purchasers of the property.[21]

Under its freshwater wetlands law, the New York Department of Environmental Conservation classifies freshwater wetlands regulated by the state (those above 12.4 acres in area) in four categories based on criteria for functional characteristics, including some social functions such as the wetland's role in protecting water supplies. Following mapping and ranking, the state notifies landowners by registered mail of wetlands on their property and provides information on the likelihood of obtaining a permit for activities in the wetland.

A number of arguments have been raised for and against ranking and its various permutations. Many wetlands scientists and policymakers accept the premise that different wetlands perform different functions and thus, for particular purposes, some wetlands are more valuable than others. Case by case permit decisions reflect these judgments. Ranking can be viewed as institutionalizing this premise, and setting priorities explicitly rather than implicitly, perhaps on a more consistent basis. To the regulated community, ranking of wetlands can provide greater certainty and predictability to the regulatory process, reduce delay, and help to avoid costly disputes over highly valued wetlands. Ranking can also help ensure that limited agency resources aren't tied up on a few proposals, while in potentially more valuable wetlands, alterations go on unnoticed.

However, some observers question the policy basis for judgments about the relative value of wetlands, particularly for wetlands high in different values (for instance, wetlands important for wildlife habitat versus those important in moderating flood flows). The relative values of wetlands may also change over time, as might our knowledge and appreciation of them. If criteria are not well specified, the rankings may be inconsistent. The process of identifying and ranking wetlands can also be very resource-intensive. If the rankings are only advisory and are not tied to a specific regulatory authority, some critics charge that little is gained through a costly process.

Others point out that, even in the absence of regulatory "teeth," advance designation can be a useful tool for educating landowners and avoiding costly conflicts over high-value systems.

Within a multiple-objective planning process, ranking systems may be of limited value because they only rank the importance of wetlands relative to other wetlands--not to the other land and water resources which may be the subject of the planning process. Other analytical tools may be needed to determine the value of wetlands as integral elements of economic and ecological landscapes.

Ranking systems tied to predetermined permit decisions are subject to a variety of criticisms. At one end of the ranking scale, some say that prohibitive designations (in other words, preservation areas where no permit would be granted) could raise legal questions about whether the regulatory agency was "taking" the property of wetland owners. Policies such as transfers of development rights could reduce this concern. At the other end of the scale, particularly in the absence of strong mitigation requirements, others see the lowest designation as sanctioning the conversion of lower value wetlands. This criticism can be reduced, if existing levels of protection under Section 404 and other state and local programs are provided. The Massachusetts system, for example, in effect raises the average level of protection for all wetlands by designating some as off limits and retaining existing permit procedures for the remainder. If, however, ranking systems evolve into a proliferation of categories or require detailed case-by-case review within all categories, some of the benefits of consistency and predictability are lost.

What Issues Should Be Addressed in Implementation?

Comprehensive plans for wetlands management are next to useless if they are not implemented. Yet, relatively little information exists about success in implementing wetlands planning projects. Evaluating this success is complicated by two factors. First, the concept of success is somewhat subjective and likely to vary according to who is doing the evaluation.

Second, existing reports on advanced planning processes contain descriptions of the process and land use issues, but provide little information on responses to plans once they are implemented. Many have not been carried out long enough to make a meaningful evaluation. Nonetheless, one can identify several challenges that are likely to arise in implementing a wetlands management plan.

As noted above, the involvement of all relevant agencies is necessary in order to arrive at a meaningful plan. However, each of these agencies may have public comment or other review procedures which might have the potential to introduce changes to the plan. In addition, new laws, regulations or policies which come into effect following completion of the plan might affect an agency's ability to carry out its commitments. These potential problems underscore the importance of agency representation by those in a position to make commitments, and clear agreements during the negotiations about what authority each agency commits to exercise to implement the plan.

Another vital implementation issue is whether resources are available to effectively implement the plan. Even if responsibilities are clearly assigned, yearly changes in budget allocations and other factors may affect the ability of agencies to follow through on long-term commitments. For example, some of the Anchorage Plan's "preservation" wetlands have been disturbed by users of off-road vehicles, but the municipal government responsible has found itself short of staff to enforce bans on such activities.

In many cases, particularly those that involve planning for an area that does not correspond with existing political jurisdiction, it is necessary to establish a new agency to oversee implementation of the plan. The San Francisco Bay Conservation and Development Commission, the New Jersey Pinelands Commission, the California Coastal Conservancy, and the Adirondack Park Agency are examples of special entities created to implement plans and to provide ongoing capability to update plans and to respond to new challenges that were not foreseen during development of the plan.

If no agency is created it is important that plans seek to assure availability of resources and incorporate mechanisms for monitoring implementation of the plan, enforcing agreements, and resolving future disputes as they arise. These roles and responsibilities might be assigned as part of an agreement on the plan.

CONCLUSION

Negotiated planning processes--those that involve the many interests in wetlands management in joint setting of goals for a particular location and its land or water resources--show considerable promise as a way of arriving at rational, coordinated, and consistent plans for wetlands conservation, restoration, and management. A variety of processes are appropriate for different planning areas and management challenges. Planning processes can be used to address wetlands management issues within the context of multiple objectives (river corridor or greenway planning, for example, which might address open space, recreation, and flood protection, among others); to coordinate the array of government programs which affect wetlands; to implement regulatory and nonregulatory programs, and to develop new policies and address issues outside of the scope of established authorities and procedures. If boundaries are set appropriately, planning processes can allow consideration, within an overall context of development and preservation, not only of wetlands, but also those uplands on which the wetlands may be functionally dependent.

However, if all relevant agencies are not involved in the planning process, or if the agencies are not willing or able to commit to exercise their regulatory authority consistent with the plan, the development of a plan could in effect add a layer of bureaucracy and confusion, rather than reducing it. Nongovernmental interests must also be involved appropriately in the process in order to assure implementation success.

Although existing authority exists in many cases for government agencies to initiate or participate in planning processes, institutional mechanisms to trigger the initiation of a process; the appropriate definition of planning area;

the selection of participants in the planning process; and the effective implementation of plans developed are lacking. Also lacking is information on the long-term success of planning processes, challenges faced in implementation, and implications of problems that arise in implementation for how to better structure the processes at the outset.

REFERENCES

1. Brower, David J. and Daniel S. Carol (Eds.), <u>Managing Land-Use Conflicts, Case Studies in Special Area Management</u> (Durham, N.C.: Duke University Press, 1987).

2. 16 U.S.C.A. Section 1452 (Coastal Zone Management Act).

3. 40 CFR, Section 230.80

4. Oregon Land Conservation and Development Commission, <u>Oregon's Statewide Planning Goals 1985</u> (Salem: Oregon Department of Land Conservation and Development, 1985).

5. Apgar, R.C., 1986. "Florida's State Land Development Plan," <u>Florida Environmental and Urban Issues</u>, vol. 13, no. 3, pp. 4-7.

6. DeGrove, J.M. and W.J. deHaven-Smith, "Resource Planning and Management Committees: A Tool for Intergovernmental Coordination," in press.

7. Harford County Zoning Code, Section 25-6.4(a)(5)(e).

8. Eugster, J.G., 1988. "Steps in State and Local Greenway Conservation Planning," Seminar on Multiple-Objective Greenways and Coordination of Wetland and Floodplain Programs, Washington, D.C.

9. President's Commission on Americans Outdoors, <u>Report to the President of the United States</u>. U.S. Government Printing Office, Washington, D.C., 1986.

10. 16 U.S.C. section 1351 <u>et seq.</u>

11. North Key Largo Habitat Conservation Plan Study Committee, 1986. <u>Final Report</u>.

12. Gosselink, J.G., R. Boumans, D, Durdick, D. Childers, D. Cushman, S. Fields, S. Hamilton, M. Koch, G. Schaffer, J. Visser, <u>Cumulative Impact Assessment and Management in the Tensas River Basin: A Pilot Study</u> (Baton Rouse: Center for Wetland Resources, Louisiana State University, 1987).

13. 16 U.S.C.A. 4601-5, et seq.

14.   P.L. 99-645.

15.   Anderson, Thistle, "Local Government Techniques for Inland Wetlands Protection," report to the EPA Office of Wetland Protection (Ithaca, NY: Cornell University Student Intern, October, 1987).

16.   Platt, Rutherford H., "Coastal Wetland Management.   The Advance Designation Approach," Environment 29(9):16-20, 38-43, November 1987.

17.   Gusman, Sam and Verne Huser, "Mediation in the Estuary," Coastal Zone Management Journal 11(4):273-295, 1984.

18.   Platt, "Coastal Wetland Management"; and Walters, Charles K., "Special Area Management Planning in Coastal Areas: The Process," in Brower and Carol, Managing Land-Use Conflicts, pp. 11-26.

19.   The Habitat Evaluation Procedure (HEP) developed by the U.S. Fish and Wildlife Service, is used to assess the value of a land, water, or wetland resource as habitat for particular species of concern.   Use of HEP yields a numerical index which can be used to compare different habitats or to assess the value of a habitat before and after an impact occurs.

      The Wetland Evaluation Technique (WET, known in an earlier version as the "Adamus Method"), was developed specifically to account for the variety of functions (not only habitat-related) that may be performed by a particular wetland.   It is not an impact assessment technique or a planning tool.

20.   Office of Technology Assessment, Wetlands, their Use and Regulation (Washington, D.C.: Office of Technology Assessment, 1984).

21.   Massachusetts Department of Environmental Quality Engineering, Massachusetts Wetlands and Waterways, November 1984.

Case Examples

1. RAINWATER BASIN

Location. The Rainwater Basin is an area of Nebraska, encompassing 4200 square miles and parts of seventeen counties. The region contains hundreds of isolated prairie wetlands and represents a narrow neck of the central flyway for migrating waterfowl which serves five to seven million ducks and geese each year.

Factors Prompting Initiation of the Program. The total area of wetlands in the Rainwater basin has been reduced to less than 25 percent of its original acreage. Fewer than 400 of the original 4000 marshes remain. As a result of the diminishing wetlands in the Rainwater Basin, waterfowl have been concentrating in increasingly greater densities in the areas that remained, causing outbreaks of density related diseases.

Many of the converted wetlands were drained to increase arable land. Since §404 pertains to discharges of material into wetlands, it has been somewhat ineffective in controlling alterations in the Rainwater Basin. Facing continuing wetland losses and limited funds for acquisition, state natural resource agencies requested management assistance from EPA.

Authorization. The authority to conduct advanced identification programs (ADIDs) is provided EPA through the §404(b)(1) guidelines, Subpart I, under the title "Planning to Shorten Permit Processing Time," and listed in 40 CFR, §230.80. EPA conducts ADIDs in cooperation with appropriate "permitting authorities," generally the Corps.

Definition of Management Area. The Rainwater Basin is a loosely defined ecoregion, consisting of numerous isolated wetland systems. It has no clearly defined boundaries.

Objective. To better protect, enhance and manage the remaining wetlands, and stop unauthorized wetland alteration, the EPA outlined several objectives:

o   collect information necessary for making wetland jurisdictional and delineation determinations;

o   designate wetlands regulated under Section 404 and those that are unsuitable for fill;

o   increase the information base the Corps and other agencies have available for making permit decisions and for taking possible future 404(c) or special case actions--404(c) authority allows EPA to preclude 404 permits in an area before applications for such permits have been filed;

o   work with federal, state, and local organizations to build a unified approach to wetlands protection and management in the Rainwater Basin;

o   increase public awareness of both the importance of these wetlands and the scope of the destruction problem;

o   educate the public on the 404 program and the need to obtain permits before dredge and fill activities;

o   involve landowners and community groups in the advanced identification project and urge community concern.

What was the result?   The process has not been completed, but is expected to result in designation of wetlands areas suitable and unsuitable as disposal sites for dredge and fill material.   Designations will not be legally binding.

Who were the parties involved?   The Rainwater Basin program is primarily a cooperative effort between Nebraska state agencies and federal agencies. Nongovernmental organizations have advisory roles.   The "Interagency Team" of federal and state agencies includes the EPA, Corps, FWS, Nebraska Game and Parks Commission, Nebraska Department of Environmental Control, and SCS. The "Advisory Committee" includes the Nebraska Natural Resources Commission, Ducks Unlimited, and the Wildlife Management Institute.

Special features.   The process has included extensive public information and education through discussions with landowners, public meetings, development of a slide show, and sponsorship of research on the economics of wetland conversion.

For more information, refer to:

1986 EMR Action Plan-Rainwater Basins Wetlands, EPA Region VII.

Feeney, A.   "EPA's Advanced Identification Program for Wetlands Draws Mixed Reaction from Conservationists," Land Letter, Vol. 5, no. 18, 1986.

Furst, F.   "A New Approach to Wetlands Protection for Nebraska's Rainwater Basin," National Wetlands Newsletter, Vol. 8, no. 4, 1986.

2.   TIMBER/FISH/WILDLIFE AGREEMENT

Location.   Washington state.

Factors Prompting Initiation of the Program.   The value of forest resources in Washington makes it the focus of environmental concern.   Yet, the value of the forest industry to the state economy is widely recognized. Several nongovernmental organizations, representing Indian interests, environmental concerns, and the forest products industry, convened to discuss acceptable methods for managing Washington's natural resources for maximum economic and conservation benefits. This effort reflects an attempt to resolve differences at the stage of planning a forestry operation, where all parties involved have the greatest degree of flexibility.

Authorization. The process was a voluntary effort convened by the Northwest Renewable Resources Center.

Definition of Management Area. The negotiating parties directed their recommendations at statewide regulatory and management programs.

Objective. Discussion focused on wildlife and fisheries resources, water quantity and quality, archaeological and cultural resources, and timber production. The wildlife resource goal was to provide the greatest diversity of habitats and species. Fishery goals were directed at maintaining long-term habitat productivity for wild fish and at the protection of hatchery water supplies. Water quantity and quality goals were aimed at meeting the needs of people, fish and wildlife. Archaeological and cultural goals emphasized developing a process to inventory, evaluate, and preserve traditional cultural and archaeological spaces. The goal for timber resources was the continued growth and development of the state's forest products industry, acknowledging its stake in the long-term productivity of both the public and private forest land base.

More specifically, the negotiators sought to:

o   set goals to meet specific needs;

o   evaluate site-specific management needs;

o   move toward problem-solving at the planning stage where all parties have more flexibility;

o   promote a management system that encourages participation and consensus-building;

o   incorporate an adaptive management system;

o   develop and promote inter-disciplinary analysis of priority issues;

o   recommend regulatory changes to the Forest Practices Board;

o   provide measures to ease disproportionate impacts of management requirements on small landowners; and

o   provide measures to achieve better enforcement.

What was the result? A principal result of the process was the cooperation developed through the negotiation process between all parties interested in Washington forest resources. The more tangible products were recommendations for changes in statutes, regulations, and management procedures, and the initiation of coordinated efforts by forest landowners and other interested parties.

Who were the parties involved?   The process involved: Indian Tribes, the Northwest Indian Fisheries Commission, Columbia River Intertribal Fish Commission, Washington Environmental Council, Audubon Society, Washington Forest Protection Association, Washington Farm Forestry Association, Weyerhaeuser, Georgia Pacific, Plum Creek Timber Company, Simpson Timber Company, Washington Department of Natural Resources, Washington Department of Ecology, and Washington Department of Fisheries and Game.

For more information, refer to:

Timber/Fish/Wildlife: A Better Future in Our Woods and Streams, prepared by the Northwest Renewable Resources Center, distributed by the Washington State Department of Natural Resources, 1987.

3.   CREST (Columbia River Estuary Study Task Force)

Location.   The Columbia River Estuary straddles the border between Washington and Oregon.

Factors Prompting Initiation of the Program.   CREST was organized by Oregon and Washington local governments to develop a long-range management plan for the Columbia River Estuary and its shorelands.   The effort was sparked by conflicts pitting development interests against resource protection advocates that underscored the lack of ecological data for informed decision-making and the lack of comprehensive planning that might facilitate development.

Authorization.   The CREST program began as an innovative process to resolve conflicts in advance.   It was initiated by local governments.

Definition of Management Area.   The study included the estuary and its adjacent shorelands.

Objective.   The CREST program was begun in response to a lack of information and planning.   It sought to identify research needs and develop a regional management plan for incorporation into local comprehensive plans. The negotiation and planning processes were designed to identify suitable activities, facilities, and dimensions for development at specific sites around the estuary.   The resulting plan would also describe the conditions under which development could occur to maintain compatibility with estuarine resources. CREST organizers felt the accomplishment of such objectives would enhance the predictability of regulatory processes.

What was the result?   The process led to creation of the Columbia River Estuary Regional Management Plan.   It was developed by local citizen planning committees with the advice of state and federal agencies, included estuary-wide policies, designated areas for development and others for resource protection, and contained standards for uses that could be permitted.

Yet, despite many attempts to reach full agreement, several disputes between local development interests and state and federal agencies were not resolved. Local positions prevailed in the locally adopted plan. The state of Oregon, however, through its State Land Use Act, requires that all local comprehensive plans, including those for estuaries, meet the approval of the Oregon Land Conservation and Development Commission (LCDC) and conform with state planning goals. The initial CREST Plan failed to meet state requirements, and negotiations were held to revise it with the assistance of an independent mediator.

<u>Who were the parties involved?</u> Central to the process was the Columbia River Estuary Taskforce (CREST), which included representatives from local governments of cities in Washington and Oregon that border the estuary. It also involved the Corps of Engineers, Oregon Division of State Lands, Oregon Department of Land Conservation and Development, EPA, National Marine Fisheries Service, Oregon Department of Fish and Wildlife, and U.S. Fish and Wildlife Service

<u>For more information, refer to</u>:

Gusman, S. and V. Huser. "Mediation in the Estuary," <u>Coastal Zone Management Journal</u> 11(4), 1984.

4.   THE PINELANDS NATIONAL RESERVE

<u>Location</u>. The project included 1.1 million acres in the Pinelands area of New Jersey.

<u>Factors Prompting Initiation of the Program</u>. The Pinelands is a unique area, rich in natural resources, particularly wetlands and groundwater. The area faced threats from proposed development, particularly of an airport, and was expected to receive pressure from urban expansion.

<u>Authorization</u>. The Pinelands National Reserve was established by the National Parks and Recreation Act (P.L. 95-625) in 1978. Congress proposed the Reserve as a three level partnership between federal, state, and local governments, whereby state and local planners would create and implement a federally approved management plan. Roughly one third of the area was stringently protected from future development. In the remaining two thirds development that did not degrade the "essential character" of the Pinelands environment would be allowed. The then-governor of new Jersey, Brendan Byrne, through executive order responded to the federal action by creating a special commission to coordinate the necessary planning. The Governor's actions were supported by the state legislature through the New Jersey Pinelands Protection Act.

Definition of Management Area. Boundaries were established by legislation, based on resource characteristics of the area.

Objective. The overall objective was protection of the unique natural and cultural resources of the Pinelands and the indigenous economy. The New Jersey Pinelands Protection Act required the Pinelands Commission (established by State Executive Order) to adopt and implement a Comprehensive Management Plan that the 7 counties and 52 municipalities in the Pinelands region must comply with. The included counties and municipalities were mandated to revise their master plans and zoning ordinances to be consistent with the Commission's Comprehensive Management Plan.

What was the result? Establishment of the preserve has allowed management that focuses on protecting the resources in the area, maintaining scientifically and legally defensible regulatory provisions, and drafting policies that would permit flexible implementation, responsive to legitimate local and individual needs.

Who were the parties involved? Management of the Pinelands is guided by the 15-member Pinelands Commission. The Governor appoints seven members to represent statewide interests, each of the seven Pinelands counties designates a local representative, and one is appointed by the U.S. Secretary of the Interior.

For more information, refer to:

Moore, T.D. "Protecting the Pinelands: The First National Reserve is New Jersey's Special Place," 1987.

Batory, J. and S. Sutro, "The New Jersey Pinelands: An Analysis of Our Country's First National Reserve." Case Study in Americans Outdoors: The Legacy, the Challenge, Report of the President's Commission on Americans Outdoors. Island Press. 1987.

5. CHIWAUKEE PRAIRIE--CAROL BEACH LAND USE PLAN

Location. The Chiwaukee Prairie-Carol Beach Area of Pleasant Prairie in Kenosha County, Wisconsin.

Factors Prompting Initiation of the Program. In Southeastern Wisconsin many public agencies and private interests are concerned about the conflict between resource preservation and urban development, and they attempt to influence land use decisions in the area. Recognizing the importance of the area's natural resource values, as well as the problems of and potential for urban development, the Town of Pleasant Prairie and Kenosha County in 1981 requested assistance in preparing a land use plan for the area that would reconcile conflicting interests.

Authorization. The community sought help from the Southeastern Wisconsin Regional Planning Commission (SEWRPC). The SEWRPC, established by Wisconsin statute, is one of six regional planning commissions in the state. The primary work of identifying areas for protection and designating sites suitable for development was carried out by the staff of the SEWRPC. Support was provided by the Wisconsin Department of Natural Resources, the Kenosha County, and the Town of Pleasant Prairie.

Definition of Management Area. Natural Resource features identify the area. It is contained within a section of town with boundaries defined by the planning agencies, based largely on the extent of urban encroachment on three sides and by the Illinois state line on the fourth.

Objective. The primary purpose of the Chiwaukee Prairie-Carol Beach Planning program was to develop a plan which would identify those lands--both wetlands and uplands--which should be protected and preserved in the public interest for their resource values, and those lands upon which urban growth should continue to be accommodated. The planning process attempted to achieve a sound balance between resource protection and urban development. It also sought a way to fairly compensate landowners whose land would have to be zoned against development to protect the natural resource base.

What was the result? The project resulted in development of a land use plan that the county and town adopted and the state approved. Acquisition of lands is underway.

Who were the parties involved? Development of the plan was undertaken by the Southeastern Wisconsin Regional Planning Commission with the support of a designated advisory committee. The advisory committee was composed of representatives from local and county governments, Wisconsin Electric Power Company, the Corps, a Property Owners Association, Kenosha Water Utility, the Committee on Coastal Management in Southeastern Wisconsin, Wisconsin Department of Natural Resources, The Nature Conservancy, and academic experts.

For more information, refer to:

Southeastern Wisconsin Regional Planning Commission Newsletter 25(2), March-April 1985.

Community Assistance Planning Report No. 88. A Land Use Management Plan for the Chiwaukee Prairie-Carol Beach Area of the Town of Pleasant Prairie, Kenosha County, Wisconsin. Prepared by the Southeastern Wisconsin Regional Planning Commission. 1985.

6.   THE PERCIVAL CREEK CORRIDOR PLAN

Location. Percival Creek stretches 3.3 miles between Black Lake and Capitol Lake through the Cities of Tumwater and Olympia, in Thurston County, Washington.

Factors Prompting Initiation of the Program. The Percival Creek corridor is rich in natural resources and recreational opportunities. Within the 3.3 miles are three distinct creek reaches. Each reach contains a unique mix of water, wetlands, and riparian vegetation that supports a diverse wildlife population.

The resources and amenities of the Percival Creek corridor survive in the midst of an urban area experiencing rapid growth and accompanying development. Due to these pressures, conflicts have arisen between upland activities and the future maintenance of the creek's natural integrity, especially the quality of its water.

Authorization. The project was initiated by the Thurston Regional Planning Council as a Special Area Management Plan. It was funded by a Coastal Zone Management Grant through the Washington Department of Ecology.

Definition of Management Area. The process was designed to cover the entire Percival Creek system, but the boundaries may have been influenced by the extent of urban encroachment.

Objective. Organizers of the program sought to develop a management plan to guide future land use decisions along the creek. Goals for the plan included:

o   providing long-term protection for the creek ecosystem, while maintaining economic vitality and allowing for economic growth;

o   resolving existing regulatory conflicts by combining shoreline development and zoning restrictions;

o   establishing predictability in management of the corridor.

What was the result? The process resulted in creation of the Percival Creek Corridor Plan, which was incorporated into the applicable city and county zoning codes. It was also integrated into the local shoreline master plan for regulating development of shorelands, as required under the Washington Shoreline Management Act.

Who were the parties involved? Development of the Corridor Plan was undertaken by the Thurston Regional Planning Council with support from an advisory committee, consisting of representatives from local jurisdictions, affected state agencies, an Indian tribe, property owners, and community groups.

Special features. Creation of the Plan required an inventory and classification of wetland resources. An interagency team of state, federal, and local wetlands experts identified and delineated the boundaries of wetlands in the management area. Inventory and classification efforts were instrumental in guiding the planning task force in developing a management plan which recognized the relative importance of each wetland and avoided critical habitat areas in siting potential road and utility crossings.

For more information, refer to:

Percival Creek Corridor Plan. Thurston Regional Planning Council. 1985.

7.   NORTH KEY LARGO HABITAT CONSERVATION PLAN

Location. North Key Largo, Florida

Factors Prompting Initiation of the Program. North Key Largo provides habitat for four species listed as endangered under the Endangered Species Act--the American crocodile, the Key Largo woodrat, the Key Largo cotton mouse, and the Schaus swallowtail butterfly. Land clearing in conjunction with development on North Key Largo threatens all four species, as does the establishment of a resident human population. The crocodile is the species most reliant on the region's wetlands, inhabiting shallow mangrove wetlands in the area. Environmental groups sued, seeking to halt development activities and proposals in the area, claiming violations of the Endangered Species Act and other federal laws.

Authorization. The Endangered Species Act prohibits activities, including development, which "harass, harm, or kill" designated species. Section 10 of the Act, however, provides a mechanism for the "incidental" taking of endangered species with a permit issued under provisions of an approved Habitat Conservation Plan which provide for the overall enhancement of the habitat. In 1985, Florida Governor Bob Graham established a study committee to prepare a Habitat Conservation Plan for the North Key Largo area. The work of the committee was financed by an appropriation from the U.S. Congress and matching funds and in-kind services provided by private interests, Monroe County, and the State of Florida.

Definition of Management Area. The area is bounded on three sides by water. Although it may not define the exact extent of endangered species habitat, a highway intersection designates the southern boundary of the management area.

Objective. The Habitat Conservation Plan was prepared as a means of reconciling the habitat needs of the endangered species in North Key Largo with the investment and development expectations of the landowners in the area. Agreement on the plan was necessary to target land acquisition objectives, ensure consistent permitting, and to enable limited development while providing overall protection to the habitat.

Objectives of Habitat Conservation Plans under the Endangered Species Act are to:

o   preserve endangered species habitat in sufficient quantity to accommodate stable reproductive populations and protect it from human activity and presence;

o   limit human activities in the vicinity of the animals' habitat to those that are compatible with the survival of the species;

o   enhance the animals' habitat by implementing mitigation strategies designed to maintain the functional integrity of specific areas; and

o   implement recovery actions necessary to improve habitat quality and enhance the survival of the species.

<u>What was the result?</u>   The Committee established a study program to research the needs of the endangered species and assess the feasibility of various management and development options.   From the information it assembled, the Committee formulated a series of discrete policy statements and management assumptions to constitute the basis and guiding principles for the Habitat Conservation Plan.

The Plan provides for the designation of areas of large contiguous tropical hardwood hammock as "conserved habitat" and limits development to a series of discrete nodes.   The Plan specifies the character, location, and magnitude of development that is authorized within the development nodes and provides that maximum densities within the nodes can only be achieved through the use of development rights transferred from lands designated as conserved habitat.   The Plan also deferred all development until after August 1, 1988 to provide a reasonable opportunity to pursue the public acquisition of land in North Key Largo.

Since the development that is authorized by the Plan will continue to have some impact on the four endangered species, the Plan provides specific management responses to each of the expected direct or indirect impacts.   The responses are to be implemented through regulations imposed by Monroe County and through private covenants and contracts between landowners, interested parties, and developers.   The Plan further provides for a series of mitigation and recovery programs to protect and enhance the environmental values of the area and to enhance the potential for survival of the four endangered species.

The Plan was negotiated among the parties in one year's time.   It is still awaiting formal adoption by the U.S. Fish and Wildlife Service.

<u>Who were the parties involved?</u>   The study committee established by Governor Graham to prepare the Habitat Conservation Plan consisted of private landowners, officials from local, regional, state, and federal agencies with jurisdiction over or an interest in either the endangered species present or the land use on North Key Largo.   It also included representatives from several environmental and public interest groups.

For more information, refer to:

North Key Largo Habitat Conservation Plan Study Committee Final Report.
1986.

8. APALACHICOLA BAY NATIONAL ESTUARINE SANCTUARY

Location. Apalachicola Bay, Franklin County, Florida

Factors Prompting Initiation of the Program. Apalachicola Bay receives waters from a drainage basin that extends into parts of Georgia and Alabama. It is one of the most productive estuarine systems in North America and remains in near-pristine condition. Because it is a National Estuarine Sanctuary, management must be characterized by intensive coordination between local, state, and federal regulatory agencies.

The movement to have the Apalachicola Bay designated an estuarine sanctuary began at the local level. Fishermen and seafood dealers, encouraged by the scientific community, pressed for designation when proposals for development on the bay's barrier islands and efforts to channelize the Apalachicola River appeared to threaten their livelihoods. Local interests received support from the Florida Department of Environmental Regulation (DER). With the help of the DER and outside technical assistance, they developed a sanctuary proposal that was accepted by the National Oceanic and Atmospheric Administration (NOAA), the administrator of the National Estuarine Sanctuary Program.

Authorization. The National Estuarine Sanctuary Program was created by the Coastal Zone Management Act (CZMA). It requires coordinated planning and management in estuarine sanctuaries.

Definition of Management Area. The lack of quantitative data documenting cause and effect relationships between land use and estuary conditions complicates efforts to determine how much of an estuary's drainage basin should be preserved to prevent its degradation. Questions concerning the emphasis to place on preserving land in the watershed, relative to managing shorelines remain largely unanswered. Nevertheless, boundaries for the Apalachicola Sanctuary were set to include the bay with its associated tidal creeks, marshes and bayous, and portions of the Apalachicola barrier islands. It encompasses roughly 193,000 acres, of which 135,000 are prior state-owned submerged lands, and 58,000 are transition zones--shorelands and tidally-influenced areas.

Objective. After the Bay was officially designated a sanctuary in 1980, a Sanctuary Management Committee was appointed. Initially the Committee tried to oversee all permit authorization, but was unable to achieve that goal. It then chose to rely, instead, on ecologically-based land use controls and special management of shoreline zones. The shoreline protection strategy contains provisions for protecting transitional areas and submerged habitats, controlling pollutants that originated on land, and guiding development in hazard-prone areas. Government and private organizations also maintain efforts to acquire sensitive and ecologically significant lands in the area.

What was the result? The cooperative management efforts eventually led to the passage by the Florida Legislature of the Apalachicola Bay Area Protection Act. The Act designated the area for special state concern and provided for state oversight on local land use planning. It also contained specific requirements for managing shoreline zones. It also established the principle that economic growth and diversification would be permitted only if it was "consistent with protection of the natural resources of the Apalachicola Bay area through appropriate management of the land and water systems."

Who were the parties involved? Discussion over the best way to manage the Bay began with local seafood dealers and fishermen, then spread to involve the Florida DER, Florida DNR, property owners, the Corps, navigation interests, and officials from the affected counties. The process led to creation of the Apalachicola Resource Management and Planning Program and, subsequently, to designation of the area as a National Estuarine Sanctuary.

For more information, refer to:

Clark, J.R. and S.T. McCreary. "Special Area Management at Estuarine Reserves," in Brower and Carol, eds., Managing Land-Use Conflicts. Duke University Press, 1987.

9. **CITY OF ANCHORAGE SPECIAL AREA MANAGEMENT PLAN**

Location. Anchorage, Alaska

Factors Prompting Initiation of the Program. The process was jointly initiated by the Corps, the Alaska Coastal Zone Management Program, and the City of Anchorage, in recognition of three factors:

o   Anchorage has considerable wetlands resources;

o   the availability of upland development sites is dwindling;

o   the Section 404 permitting requirements are uncertain.

Authorization. The 1980 amendments to the CZMA encourage federal, state, and local agencies to develop SAMPs where appropriate. The Corps can initiate SAMPs to facilitate the Section 404 regulatory process.

Definition of Management Area. The boundaries were established on the basis of existing local jurisdiction, including only the City of Anchorage.

Objective. The cooperating parties sought to improve predictability in permitting, educate the public on the relative functions and values of wetlands, and, where possible, link wetland values to appropriate degrees of management.

What was the result? The process resulted in a final document which identifies wetland areas suitable for preservation, conservation, or development. Designated preservation sites have no legally binding protection, although both the City and Corps agreed not to approve permits in those areas. The effort produced general permits to issue in areas suitable for development.

Who were the parties involved? Development of the management plan involved the Corps, City of Anchorage, EPA, FWS, National Marine Fisheries Service, Alaska Department of Fish and Game, Alaska Department of Environmental Conservation, Alaska DNR, Alaska Department of Transportation and Public Facilities, the Real Estate Association, and the Trustees of Alaska (an environmental group).

For more information, refer to:

Information was provided by David B. Barrows, U.S. Army Corps of Engineers, Washington, D.C., 1987.

10. HACKENSACK MEADOWLANDS

Location. The Hackensack Meadowlands lie just across the Hudson River from Manhattan in northeastern New Jersey.

Factors Prompting Initiation of the Program. The Meadowlands is an extensive urban wetlands system that faces tremendous pressure as a site for highways, industrial facilities, and other development. Two distinct phases of planning have occurred: 1) coordinated planning for orderly development by the Hackensack Meadowlands Development Commission (HMDC), which began in 1968; and 2) integration of an advanced identification program for wetlands into HMDC planning through cooperation with EPA and the Corps, which began in 1985.

Authorization. The HMDC was established by the State of New Jersey in 1968 to protect the environment of the Meadowlands, promote orderly development, and provide a location for solid waste disposal. The HMDC promulgated a Master Plan in 1972 and has since attempted to balance environmental and development interests. Some environmental groups, however, have criticized HMDC decisions about wetlands as inconsistent with objectives of the federal Clean Water Act, and in late 1985 the Commission began efforts to revise its Master Plan.

At the same time, because of the Meadowlands' urban location, the strength of development pressure, and questions over the HMDC's effectiveness in protecting wetlands, EPA and the Corps began a cooperative program under §230.80 of the 404(b)(1) guidelines to identify wetlands suitable and unsuitable for receiving discharges. The advanced identification (ADID) results were intended to be incorporated into the development of the revised Master Plan, and the agencies have contemplated issuance of an Environmental Impact Statement (EIS) by the Corps on proposed acceptance of wetland discharges in accordance with the revised Plan.

Definition of Management Area. The Hackensack Meadowlands District was legislatively established by the State for coordinated land use planning. The District contains 19,730 acres of land in 14 New Jersey townships and in 1972 included 10,524 acres (as identified by the HMDC) of estuarine wetlands. Approximately 8000 acres of wetlands remain today.

Objective. The HMDC was created to carry out environmental resource inventories and area-wide planning in an effort to reduce conflicts between wetlands protection and development. Under the 1972 Master Plan it has initiated innovative planning and cost-sharing techniques, aimed primarily at preserving open space, but also at limiting pollutant discharges into wetlands, and at equalizing benefits and tax revenue losses across the 14 affected municipalities. In revising the Master Plan, the HMDC originally intended to integrate data gathered by the ADID effort.

Through its involvement in the Meadowlands ADID, EPA has hoped to: 1) relay upfront information on the value of Meadowlands wetlands, and the potential significance of development impacts; 2) address potential cumulative wetlands impacts; 3) identify wetlands appropriate for mitigation efforts; and 4) facilitate the §404 permit process.

What was the result? Since 1985, the two processes--HMDC management and the ADID program--have proceeded in parallel. The time required for ADID data gathering and analysis has slowed integration. Differences in the mandates of the agencies have also made coordination difficult. The HMDC suggests that some federal decisions and attempts to enforce mitigation requirements might be inconsistent with the HMDC Master Plan and its revisions. For example, in August of 1987 EPA announced a proposal to issue a §404(c) denial of a Corps §404 permit that the HMDC had approved in the belief that the disputed area was not wetlands. The HMDC also maintains that, in reviewing mitigation requirements, it lacks authority to consider practicable alternatives to wetlands alterations when alternative sites lie outside the Meadowlands District.

The HMDC now plans to issue a draft of its revised Master Plan in early 1988 before ADID analyses are complete.

Who were the parties involved? The attempt at integrating the ADID process into the HMDC revised Master Plan has involved the HMDC, EPA, Corps, FWS, NMFS, and the New Jersey Department of Environmental Protection.

For more information, refer to:

Anderson, T. "Local Government Techniques for Inland Wetlands Protection," report to the EPA Office of Wetland Protection, Washington, D.C., 1987.

Baldwin, M.F. "Interim Report to Urban Land Institute Advisory Group on Federal Permitting," (draft) prepared for the Urban Land Institute, 1987.

"Advanced Identification Study of Critical Wetlands: Hackensack Meadowlands, New Jersey," Information provided by Brenda Davis, Office of the Governor, State of New Jersey, prepared with assistance from EPA Region 2, 1987.

NONREGULATORY PROGRAMS PROMOTING WETLANDS PROTECTION

Abby Goldsmith and Edwin H. Clark II

The essential characteristic of nonregulatory wetland protection programs is that the decision about what should be done with the property ultimately lies with the land owner. Under regulatory approaches, that decision is shifted, at least in part, to the regulatory authority. In practice, however, the distinction between the two may become blurred. For instance, many nonregulatory approaches require that both the government and the land owner agree on how the land is to be protected or managed before the land owner can benefit from the program. And in some cases the nonregulatory program may be designed to complement a regulatory approach.

Federal, state, and some local governments have adopted a number of different types of nonregulatory programs which result in the protection of wetlands. Some of these involve the government (or some semi-government or private protection organization) acquiring full or partial title to the land. Some provide financial inducements--for instance, tax credits or government payments--to the land owner for protecting or managing the land in a desired manner. Some rely primarily upon education and persuasion.

Some of the existing nonregulatory programs were established solely for the purpose of protecting wetland areas. Many, however, have broader goals, and the protection of wetlands is only a part of or even incidental to the broader purpose. And finally, these programs have tended in the past to focus primarily on protecting existing wetlands from alteration, but the approaches, and in some cases the existing programs, could also be used to encourage private restoration and enhancement efforts as well.

The following discussion of nonregulatory programs focuses primarily on describing alternative approaches and providing examples of where and how

---

The authors are former junior associate and former vice president, respectively, The Conservation Foundation, Washington, D.C.

they have been used. The appendix to this chapter briefly summarizes a number of examples or "success stories" of nonregulatory approaches. Unfortunately, very little information is available which would allow an analysis of how effective and efficient such programs are in providing permanent protection to the resource.

ACQUISITION

The most permanent method of nonregulatory protection is usually acquisition--either by the public sector or a private, semi-public organization acting in the public interest. Acquisition alone, however, does not guarantee that the wetlands will be protected. The acquiring organization may not manage the land in such a way as to protect all of its wetland functions, or events outside the boundary of the property--such as the diversion or contamination of the property's water supply--may also reduce these values.

Acquisition can be complete, or "in fee-simple", which involves acquiring full ownership of the land and all the rights which go with such ownership. Alternatively, it can be partial, involving only some of the rights, as in a conservation easement. In less-than-fee ownership the original owner retains the basic property ownership (and liability), but gives up the right to use or manage it in specified ways. The owner, for instance, may sell the development rights to the land, in which case that owner and all subsequent owners no longer have the right to build housing or other development on the land. A conservation easement also requires the owner to maintain the land in an undeveloped state. The conditions and restrictions of less-than-fee acquisition can be tailored to the specific needs both of the acquiring organization and the land owner.

Less-than-fee acquisition has the advantage that the original land owner retains responsibility for managing the land and most of the liabilities associated with land ownership. It may also be less expensive than fee-simple acquisition, although in many instances the cost of a conservation easement is almost as high as the cost of fee-simple acquisition. Less-than-fee acquisition also limits the uses the acquiring organization can make of the land, and requires some vigilance on the part of that organization to ensure that the original and subsequent land owners do not violate the conditions of the easement.

In both fee-simple and less-than-fee acquisition, the terms of the transfer can also be negotiated to serve the interests of the acquiring organization and the original land owner. For example, · the purchase can be immediate or delayed, temporary (a lease), or permanent. In some cases, the land is left for some length of time under the management of the original owner through a "lease-back" or a retained life estate. In all these cases, the new owner may impose stipulations on the use of the land while the original owner remains.

Federal Acquisition

The principal owners and managers of wetlands at the federal level are the U.S. Department of the Interior (DOI), including the Fish and Wildlife Service (FWS), National Park Service (NPS), and the Bureau of Land Management (BLM); the U.S. Department of Commerce, specifically the National Oceanic and Atmospheric Administration (NOAA); and the U.S. Department of Agriculture (USDA), specifically the U.S. Forest Service (USFS). Other federal agencies such as the Bureau of Reclamation (BuRec) in the DOI, the U.S. Army Corps of Engineers (Corps), and the U.S. Department of Defense (DOD) also have wetlands on their lands. In many cases, however, these agencies own and manage their lands for reasons unrelated to any wetland values they may provide. Typically, the agencies do not even have an inventory of their wetlands, and may manage the land in such a way as to diminish these values. In some cases, to reduce this problem, the DOI and the USFS have contracted with Ducks Unlimited, a nonprofit organization, to manage some of the wetlands these agencies own.

The federal government has no program that focuses solely on acquiring new wetlands. However, the following programs do acquire substantial wetland areas to protect wildlife habitat, open space, or some other value that wetlands provide.

* The National Wildlife Refuge System, a 90-million acre nationwide network of lands and waters administered by the FWS, is set aside chiefly for wildlife conservation. Since three-fourths of the refuges were established for the protection of migratory waterfowl, millions of acres of wetlands are protected under this system. The majority of the funds for the purchase of National Wildlife Refuges come from the Migratory Bird Conservation Fund.[1]

* The National Estuarine Sanctuary Program,[2] administered by NOAA, establishes a national system of estuarine sanctuaries representative of biogeographical regions and estuarine types in the United States. These sanctuaries, of which 16 had been designated by April 1986, are established and managed through a cooperative federal-state effort for long-term research, education, and interpretation. The National Marine Sanctuary Program, a similar effort for marine areas also includes wetlands because submerged lands are some of the target areas.

* The NPS protects an unknown number of wetlands within national parks, recreation areas and other types of park service properties. Wetlands may also be protected on other federal lands, for example, within wilderness areas or wild and scenic river corridors managed by the NPS, the BLM, or the USFS.

* The Canadian Minister of the Environment and the U.S. Secretary of the Interior signed a joint agreement in May 1986 to restore, protect, and improve over 6 million acres of waterfowl habitat by the year 2000. The North American Waterfowl Agreement recommends that federal, state and local governments and private organizations in the United States spend $1.3 billion (1985 U.S. dollars) and that Canadian governments and organizations spend $375.5 million to carry out the objectives of the agreement. Contributions totaling $8 million have been raised through an innovative multiple matching effort. State wildlife agencies contributed a

total of $1 million dollars, Ducks Unlimited matched the states' $1 million, the National Fish and Wildlife Foundation matched the $2 million sum, and Habitat Canada matched the United State's total of $4 million.

In the past, some of these programs have tended to acquire lands on somewhat of an *ad hoc* basis rather than establishing a clear plan establishing acquisition priorities. Two relatively recent initiatives have attempted to correct this problem:

o   The Emergency Wetlands Resources Act of 1986 (EWRA)[3] contains a provision for establishing a National Wetlands Priority Conservation Plan which will guide acquisition efforts.

o   The FWS has designed a 10-year acquisition plan which aims to protect more than 2.6 million acres of waterfowl habitat through purchases of land or conservation easements at an estimated program cost of at least $563 million.

Some of the funds for these acquisition initiatives come from general revenues. However, most are funded by one of the following special purpose programs:

o   The Migratory Bird Conservation Fund is reserved for the purchase of small wetlands and prairie potholes for "waterfowl production areas". Funding comes from the sale of duck stamps which all migratory bird hunters over the age of 16 must purchase. The Wetlands Loan Act allows Congress to appropriate advance loans against the sale of future duck stamps. Provisions of the EWRA doubles the price of the federal duck stamp over the next five years with most of the proceeds earmarked for wetland acquisition, and forgave the loans that had accumulated from previous expenditures.

o   Another provision of the EWRA authorizes entrance fees at certain national wildlife refuges, with 70 percent of the proceeds channeled into the Migratory Bird Conservation Fund.

o   The Land and Water Conservation Fund, funded primarily from receipts for off-shore oil and gas leasing and development, is spent to acquire recreational lands and natural areas which can include wetlands. The EWRA specifically includes wetlands as types of lands that can be acquired with these funds.

o   The Pittman-Robertson Federal Aid in Wildlife Restoration Act[4] and the Dingell-Johnson Federal Aid in Fish Restoration Act[5] authorize federal matching grants to states for wildlife and fish habitat restoration. Funds come from excise taxes on hunting and fishing equipment, which totaled approximately $243 million in 1985.

State Acquisition

States also acquire wetlands for wildlife refuges, as part of their state park systems, or under other programs, either out of their own funds or with monies made available for this purpose by the federal government. Some states have extensive acquisition programs which include fund raising, planning, and management components. Some examples are:

o   Through purchase and donation, Florida has acquired hundreds of thousands of acres, much of it wetlands or areas adjacent to wetlands. In the next ten years, Florida's state agencies, regional water management districts, and local governments will have the capability to generate over $1 billion to acquire more land. The major funding sources are bonds, general revenue (made up largely of state taxes), documentary stamp taxes, severance taxes, and tourist impact taxes with additional funds coming from ad valorem taxes and revenues from state forests and hunting permits.

o   In addition to purchasing land at the state level, New Jersey's Green Acres program provides grants and low interest loans to counties and communities for the acquisition or development of open space for outdoor recreation. A bonus is granted if the lands are environmentally sensitive. Over 650,000 acres of land have been acquired, a substantial amount of which are inland wetlands.

o   The California Coastal Conservancy, funded by state general obligation bonds and devoted primarily to resolving conflicts over coastal resources, manages a Resource Enhancement Program which preserves wetlands through acquisition, restoration, and the prevention of further degradation. In addition, California's Land Bank Act creates a trust to acquire real property or any interest in real property for preservation or restoration of wetlands.

Many states also have special programs for raising funds for the acquisition of wetlands in addition to receiving direct appropriations for land acquisition. Some of the programs do not exclusively protect wetlands but wetlands are included in an effort to protect values that they provide.[6]

o   Over half the states have their own waterfowl stamp that hunters must purchase in addition to the federal stamp, with much of the funds channeled toward habitat acquisition.

o   Thirty-two states have check-offs for nongame wildlife on their income tax forms. In 1983, proceeds from these sources totaled about $9 million.

o   Documentary and severance tax proceeds go to land acquisition in Florida, Tennessee, South Carolina, Maryland, Arkansas, and Washington.

o   In Missouri, one-eighth of one percent of the state sales tax is earmarked for the Department of Environmental Conservation, a large portion of which goes to land acquisition. This totals about $50 to $60 million annually.

o   California, Minnesota, Rhode Island, Connecticut, and New York have approved millions of dollars of bonds for land acquisition.

o   The Wyoming Game and Fish Department has a wetland avifauna team comprised of state and federal agency biologists who meet annually to identify and rank high priority wetlands for acquisition, improvement, and development programs. The coordinator of this program seeks outside and internal funding sources to complete projects.

State wetlands acquisition policies are also influenced by federal programs. The EWRA contains provisions that require states to consider wetlands in their public acquisition programs and to establish a state priority plan for acquisition. The Coastal Zone Management Act[7] (CZMA) encourages and funds states to develop coastal management plans which include wetland protection measures. The states are authorized to receive matching grants for wildlife conservation by the Pittman-Robertson, Dingell-Johnson, and the Fish and Wildlife Conservation Acts,[8] and for recreation and open space through the Land and Water Conservation Fund. These funds can be used for land acquisition, as well as research, education, management, restoration, and development of facilities.

Local Government Acquisition

Like state governments, local governments may acquire wetlands to protect open space, wildlife habitat, and water quality. Funds for these activities are generated through appropriations from general revenues (usually based on property tax receipts), special purpose bonds, and intergovernmental transfers. For example, Suffolk County, New York has approved a $65 million bond for natural area acquisition.

Private Acquisition

Private organizations devoted to the preservation of wetlands for open space, wildlife protection, hunting, fishing, and other purposes have played a large role in land acquisition. Organizations such as The Nature Conservancy (TNC), Ducks Unlimited, The Trust for Public Land, and the National Audubon Society (Audubon) have acquired substantial amounts of wetlands, often using creative financing techniques. Local land trusts throughout the United States have developed similar strategies to assist landowners in protecting valuable lands.

Funds for private acquisition come from cash donations, membership fees, foundation grants, mitigation fees, or other techniques. Ducks Unlimited also has a stamp program for raising funds. In addition to outright purchase, private organizations can acquire land through donations or exchanges.

Joint Efforts

Often a cooperative effort involving both the public and private sectors is needed to acquire a parcel of land. Since each of them will have access to different resources, a joint effort can often protect an area that might otherwise be unattainable. For example, a nonprofit organization may have the resources to purchase a parcel of land as soon as the opportunity arises, and may be able to purchase it at a lower cost than a government agency. Thus, the organization can buy a piece of property quickly and then resell it to a government agency when appropriations are forthcoming. Nonprofit organizations such as TNC and Audubon are often better able to carry out exchanges since they are not hampered by government restrictions on selling land and can, unlike a state, work out interstate exchanges. Certain agencies and organizations such as the California Coastal Conservancy and TNC specialize in negotiating acquisition agreements that involve a number of parties. For example:

o   Although the Ohio Power Company offered its Sandusky Bay property, valued at $4.7 million, as a bargain sale for $2.8 million to TNC, the organization alone could not come up with the total sum. The state of Ohio appropriated $2 million, contributed another $300,000 from general funds and the Richard King Mellon Foundation provided a loan for the remainder. The area is now protected by TNC as one of Ohio's largest public wildlife areas.

o   The California Coastal Conservancy acquired 7,130 acres of the Sinkyone Wilderness jointly with the California Department of Parks and Recreation, the Save the Redwoods League, and the Trust for Public Land.

TAX CREDITS AND EXEMPTIONS

All levels of government can adopt provisions in their tax codes to encourage the protection of wetlands by reducing the tax burden on property owners who protect or manage their land in designated ways.

These provisions may support acquisition programs (resulting in the permanent protection of wetlands) by providing tax benefits to owners who sell or donate wetlands to the government or to a qualified conservation organization. Income tax codes, for instance, may allow deductions for charitable contributions, involuntary conversions, and some types of land exchanges.

Other types of tax breaks, for instance reductions in state or local property taxes, do not require that the owner transfer any part of the land title. Such programs may encourage the temporary protection of the resource, but do not ensure its permanent protection. If, however, a land owner does provide permanent protection by transferring the development rights on a parcel of land to a government or nonprofit conservation organization, this should result in reduced property tax payments reflecting the reduced market value of the land. Such benefits resulting from easement transfers should occur regardless of whether the tax code has any special provisions for open space protection.

Most of the existing tax exemptions are not focused on wetlands alone, but apply to a wide range of natural areas and open space.

Federal Tax Incentives

The federal tax code allows landowners who donate land or easements to qualified conservation organizations to deduct the value of their donation as a charitable contribution in computing their income taxes. Other tax incentives promoting land or easement transfers are:

o When an individual or corporation sells property to a qualified conservation organization at less than market value (as a bargain sale), the donor not only saves in the form of reduced capital gains or income taxes on the appreciated market value, but may be able to claim an income tax deduction by listing the difference between the market value and the purchase value as a contribution.

o Involuntary conversions for destruction or condemnation of property give the taxpayer the benefit of being able to defer tax liability on the sale.

o A land owner can defer any tax by exchanging land for land of equivalent value rather than selling it.

The Tax Reform Act of 1986,[9] which reduces tax rates, may change the degree of charitable giving. Some argue that the reduction of the rate in the highest tax brackets will encourage charitable contributions since, if taxpayers pay lower taxes, they will have more money to contribute. On the other hand, the after-tax cost of charitable contributions will be higher than it used to be because there will be less of a tax break. Also, the new Alternative Minimum Tax Rules now disallow the deduction for the appreciation portion of contributed property. On the whole, it is too early to tell what the net effect of the Tax Reform Act will be on charitable giving.

State Tax Incentives

More than half of the states have tax programs that encourage the protection of open space including wetlands. Tax advantages for conservation can include a reduction in property tax, income tax, gift tax, inheritance tax, or capital gains tax. For example:

o   Property tax abatement is offered to land owners who retain their wetlands in Iowa, Minnesota, and New Hampshire.

o   Minnesota exempts wetlands not receiving other compensation from local property taxes. The state also gives property tax credits on tillable land to land owners who agree not to drain wetland property.

o   In New York, land owners who have been denied permits to develop wetlands are offered a reduction in property tax.

o   Property tax incentives for protecting open space, which can apply to wetlands, exist in Connecticut, Delaware, Maine, New Hampshire, North Carolina, Rhode Island, Tennessee, Vermont, and Virginia.

o   In Connecticut, Maine, Oregon, and Vermont, wetlands are protected under other categories such as recreation, agriculture, or timberlands, which make them eligible for property tax incentives.

o   In Delaware, Maryland, New Jersey, Rhode Island, and South Carolina, land owners can receive property tax reductions for granting conservation easements.

o   Delaware, Maryland, North Carolina, Oregon, Rhode Island, Vermont and Virginia, offer a charitable deduction from state income tax for donation of interests in land. Some of the laws require that the donation be made to a qualified conservation organization.

The incentives provided by property and most other types of tax exemptions, of course, depend upon the market value of the land. In rural areas where wetlands may have a very low market value, tax exemptions may make little difference in total tax payments, and therefore, provide limited incentive for wetlands protection. In areas with higher property values, however, these incentives may be important.

Local Tax Incentives

Local governments can also provide tax benefits by lowering property taxes on lands on which conservation efforts take place. In some cases, the states provide assistance to local governments to encourage this. For example, in Iowa, New York, Pennsylvania, and Vermont, the states reimburse localities for the reduction in the tax base that results from lower property taxes.

SUBSIDIES FOR WETLAND PROTECTION

In some cases, governments and private organizations may pay land owners for setting aside land for conservation purposes even though the government does not acquire any interest in the land. Most of the existing subsidy programs provide only temporary protection to the land. Some operate on a year-to-year basis. Others may involve an agreement with the land owner to protect the land for several years, and these agreements may be renewed when the initial period is up. Typically, the land owner is free to do whatever he or she wants with the land when the agreement period is completed or the subsidies are no longer paid. Ensuring that the land owner adheres to the conditions of the subsidy agreement may involve periodic inspections by the implementing agency.

The USDA's Water Bank Program, authorized in 1970 and expanded in 1980, pays farmers to keep wetlands out of production and shares the costs for certain conservation practices. These payments are negotiated on the basis of five year contracts. The program operates primarily in migratory waterfowl flyways. By 1985, Congress had appropriated nearly $130 million for the Water Bank Program, protecting 605,977 acres of land. However, appropriations in 1986 and 1987 were at an all time low of $8,371,000, compared to an authorization of $30 million. The USDA also has helped finance the construction of millions of farm ponds in the United States which have often created new wetlands where none existed before.

The USDA's Conservation Reserve Program, authorized by the Food Security Act of 1985, may also protect some wetlands, at least indirectly, as farmers set aside highly erodible lands for at least 10 years. Under certain conditions, the lands could be converted to wetlands since shallow water is an approved cover type. (Under current policies this could only occur with lands subject to unusually high wind erosion.) The program may also curb indirect alteration of wetlands by reducing sediment and pesticide runoff from adjacent lands which are set aside in the conservation reserve. Some parties favor expanding the potential for wetlands protection under this program by also allowing the conservation reserve to be used to protect wetlands either directly or indirectly by protecting regional water supplies or preventing serious nonpoint-source water pollution problems.

The Farm Debt Restructure and Conservation Set-Aside provision of the Food Security Act also allows the Farmers Home Loan Administration (FmHA) to provide debt relief to land owners if they are willing to set aside wetlands for 50 years, or undertake other conservation measures. However, very little use has been made of these provisions.

In Wyoming's rangeland stewardship project, federal and state agencies give financial assistance to landowners completing habitat improvement projects. The land improvement plan is designed by a committee composed of federal and state biologists and local land owners.

Subsidies by Private Organizations

Ducks Unlimited and other clubs make rental payments to land owners to set aside their land for conservation purposes, or hunting and/or fishing. This differs from a conservation easement in that the land owner maintains full title to the land and all rights on it.

TRANSFERABLE DEVELOPMENT RIGHTS

Another mechanism which state and local governments can use to provide a financial reward to land owners who agree to protect their wetlands is to allow them to sell the development rights to other land owners. If, for instance, zoning or other development regulations allow no more than an average of one house per acre, a transferable development rights scheme will allow a land owner wishing to preserve, say, 50 acres of wetlands, to sell the rights to build the 50 houses that could have been constructed on this land to another land owner. The purchaser can then use these rights to build more houses on his or her land. Under such a scheme, the seller receives some financial reward for protecting the land at no financial cost to government.

Such schemes have been adopted by some local governments, such as Montgomery County, Maryland, to protect open space including wetlands. However, as appealing as they may appear in theory, they often have not worked particularly well in actual practice.

EDUCATION AND RESEARCH

Public education efforts can play an important role in encouraging wetlands protection by making land owners, local governments, and the general public more aware of the values that wetlands provide, the threats to this resource, the rate at which these lands are being lost, the relative importance of particular types of wetlands, the effect of certain activities and policies on wetland functions, and the nature of the programs which exist to protect them. Such education efforts operating by themselves can be effective by directing more attention to the need for wetlands protection by individuals, nonprofit organizations, and governments. They are also important in increasing the effectiveness of other regulatory and nonregulatory programs for wetlands protection.

More information (which may often require additional research) on wetlands hydrology and ecology, on wetlands management techniques, and on methods for successfully restoring and creating wetlands will help people adopt more effective land management techniques. Such education and technical assistance efforts are particularly important in promoting voluntary wetlands restoration and creation efforts. These can be complicated undertakings, often requiring hydrological modifications, and are likely to fail if not undertaken and managed properly.

Public information can be provided through specific educational outreach programs and through existing institutions such as state game and fish information and education branches, private conservation organizations, government and university extension services, and local conservation districts.

Public Activities

Federal, state, and local agencies conduct research, provide grants to research organizations, fund educational programs, and dispatch extension agents to educate land owners on the values of their land. Local governments can plan for the wise use of wetlands by including them in land use plans. Below are some examples of a few education programs conducted by the public sector:

o   Kentucky's adopt-a-wetland program includes education on wetland management and conservation and initiates projects to enhance specific wetland areas.

o   The Washington State Department of Ecology has developed a clearinghouse for information regarding the preservation of wetlands in the state. This includes a guide for land owners and government officials outlining exactly what individuals can do with wetlands on their property.

o   Canada has a land owner's guide, as do some state agencies, to improve wildlife habitat on private lands. This information is distributed free to land owners and deals with developing and improving wetlands.

Private Efforts

Private organizations contribute to efforts to encourage the conservation of wetlands through wetland inventories, scientific and policy research, and public education and outreach programs. They also disseminate information to their members on government activities and their consequences with regard to wetlands.

The Nature Conservancy cooperates with state agencies in developing an ecological inventory of the state's natural resources, including wetland flora and fauna, and in setting priorities for their protection. This national, natural heritage network covers 47 states. When the inventory determines a priority area on private land, TNC informs the land owner and, if the land owner is willing, enters into an agreement that the land owner will not alter the land and will contact TNC first should he or she decide to sell the property.

Other conservation organizations at the national and local level also undertake significant education activities. The National Wildlife Federation, the National Audubon Society, the Environmental Defense Fund and other environmental organizations, for instance, emphasize the importance of protecting wetlands in many of their publications, films, and other activities. The National Wildlife Federation's Corporate Conservation Council has adopted and provided substantial publicity for its wetlands conservation policy, and recognizes outstanding protection efforts with a prestigious annual award.

In another effort, a group of private corporations and environmental organizations have formed a cooperative effort called the Wildlife Enhancement Council to promote the conservation and improved management of wildlife habitat, including wetlands, on corporate property.

CONCLUSIONS

All levels of government have instituted numerous different types of nonregulatory programs which can help protect wetland areas. Although many of these programs have a broader purpose than protecting wetlands alone, several have resulted in the protection of substantial amounts of wetland acreage. Many of the programs have the disadvantage, in a time of tight budgets, that they require increased government expenditures or result in a decrease in tax receipts. A further drawback for many is that they only provide temporary protection.

Nevertheless, nonregulatory programs have been a key component of the nation's wetland protection efforts in the past and are likely to continue to play an important role in the future. There are substantial opportunities for expanding these programs at all levels of government. Their effectiveness also could often be enhanced by better coordination among the different programs. The North American Waterfowl Agreement is a notable effort to this end. Finally, actively attempting to integrate nonregulatory and regulatory programs often could substantially improve the effectiveness and acceptability of each.

REFERENCES

1. The Migratory Bird Conservation Act of 1929 (16 U.S.C.A. 715) and the Migratory Bird Hunting and Conservation Stamp Act of 1934 (16 U.S.C.A. 718 *et seq.*) authorizes these purchases and establishes the federal duck stamp as the funding mechanism for them.

2.   16 U.S.C.A. 4601-4 to 4601-11.

3.   16 U.S.C.A. 3901.

4.   16 U.S.C.A. 669 et seq.

5.   16 U.S.C.A. 777 et seq.

6.   For more information on state programs see C. Deming Cowles et al., State Wetland Protection Programs - Status and Recommendations, prepared for the U.S. Environmental Protection Agency, December 1986; and Appendix 4-A.

7.   16 U.S.C.A. 1451-1464.

8.   16 U.S.C.A. 2901 et seq.

9.   26 U.S.C.A. 1 et seq. (PL 99-514).

Examples of Nonregulatory Programs

This appendix provides a number of examples of the use of nonregulatory approaches and other innovative strategies to protect or restore wetlands. The information on these "success stories" was obtained during the life of the Forum from publications, information provided by members, and other sources. This listing is only indicative, however. A more extensive research effort would undoubtedly have identified many more. Because no attempt was made to verify the accuracy of the information provided or to evaluate the actual effectiveness of the programs described, the reader is referred to the responsible organization to obtain further information. The information is organized as follows:

Acquisition Programs
Planning Acquisition Programs
Funding Programs
Tax Incentives
Subsidies
Transfer of Development Credits
Education
Conflict Resolution
Integrating Regulatory and Nonregulatory Programs
Examples of Innovative Restoration and Enhancement

ACQUISITION PROGRAMS--Federal

National Wildlife Refuge System

A 90-million acre nationwide network of lands and waters administered by the FWS, is set aside chiefly for wildlife conservation. Since three-fourths of the refuges were established for the protection of migratory waterfowl, millions of acres of wetlands are protected under this system. The majority of the funds for the purchase of national wildlife refuges come from the Migratory Bird Conservation Fund[1] and advance loans authorized under the Wetlands Loan Act.[2]

Waterfowl Production Areas

The FWS has purchased conservation easements using a one-time lump sum payment. In exchange, owners agree not to burn, drain, level or fill wetlands. This program operates in perpetuity, primarily in the prairie pothole region of the Dakotas, Minnesota and Montana. Under this program, the FWS has acquired about 25,000 easements just in the Dakotas.

The FWS also has purchased conservation easements from hunting clubs, primarily within the Central Valley of California, to increase wintering waterfowl habitat. Land owners agree to maintain natural cover and provide seasonal flooding.

National Estuarine Research Reserves, NOAA

This program establishes a national system of estuarine sanctuaries representative of biogeographical regions and estuarine types in the United States. These sanctuaries--16 had been designated by January 1988--are established and managed through a cooperative federal-state effort for long-term research, education and interpretation. The National Marine Sanctuary Program, a similar effort for marine areas, also includes wetlands because submerged lands are some of the target areas.

The North American Waterfowl Agreement

The Canadian Minister of the Environment and the U.S. Secretary of the Interior signed a joint agreement in May 1986 to restore, protect, and improve over 6 million acres of waterfowl habitat by the year 2000. The North American Waterfowl Agreement recommends that federal, state and local governments and private organizations in the United States spend $1.3 billion (1985 U.S. dollars) and that Canadian governments and organizations spend $375.5 million to carry out the objectives of the agreement. Contributions totaling $8 million have been raised through an innovative multiple matching effort. State wildlife agencies contributed a total of $1 million dollars, Ducks Unlimited matched the states $1 million, the National Fish and Wildlife Foundation matched the $2 million sum, and Habitat Canada matched the United States' total of $4 million.

San Pedro River, Arizona, BLM

BLM is involved in acquiring new and critical riparian areas through land exchanges with states and private individuals. In Arizona alone, BLM has acquired more than 157,000 acres of prime riparian habitat during the last two years. The most significant of these acquisitions is a 43,000 acre tract along the San Pedro River in southeastern Arizona. The area serves as a migration corridor for tropical wildlife species moving into and out of Mexico and provides habitat for hundreds of other wildlife species.

ACQUISITION PROGRAMS--State and Local

Florida Land Acquisition Programs

Through purchase and donation, Florida has acquired hundreds of thousands of acres, much of it wetlands or areas adjacent to wetlands. In the next ten years, Florida's state agencies, regional water management districts, and local governments will have the capability to generate over $1 billion to acquire more land. The major funding sources are bonds, general revenue (made up largely of state taxes), documentary stamp taxes, severance taxes, and tourist impact taxes with additional funds coming from ad valorem taxes and revenues from state forests and hunting permits.

New Jersey Green Acres

In addition to purchasing land at the state level, New Jersey's Green Acres program provides grants and low interest loans to counties and communities for the acquisition or development of open space for outdoor recreation through its Green Trust program. A bonus is granted if the lands are environmentally sensitive. As of December 1987, approximately 80,000 acres of wetlands had been acquired through this Green Acres and Green Trust.

Pinelands Acquisition

In 1904, New Jersey bought 1,532 acres to establish a state forest. Nearly 50 years later, the 96,000 acre Wharton Tract was purchased with special state revenue appropriations. Although the advent of the Green Acres program in 1961 accelerated acquisition, it became clear that the region could not be protected solely by state land acquisition and that a comprehensive preservation program with regulation and acquisition guided by sound planning was required. Federal legislation designated the Pinelands as the nation's first national preserve and provided special funds for planning and acquisition. Over 25,200 acres have been purchased with federal and Green Acres funds since the 1979 legislation, bringing the state open space holdings there to 248,036 acres.

Higbee Beach, New Jersey

In 1974, New Jersey initiated the process of acquiring the Higbee Beach. Combining the resources of the FWS's short-lived funds for the endangered species program and the state's own Green Acres funds, over $1 million was raised to purchase 416 acres. The area was assigned to the Division of Fish, Game and Wildlife for management, and operating money is generated by the state income tax check-off for endangered and nongame species.

Puget Sound, Washington

The Puget Sound Water Quality Authority recommended that $2.5 million be spent to acquire the remaining pristine wetlands in Washington State. TNC, the Washington Department of Ecology, and Snohomish County all initiated programs to accomplish this.

Carquinez Shoreline Park, California

The California Coastal Conservancy provided a repayable grant of $1.3 million to enable the East Bay Regional Park District to preserve the last scenic undeveloped shoreline in one of the fastest growing counties in California. The grant allows the consolidation of 336 acres for a new 2.5 mile shoreline park along the Straits at the eastern end of San Francisco Bay. The Port Costa Conservation Society, a local nonprofit organization, played a key role by successfully soliciting the donation of eighty acres of ridge land that, with technical assistance from the Coastal Conservancy, could be incorporated into the new park.

Tulsa, Oklahoma

Recent floods raised the awareness of the need for flood protection in Tulsa. During this opportune period, Tulsa looked to multiuse purposes for wetlands acquisition to gain support from many different groups for the Tulsa Flood Control District's acquisition program. For example, a hiking trail was planned next to the existing creek as part of the acquisition program to gain the support of hikers, bikers, joggers, and outdoor enthusiasts.

ACQUISITION PROGRAMS--Private Organizations

Ducks Unlimited

Ducks Unlimited has acquired 3 million acres in the United States and Canada, and spent $34-$37 million in 1984 on wetland creation and restoration. Audubon has acquired 200,000 acres of wetlands and wet meadows.

The Nature Conservancy's National Wetlands Conservation Project

Launched in 1983 with a $25 million grant, this project is a $55 million private/public effort to protect outstanding examples of an array of aquatic systems. As of 1986, over 150,000 acres had been brought under protection through this program.

Stone Harbor, New Jersey

A fund-raising campaign through the World Wildlife Fund resulted in the money needed to purchase more than 6000 acres in the Cape May marshes of New Jersey in 1968. Support by private donations and research grants enabled the construction of a facility to house a museum and a library.

San Juan Preservation Trust, Washington

This local land trust in Washington State includes the preservation of vital wetlands as part of its mission. The most recent addition was 7.5 acres of a 20-acre freshwater marsh on Orcas Island. An easement on this property prohibits any development which would impact the wetlands. Public access is limited to educational and scientific visits but the adjacent county road provides visual access. The site is monitored by volunteers working for the trust and funds for management of the site come from an endowment fund administered by the Trust. The Trust is currently working with an adjacent land owner to see that the remaining marshland is included in the preserve.

Yakima River Greenway Foundation, Washington

The goal of this trust is to preserve, enhance and maintain a 3,600 acre river corridor adjacent to the Yakima urban area as a living resource for future generations. Currently, half of the corridor is in public ownership and the Foundation has acquired and manages 300 of the remaining 1,800 acres.

Hood Canal Land Trust, Washington

The Trust owns title to 88 acres of marsh and upland area. The latest acquisition involved a 72-acre parcel including 1,480 feet of shoreline, a four-acre tidal lagoon, a creek running through a deep ravine, and forested uplands. The original land owners remained on the property. While they were interested in seeing the important natural features of the property protected, they also wanted to make enough money from their investment to retire comfortably. The resulting arrangement was a combination of land donation (32 acres) and conservation easement (40 acres). The arrangement includes provisions that allow some development in certain upland areas.

Union Camp Corporation Land Legacy Program

This forest products company's program has donated about 78,000 acres valued at more than $23 million to TNC and other nonprofit groups for preservation purposes. Their approximately 50,000 acre Great Dismal Swamp property in Virginia served as the core area around which the Great Dismal Swamp National Wildlife Refuge was established.

American Forest Foundation

This Foundation was established by the forest products industry for donations of ecologically important sites, including wetlands. These donations of land provide tax advantages to corporations. The Foundation then sells the lands to conservation organizations and uses proceeds to support environmental education and the American Tree Farm System. Begun in 1986, the Foundation has already received 7,300 acres of wetland sites.

Sundusky Bay, Ohio

Although the Ohio Power Company offered its Sandusky Bay property, valued at $4.7 million as a bargain sale for $2.8 million to TNC, it took a joint effort to secure the funds. The state of Ohio appropriated $2 million and contributed another $300,000 from general funds, and the Richard King Mellon Foundation provided a loan for the remainder. The area is now protected by TNC as one of Ohio's largest public wildlife areas.

Cache River Basin, Arkansas

For the past twenty years, the Cache Basin in northeastern Arkansas, which draws the largest concentration of mallards in the nation, has been imperiled by channelization. Thus, the FWS proposed safeguarding 92,000 acres of the basin. While the FWS worked out the details, TNC purchased 1000 acres using a $300,000 matching grant from the Richard K. Mellon Foundation. The next year the Migratory Bird Commission approved the initial acquisitions. As of late 1986, 4,565 acres had been purchased by TNC and transferred to the FWS.

Coachella Valley Preserve, California

Local communities, California, the FWS, and BLM participated in land exchanges and used mitigation fees from developers to preserve a 13,000 acre sand dune habitat.

Roanoke River, North Carolina

Among the sources tapped to preserve this riparian area were the donation of land from Union Camp Corporation, a bargain sale from True Temper, Inc., funds from the North Carolina legislature to Wildlife Resources Commission, DOT's purchase from a mitigation bank, proceeds from the nongame tax check-off, interest from North Carolina's state Wildlife Endowment Fund, MARSH (Ducks Unlimited) money, and interest-free loans from TNC's Wetlands Conservation Project.

Mashpee River, Massachusetts

The Town of Mashpee on Cape Cod purchased 250 acres along their river bank that was slated for development. A total of $4.05 million was generated by the state, TNC and other nonprofit groups.

Ash Meadows, Nevada

The Nevada delegation supported an emergency appropriation to purchase this oasis in the Mojave desert that was threatened by development. The developer sold its 12,613 acres to TNC for $5.5 million, including a $1 million loan made at 5 percent interest by TNC at closing. The land was conveyed to FWS.

Block Island, Rhode Island

Land owners challenged TNC to raise the funds to purchase some of their land at bargain sale in exchange for the donation of the rest. The town passed a $1 million bond issue for land acquisition; Senator John Chafee secured matching federal funds; TNC raised more than $1.5 million from private sources; and a $7 million loan was secured from the Richard King Mellon Foundation.

Chimon Island, Connecticut

The owner sold Chimon Island to TNC--rather than to a counter bidding developer--for $1.1 million, the asking price was $2.5 million. TNC transferred it to the FWS to be included in the Connecticut Coastal National Wildlife Refuge.

Platte River, Nebraska

The Platte River Whooping Crane Critical Habitat Maintenance Trust was established as part of an out-of-court settlement. TNC has helped the Trust in safeguarding more than 4,000 acres in a portion of the Platte that the cranes frequent.

Peach Point, Texas

The six petrochemical companies that owned this property joined together and donated 7,000 acres at Peach Point and arranged for another 1,500 acres to be purchased by TNC at low cost. Through a lease and sale agreement, TNC has transferred Peach Point to the Texas Parks and Wildlife Department for protection as a wildlife management area.

Mad Island, Texas

This property on the Texas Gulf coast was acquired from private land owners through a tax free exchange. Since the tax was deferred on this exchange, the seller was able to make a partial gift of the property.

Sampson Island Dedication, South Carolina

This 2,696 acres of predominantly freshwater tidal marsh was dedicated to the State of South Carolina. The acquisition was made possible through the conservation concerns of the donor in cooperation with the South Carolina Nature Conservancy. The South Carolina Wildlife Department now manages the property, which expanded the state's largest waterfowl management area, Bear Island, to 11,055 acres.

Botany Bay, South Carolina

The South Carolina Nature Conservancy purchased a 493 acre barrier island (60 percent of the area was wetlands), which had been zoned to permit a 300 unit residential development. TNC resold the island, subject to a conservation easement, to a private conservation minded corporation. The conservation easement allows only 12 homes to be built and will restrict activities on the island, leaving the marshes, forests, and beaches undisturbed.

Tilghman Natural Area, South Carolina

Acquisition of the unique 500 acre bottomland hardwood forest was made possible through cooperative efforts of the Governor's Office, the South Carolina Wildlife Department's Heritage Trust Program, the South Carolina Nature Conservancy, and local land owners. The initial purchase was made by TNC. The related land owners sold their property well below market value and donated conservation easements. The Wildlife Department will ultimately purchase and manage the property as a State Heritage Preserve.

Springfield Marsh Project, South Carolina

The South Carolina Marine Resources Department, in cooperation with South Carolina Ducks Unlimited, purchased 696 acres of old rice field impoundments in order to restore them to multiple-use waterfowl habitat. All funds were provided by South Carolina Ducks Unlimited through their MARSH

Program. The property is now managed by the South Carolina Wildlife Department.

Larsen Audubon Sanctuary, Connecticut

When this Birdcraft Sanctuary fell victim to Connecticut turnpike construction, Larsen's offered Audubon 35 acres provided they develop it into a managed area that would serve as a model of habitat manipulation. The contributors were so pleased with the result that succeeding grants brought the sanctuary to nearly 200 acres, visited annually by more than 10,000 people.

PLANNING ACQUISITION PROGRAMS

Wyoming's Wetland Avifauna Habitat Project

Begun in 1985, this program brings together biologists from the BLM, FWS, Soil Conservation Service, and Wyoming Game and Fish to identify, protect, and enhance statewide wetland habitat. Priority lists are developed at an annual meeting and funding sources are identified and coordinated to complete the highest ranking purchase. Since the program's inception, two projects have been initiated through the Ducks Unlimited MARSH program cost-sharing project.

National Wetlands Priority Conservation Plan

The Emergency Wetlands Resources Act of 1986 contains a provision for establishing a National Wetlands Priority Conservation Plan which will guide acquisition efforts.

The FWS has designed a 10-year acquisition plan which aims to protect more than 2.6 million acres of waterfowl habitat through purchases of land or conservation easements at an estimated program cost of $563 million.

The Ramsar Convention on Wetlands of International Importance Especially as Waterfowl Habitat

The Ramsar Convention has 45 member countries who are obligated by a treaty to designate at least one suitable wetland on the List of Wetlands of International Importance (the List now numbers some 357 sites covering more than 22 million hectares), to contain wetland conservation considerations in their national planning initiatives, and to promote the "wise use" of wetlands in their areas.

Waterfowl Management Plans

The Office of Migratory Bird Management in the DOI works with states to prepare management plans for waterfowl populations in each flyway. An element of these plans is the protection of migratory waterfowl habitat.

Western Hemisphere Shorebird Reserve Network

An international collaborative venture of the National Audubon Society, International Association of Fish and Wildlife Agencies, the World Wildlife Fund, and Manomet Bird Observatory to link sites critical to shorebird migrations across the Americas. To date, 36 state wildlife agencies and five countries have joined the effort.

FUNDING PROGRAMS--Federal

Migratory Bird Conservation Fund

This fund is reserved for the purchase of small wetlands and prairie potholes for "waterfowl production areas." Funding comes from the sale of duck stamps which all migratory bird hunters over the age of 16 must purchase. The Wetlands Loan Act allows Congress to appropriate advance loans against the sale of future duck stamps. A provision of the EWRA doubles the price of the federal duck stamp over the next five years with most of the proceeds earmarked for wetlands acquisition.

Entrance Fees at National Wildlife Refuges

Another provision of the EWRA authorizes entrance fees at certain national wildlife refuges with 70 percent of the proceeds channeled into the Migratory Bird Conservation Fund.

Land and Water Conservation Fund

This is funded primarily from receipts for off-shore oil and gas leasing and development and is spent to acquire recreational lands and natural areas which can include wetlands. The EWRA lifted restrictions of the use of LWCF to purchase waterfowl habitat.

Pittman-Robertson Federal Aid in Wildlife Restoration Act[3] and the Dingell-Johnson Federal Aid in Fish Restoration Act[4]

These Acts authorize federal matching grants to states for wildlife and fish habitat restoration. Funds come from excise taxes on hunting and fishing equipment, which totaled approximately $243 million in 1985.

FUNDING PROGRAMS--States

More than half the states have their own waterfowl stamp in addition to the federal one; 32 states have check-offs on their income tax forms for nongame wildlife (generating a total of $9 million in 1983).

Documentary taxes and severance taxes are used for land acquisition in Florida, Tennessee, South Carolina, Maryland, Arkansas and Washington.

In Missouri, a one-eighth of one percent state sales tax is earmarked for the Department of Environmental Conservation, a large portion of which goes to land acquisition. This totals about $50 to $60 million annually.

Minnesota, Rhode Island, Connecticut, California, New York, and many other states have approved millions of dollars of bonds for land acquisition.

California uses racetrack wager revenues and duck stamps to help finance the operations of one of the wetland acquisition agencies. Also on the ballot is a proposal to use cigarette tax revenues to fund wetland acquisition as well as some operations of the state park system.

New Jersey's Waterfowl Stamps and Prints

In less than two years after the waterfowl stamp had been instituted, the sale of stamps to hunters and the sale to collectors of the stamp and artist's prints, netted the state more than $717,000. Of this amount, New Jersey had committed $284,494 for the acquisition of eight south Jersey wetland parcels which provide perpetual habitat for New Jersey's native and migratory waterfowl. By the time the fourth stamp and print were issued, the proceeds from the previous stamps had totaled over $1,000,000 and 5,000 acres of waterfowl habitat had been purchased or donated.

Alaska's Waterfowl Conservation Stamp Program

This program has generated over $900,000 in its three years of existence to be used specifically for wetlands purchase, enhancement or management. No direct purchases of wetlands had occurred as of the end of 1987.

Wyoming Game and Fish Wildlife Trust Account

Money deposited into this trust account comes from sale of the Game and Fish Department conservation stamps required with license purchases, interest accrued on license application monies, sales of Department publications, and gifts and donations. Interest from this account can be used for the preservation and enhancement of Wyoming wildlife through the acquisition, maintenance and improvement of wildlife habitat. Monies from the accrued interest are spent on high priority wildlife habitat areas identified through the Wildlife Land Use Management Plan and approved through an in-house enhancement procedure.

California's Land Bank Fund

The Land Bank Fund receives money from developers or land owners who hold title to land clouded by state claims. The funds paid to acquire full interest to the land is appropriated to the State Lands Commission, which acts as a Land Bank Trustee, who acquires real property or any interest in real property for the purposes of public trust title settlements and for mitigation with respect to improvements to real property which adversely impact existing or former wetlands.

Suffolk County Bonds

Suffolk County, New York has approved a $65 million bond for natural area acquisition.

Ducks Unlimited Matching Aid to Restore States Habitat (MARSH)

This program, initiated in 1985, provides money to state wildlife agencies based on the amount volunteers in that state raise. Funds can be provided as an outright grant or as matching money for acquisition, development and enhancement of waterfowl habitat.

TAX INCENTIVES

Several states, including Iowa, Minnesota, and New Hampshire, offer property tax abatement to land owners who retain their wetlands.

Minnesota exempts wetlands not receiving other compensation from local property taxes. The state also gives property tax credits on tillable land to land owners who agree not to drain wetland property.

In New York, land owners who have been denied permits to develop wetlands are offered a reduction in property tax.

Property tax incentives for protecting open space, which can apply to wetlands, exist in Connecticut, Delaware, Maine, New Hampshire, North Carolina, Rhode Island, Tennessee, Vermont, New Jersey, Illinois, and Virginia. Under some of these provisions, such as in Illinois and New Jersey, if a land owner terminates the voluntary open space classification, he must pay retroactive property taxes based on the normal use assessment rate, plus interest for up to three years.

In Connecticut, Maine, Oregon, Illinois, California, and Vermont, wetlands are protected under other categories such as recreation, agriculture, or timberlands which make them eligible for property tax incentives.

Delaware, Maryland, New Jersey, Rhode Island, and South Carolina have special provisions guaranteeing land owners property tax reductions for granting conservation easements.

Delaware, Maryland, North Carolina, Oregon, Rhode Island, Vermont, and Virginia offer a charitable deduction from state income tax for donation of interests in land. Some of the laws require that the donation be made to a qualified conservation organization.

Iowa, New York, Pennsylvania, Minnesota, and Vermont reimburse localities for the reduction in the tax base that results from lower property taxes.

SUBSIDIES

The Conservation Reserve Program (CRP). The Federal Government

Although highly erodible lands are targeted in this program, wetlands benefit because: 1) shallow water is an approved cover type for cost-sharing on cover establishment; 2) wetlands are interspersed with highly erodible land; and 3) erosion from upland areas is reduced.

Other supplemental payments in the Conservation Reserve Program (CRP) ("Piggyback Agreements") may be paid by the FWS to encourage land owners with wetlands to participate in the CRP and to secure special land management rights so that waterfowl production can be maximized. Approximately 60,000 acres are currently involved.

Farm Debt Restructure and Conservation Set-Aside Program

Under a provision of the Food Security Act of 1985, a land owner can cancel part of a debt from an FmHA loan by granting a 50-year (or more) conservation easement to the government. Another provision allows the Secretary of Agriculture to grant or sell conservation easements on lands in their receivership to a state or local government or private nonprofit organization. An Executive Order places the affirmative responsibility on the FmHA to place protective deed restrictions on wetland areas. A Memorandum of Understanding says FWS and the state wildlife agencies will inventory these lands. (Currently 1.7 million acres are in the FmHA inventory.)

Water Bank Program, U.S. Department of Agriculture

Authorized in 1970 and expanded in 1980, the Water Bank Program pays farmers to keep wetlands out of production and shares the costs for certain conservation practices. The program operates primarily in migratory waterfowl flyways. By 1985, Congress had appropriated nearly $130 million for the Water Bank Program, protecting 605,977 acres of land. Although $30 million can be appropriated annually for this program, congressional appropriations declined to an all time low of $8,371,000 in fiscal years 1986 and 1987. In 1988, the Water Bank Program is currently working under a continuing resolution, awaiting guaranteed funding.

Wyoming's Rangeland Stewardship Program

Holders of grazing permits and public land leases are eligible for incentives from the federal government by practicing stewardship that improves range conditions. These incentives may include payment of up to 50 percent of the amount due the federal government from grazing permits, applied toward range improvement work. Development and improvement of wetlands located within the stewardship area could be used to satisfy this objective.

Reinvest In Minnesota (RIM)

A state land conservation program, designed especially for lands that are ineligible (because of size) for the CRP, has as one of its three options a Wetland Reserve Program. Under this program, land owners receive payment based on cash rental rate for a permanent easement on wetlands, including previously drained wetlands, and on land adjacent to wetlands. As of 1987, previously drained wetlands can be retired and restored.

California Coastal Conservancy Programs

The California Coastal Conservancy works with coastal ranchers in several projects in which public funds are joined with land owner efforts through written agreements to protect streams and other watershed resources. For example, public funds are used to construct fences to keep cattle out of stream corridors with the agreement that the rancher will maintain the fences.

Acres for Wildlife, South Dakota

South Dakota provides economic incentives to land owners who agree to set aside acreage from agricultural production in favor of producing undisturbed land parcels for wildlife habitat.

Ducks Unlimited

Ducks Unlimited and other clubs make rental payments to land owners to set aside their land for conservation purposes, or hunting and/or fishing. The land owner maintains full title to the land and all rights on it.

Resource Enhancement Program, California Coastal Conservancy

The California Coastal Conservancy undertakes enhancement of threatened or damaged coastal and related resources and provides grants to state and local public agencies and non-profit organizations to develop and implement enhancement projects. The Conservancy has preserved and enhanced over 7,000 acres of wetlands, dunes, and coastal habitats from 1978-1986 at a cost of $19 million. A WEP, which is designed to preserve wetlands by integrating effects of the entire watershed, is part of this.

Assistance for Restoration in the Conservation Reserve Program

Because restoring wetlands (establishing shallow water cover) on CRP may be more expensive than establishing vegetative cover, the FWS has initiated a program providing supplemental funding to land owners agreeing to the wetland restoration option.

TRANSFER OF DEVELOPMENT CREDITS (TDCs)

The **California Coastal Conservancy** is working to implement or design TDCs in the counties of Sonoma, Santa Cruz, Monterey, and San Luis Obispo that provide a voluntary, market-based method for eliminating development threats to scenic or environmentally sensitive areas while enabling property owners to obtain a fair return on their investments.

EDUCATION

Land Owner Education Program, Washington State

Washington State's <u>Wetlands Acquisition and Preservation: A Guide for Land Owners and Government Officials</u> is part of a clearinghouse for information regarding the preservation of wetlands in Washington. It is managed by the Wetlands Section, Shorelands and Coastal Zone Management Program, Washington State Department of Ecology. The document outlines options available for individuals who want to know exactly what they can do with wetlands on their property and includes information on the many organizations in the state that assist land owners in protecting their land. The document may cut down on destruction due to ignorance and increase protection efforts by land owners.

Alaska Handbook

The Alaska Department of Environmental Conservation, in cooperation with the Corps, completed a handbook in 1982 to assist applicants planning projects in wetlands. It describes the conditions when a permit may be required, guides them through the application process, provides alternative designs to promote water quality protection, and lists names of government contacts for more information. A supplemental brochure was prepared to increase circulation of the material to the public.

Kentucky Adopt-A-Wetland Program

In the Kentucky Adopt-A-Wetland program, a group of citizens take responsibility for monitoring activities at a particular site, giving the community a sense of ownership of the wetland. The program provides education on wetland management and conservation and initiates projects appropriate to particular problems at the specific wetland. The program may also help with the management and enforcement problem, at least for certain wetlands.

Wyoming's Public Information and Education Programs

"Wyoming Wildlife-Worth the Watching" is designed to promote nonconsumptive use of all wildlife resources. Wetlands are targeted because they are a prime habitat type accommodating nonconsumptive uses. The "Wild Times" newsletter is a monthly periodical distributed to Wyoming school children, with information on wildlife management and understanding of wildlife habitat factors.

Florida Forestry Manual

In the state of Florida, where virtually all forestry activities occur in wetlands, the forest products industry has produced a manual of voluntary Best Management Guidelines for forested wetlands. The guidelines are an effort to educate foresters and other natural resource managers to recognize and manage for the multiple values and benefits that wetlands provide.

South Carolina's Water Watch Program

The "Water Watch Program" is a public education program administered by the Governor's office. Objectives of the program are: (1) to encourage citizens to "adopt" a stream, lake or wetland and to make a long-term commitment of stewardship for the area; (2) to increase citizens' awareness of and involvement in water and aquatic resource management; and (3) to establish a working partnership among citizens, industries, and state and local governments leading to better aquatic resources management. Much of the educational effort in this program is geared towards making the public more aware of wetland values and functions and opportunities for conservation.

The Nature Conservancy's National Natural Heritage Network

The network is an ongoing, computer-assisted ecological inventory operated in cooperation with an arm of state government. This program operates in 47 states. In coordination with their inventory program, TNC informs land owners of environmentally important resources on their land. If the land owner is willing, he or she enters into an agreement that the land will not be altered and that TNC will be contacted first if the property is to be sold.

Canada's Land Owner Education Guide

Canada has a land owner's guide to improve wildlife habitat on private lands. This information is distributed free to land owners and deals with developing and improving wetlands.

BLM Riparian Area Management Brochure

This brochure, distributed to the public, describes the characteristics and values of riparian areas, what BLM is doing to manage them, and what individuals can do to help.

BLM Demonstration Project

The BLM Director has required that each District develop a riparian demonstration area where the best management practices and instream habitat improvement work will be implemented.

CONFLICT RESOLUTION[5]

Sinkyone Wilderness, California Coastal Conservancy

The California Department of Parks and Recreation acquired 3,500 acres for the Sinkyone Wilderness State Park in 1973. Georgia Pacific continued to log 7,100 acres of virgin redwoods on adjoining land until 1983 when they were stopped by a lawsuit. The resentment bred from the lawsuit hindered further efforts to acquire the land until the California Coastal Conservancy coordinated an advisory committee to settle the conflict. In the final arrangement, Georgia Pacific offered the land at a bargain sale, with the Trust for Public Land (TPL) initially purchasing the entire parcel (appraised at over $10 million) for $4.9 million. The State Department of Parks and Recreation will purchase 2,950 acres from TPL at a cost of $2.8 million to expand the state park; Save the Redwoods League contributed $1 million toward the state park and additional acres; and the Coastal Conservancy advanced the $1.1 million remainder, to be paid back wholly or partially by the resale of approximately 3,800 acres to the timber sector.

Los Penasquitos Lagoon, California

A component of the Los Penasquitos (in the city of San Diego) Lagoon Enhancement Plan was to expand existing park and open space areas and put into public ownership all significant wetlands and related critical habitat and buffers not currently part of the surrounding state reserve. The two major parcels recommended for addition to the reserve were owned by San Diego Gas and Electric Company, and a smaller one was owned by Sorrento Associates. As a result of intense negotiations spearheaded by the Conservancy, the San Diego Gas and Electric Co. agreed to sell its property to the State Department of Parks and Recreation. This $2.85 million acquisition will be funded by State Parks, with the City of San Diego making its contribution by allowing San Diego Gas and Electric to postpone for several years the undergrounding of utilities. The Conservancy also reached an agreement with the Sorrento Valley Associates to purchase their property.

The Land Bank Concept

In California, the public versus private boundary problem in tidelands and submerged lands has become both an impediment to the orderly development of private property and has discouraged the public's use of its waterways. Instead of engaging in litigation, the State Lands Commission seized upon a statute allowing the state to trade away such interests in small parcels no longer needed for "public trust" purposes, with the state receiving equal or greater land value. Several such title settlement exchanges have been consummated by using the Point Edith 696-acres as a "land bank". The State Lands Commission, by agreement with the TPL, established a 441-acre land bank which has now been expended through these title settlement exchanges. Some wildlife mitigation agreements also represent withdrawals from this land bank. The entire 696-acre wildlife area was thus created with no other expenditure of public funds.

INTEGRATION WITH WETLAND REGULATORY PROGRAMS

California Coastal Conservancy

The Conservancy is a "sister agency" to the California Coastal Commission which regulates development in the coastal zone and works with coastal jurisdictions to prepare local coastal programs which outline the local plan for development and resource conservation. The Conservancy uses non-regulatory means to resolve conflicts that occur when demands on coastal resources collide, and provides varied technical and financial assistance to local governments in implementing projects to carry out LCPs. The Conservancy is often called upon when an impasse has occurred, usually between the public's need for resource conservation and the rights of private land owners. The Conservancy is funded primarily by general obligation bonds. As of 1986, the Conservancy had committed or spent $74,667,150 on a total of 407 projects, valued at over $200,609,480.

INNOVATIVE RESTORATION, ENHANCEMENT, AND MANAGEMENT EFFORTS

Ducks Unlimited management of public lands

The USDA and the DOI signed an agreement with Ducks Unlimited for that organization to expand its efforts to preserve wetlands on public lands.

Tomales Bay, California Coastal Conservancy Watershed Enhancement Program

The Bay was significantly affected by sediment, some of which filled in adjacent wetland habitats, accelerated by 1982 storms. Erosion control techniques employed in the watershed include revegetation, streambank destabilization and construction of sediment traps.

Pescadero Marsh, California

The State Department of Parks and Recreation owns and manages the Pescadero Marsh but the marsh is filling in with sediment produced by erosion in the upstream watershed. The California Coastal Conservancy finances projects in the watershed to control sedimentation and the Department of Parks and Recreation will finance wetlands enhancement projects on its property.

HARD Marsh, California

The California Coastal Conservancy provided a $57,620 grant in the Hayward Area Recreation District (HARD) to improve tidal access to an 82-acre salt marsh in the 1,800 acre Hayward Shoreline Park on San Francisco Bay. The marsh had been without tidal water for more than a year. Consequently its value to the scores of shorebirds and waterfowl that depend on it had severely declined. The park district dredged a channel and installed tide control structures that will regulate the inflow of bay water throughout the marsh.

Camp Creek, Oregon

On this stream in eastern Oregon, livestock access was limited and alternative water sources were provided. This management technique resulted in the stream revegetation of the stream banks and a year-round flow where the stream once dried up during the hot summer months.

John Day River, Oregon

BLM planted juniper trees along the banks of this river to prevent further erosion and trap soil.

Beaver repair

In Wyoming, BLM is using beaver to rehabilitate eroding streams. Scarce building materials such as willow and aspen are delivered to the streams where they are used by beavers as foundations for sturdy dams that can survive floods and build up stream banks and water tables. In some cases beavers have been trapped and moved into areas where their assistance is needed.

Swan Lake, Minnesota

Because the lake was deteriorating as a waterfowl and wildlife refuge, local sportsmen banded together to form the Swan Lake Wildlife Association. With local volunteers, they began clearing vegetation to create nesting sites. To strengthen these efforts, at the encouragement of the state's Department of Natural Resources, TNC obtained an interest free loan from R.K. Mellon to purchase a 184-acre farm on the lake. The department has pledged to purchase half the property and local sportsman clubs are also helping to repay the loan. Funds for restoration are being provided by the legislature and the RIM program.

REFERENCES to Appendix

1. The Migratory Bird Conservation Act of 1929 (16 U.S.C.A. 715) and the Migratory Bird Hunting and Conservation Stamp Act of 1934 (16 U.S.C.A. 718 et seq.) authorizes these purchases and establishes the federal duck stamp as the funding mechanism for them.

2. 16 U.S.C.A. 4601-4 to 4601-11.

3. 16 U.S.C.A. 669 et seq.

4. 16 U.S.C.A. 777 et seq.

5. See also Appendix 3-A in "Advance Planning for Wetlands Protection and Management."

DEFINING AND DELINEATING WETLANDS

Dan Willard, Michele Leslie, and Robert B. Reed

Different government programs use a variety of different and sometimes inconsistent definitions of wetlands in carrying out their missions. These differences are sometimes confusing to wetlands owners and can generate inconsistencies in wetlands management efforts. It can be particularly frustrating to a landowner not to be able to determine whether or not a particular piece of land is subject to a regulatory program. The frustration understandably rises when it might be subject to two or more government programs, but a separate determination has to be made for each because they use different definitions. Unfortunately, this problem is not easy to solve.

CAUSES OF VARIATIONS AMONG DEFINITIONS

Definitions of wetlands are concepts; wetlands themselves exist as a physical reality. The correspondence between the concept and the reality is necessarily imperfect. Definitions attempt to describe a thing using selected attributes and to exclude other things dissimilar in those attributes. These attributes, and thus the resulting definitions, vary according to the purpose for which they were developed--for instance, the differing needs of regulatory and scientific purposes create obviously distinct definitions.

Precise definitions of wetlands also are inherently inaccurate. Wetlands are transitional features that vary widely in composition and function, both spatially and temporally. This natural variability and complexity exacerbates the proliferation of definitions, terms, and interpretations.

Dan Willard is Director, Environmental Programs, Indiana University. Michele Leslie is former Associate, and Robert B. Reed is former Research Fellow, respectively, The Conservation Foundation.

More than 50 different definitions of "wetlands" are in use in the United States (see Appendix 5-A for annotated listing). Although many of these definitions are basically similar, and their interpretation in the field has been converging in recent years, they do reflect a wide range of institutional perspectives and professional orientations.

In general, the definitions in use are based upon conditions in three categories: soil, water, and vegetation (see Appendix 5-B). Some definitions, especially those developed for regulatory purposes, may include other factors such as location or a minimum size criterion. It is notable that none of the identified definitions are based on functional or performance criteria, such as flood control capability, provision of habitat for fish and wildlife, or capacity to improve water quality.

Definitions also may vary by locale, based on local concerns, scientific studies of wetland functions, and legal battles. People in various regions of the country have different needs for wetland functions and, thus, have different perceptions of wetlands value. For example, many coastal states define only those wetlands related to the ocean: tidal wetlands, salt marshes, and the like.

In addition, definitions vary by the tools available to define local wetlands. For example, some definitions depend on the distribution of specific plants, some focus on specific soils, and others on specific actions of the water (such as mean high tide). These all represent the varied perceptions of wetlands viewed through the eyes of biologists, hydrologists, engineers, soil scientists, or politicians.

Definitions also reflect the needs of the definers--their purposes for creating the definition. For example, the U.S. Fish and Wildlife Service (FWS), which is a resource conservation agency, has adopted a comprehensive definition of wetlands that maximizes opportunities to carry out its responsibility to inventory the nation's wetlands (Section 208(i), Clean Water Act). As presented by Cowardin et al. (see Appendix 5-A), this definition is as follows:

Wetlands are lands transitional between terrestrial and aquatic systems where the water table is usually at or near the surface or the land is covered by shallow water... Wetlands must have one or more of the following attributes: (1) at least periodically, the land supports predominantly hydrophytes, (2) the substrate is predominantly undrained hydric soil, and (3) the substrate is nonsoil and is saturated with water or covered by shallow water at some time during the growing season of each year.

Under this definition, wetland soils, hydrology, or vegetation may signal the presence of a wetland. Thus, it is a relatively broad and inclusive definition.

The U.S. Army Corps of Engineers (Corps) and the U.S. Environmental Protection Agency (EPA), however, use a more restricted, legal definition of wetlands in their regulations covering dredge and fill permits under Section 404 of the Clean Water Act (33 CFR 323.2; 40 CFR 230.3):

The term "wetlands" means those areas that are inundated or saturated by surface or ground water at a frequency and duration sufficient to support, and that under normal circumstances do support, a prevalence of vegetation typically adapted for life in saturated soil conditions. Wetlands generally include swamps, marshes, bogs and similar areas.

The FWS definition, seeking to be expansive with its scientific perspective, recognizes any of the attributes of water, vegetation or soil as an indication of the presence of a wetland (appropriate hydrologic conditions must exist, but may not necessarily be readily apparent). Under the Corps/EPA definition, however, the area usually must exhibit all three attributes--soil, water, and vegetation.

Regulations developed to implement the "Swampbuster" provisions of the 1985 Food Security Act use a definition which is different than, but similar to that used by the FWS. Thus, at the federal level, there are two basic definitions in use whose differences reflect their different purposes: inventory and regulation.

DIFFERENCES IN CLASSIFICATION

Differences in general definition have in turn resulted in some fundamental differences in wetlands classification frameworks. In cases where a comprehensive definition is applied, a wider number of environment types tend to be viewed as wetlands. For example, the definition provided by Cowardin et al. (see Appendix 5-A) covers areas with wetland soils where wave action or extreme water level fluctuations prevent the growth of vegetation, such as mudflats; areas with wetland vegetation but without wetland soils, such as the edges of impoundments; areas totally without soil but having wetland plants, such as the spray zone of rocky shores; and areas without soil or vegetation, such as gravel beaches. (The U.S. Fish and Wildlife Service has addressed wetlands and deep water habitats in a single classification scheme, blurring the distinction between the two environment types.) In contrast, a narrow definition of wetlands would tend to exclude types of environments not clearly in the mainstream of vegetated marshes, swamps, and bogs. (Examples of disputed classifications include tundra and forested floodplain areas.)

PROBLEMS DEFINING BOUNDARIES

The proof of a definition lies in its boundary. An abstract definition of wetlands is not difficult to apply when one is sinking slowly into the middle of a marsh or swamp or is surrounded by alligators. However, controversy is likely to arise in defining the boundary or locating the edges of a wetland.

Different methods for interpreting a single definition on the ground can give rise to confusion and inconsistency. For example, the Corps and EPA have used different delineation methodologies in applying their definition. Recognizing the potential for inconsistencies that this may cause, the two agencies have established field testing programs for their methods with the goal of converging on a single methodology. A parallel, independent study sponsored by the National Association of Home Builders now underway involves comparing delineations generated by applying the two methodologies to the same site in several different locations around the country.

Even given equivalent definitions and methods for applying them, certain kinds of wetlands are difficult to delineate definitively. Many definitions recognize that wetlands are transitional natural features (see FWS above). This transitional quality makes boundaries uncertain and providing guidance in locating boundaries difficult. Because wetlands protection essentially attempts to protect the functions of those wetlands, many suggest that the boundaries should include that which is necessary to protect the function of the wetland. Although maintenance of buffers is a significant policy question, defining the location of such a buffer presents similar boundary problems. Including the area upon which the wetland is functionally dependent may extend the boundary far beyond the limits demarcated by water, soil or vegetation. It could, for instance, encompass the entire surface and groundwater supply area that supports the wetland. Another problem is that simple, reliable, and inexpensive methods for determining the functional limits of wetlands are not readily available in many cases. Until such techniques are developed or made cost-effective, delineating boundaries will continue to depend upon physical and biological descriptors.

The problem of defining the boundary is complicated by the fact that the physical and biological characteristics of wetlands are dynamic. Plant boundaries can change in a season, water levels in hours, and soils over years. Wetlands are naturally in a state of change, and these metamorphoses frustrate and confuse regulators and landowners subject to regulation. Boundary delineations must, therefore, reflect the time period for which the boundary applies. Boundaries can be drawn to apply for a year, a decade, or a century. Under its regulations, for instance, the Corps does not consider an area to be a wetland if it has not displayed all the characteristics required by the Corps/EPA definition within the previous five years. This definition of "normal" has resulted in reported efforts to intentionally modify one of these parameters, particularly the natural vegetation, for a five year period in order to remove a wetland area from regulatory jurisdiction.

Wetlands provide transitions between upland and aquatic environments, which may occur gradually over many miles, as in the Mississippi delta, or abruptly, as in the river systems of the West. The transition is irregular and non-continuous, with spots of higher or lower ground intermingled. The vegetation reflects this mosaic with upland and aquatic plants often interspersed with plants adapted to wet and dry cycles. Furthermore, the distribution of plants can be unpredictable. Individual plants vary enough physiologically to sometimes live in areas where we think they should not be able to survive. Many wetland plants establish themselves in one area and reproduce by sending runners out to invade higher and lower areas. And, all this changes as conditions change.

Given the transitional nature of wetland boundaries, experts have difficulty determining where the system changes from wetland to upland. Many different practices occur across the United States. Some, based on vegetation, tend to describe boundaries limited by the upward extent of wetland species. Others use the lower extension of terrestrial plants. Commonly, states use definitions which say that wetlands extend as far as either aquatic or wetland plants continue to be prevalent or predominate. Such definitions require trained field personnel who use plant ecological techniques with various statistical analyses which determine when wetland or aquatic plants predominate. It also requires methods, which are based on professional judgment, for determining what are wetland plants and what are not. The federal government has developed interagency detailed lists of plant species that are widely used by federal and state agencies for making wetland determinations. The lists were made through a Delphi process, based on observations by experts within the region.

Similarly, soil delineation, itself an approximate art because of the layering of soils, has provided boundaries based on the upper limit of wetland soils, the lower limit of terrestrial soils, or the predominance of wetland soils. Wetland soils are described by the U.S. Department of Agriculture (USDA) Soil Conservation Service's (SCS) documents on "Wetland Soils."

The frequency with which the land must be covered by water in order to qualify as a wetland can also a subject of controversy. In some cases the issue can be further confused because the regulatory jurisdiction is determined as much by legal concepts such as "waters of the United States" as by scientific determinations.

Finally, although some regulations may exclude small, isolated wetlands from coverage, the practical problems in setting boundaries to meet the requirements of federal and state management and regulatory programs applies to all wetlands regardless of size.

CONCLUSIONS

Fundamental differences in individual and institutional perspectives and missions lead to corresponding differences in wetlands definitions. These definitions have in common a reliance on structural indicators relating to soil, water, and/or vegetation. None rely on functional indicators, such as flood protection capacity, although preserving functional benefits is usually the underlying purpose of management and regulatory efforts. It is unlikely, however, that any single definition could be developed that could satisfy all types of individual or institutional interests. It may be possible to determine which purposes are being covered by essentially similar definitions and, thus, both narrow the number of definitions in use and clarify the circumstances under which they should apply.

Drafters of wetlands definitions must address several problems, including: clarifying the purpose for which the definition will be used; selecting attributes; determining whether one or more attributes must be present; defining the boundary (including whether the area on which the wetland is functionally dependent should be included); and accounting for changes over time.

Because of the uncertainty inherent in defining wetland boundaries with almost any definition, fewer or better definitions are not likely to solve a major dilemma of the landowner--how to determine whether a particular piece of transitional land is in a wetland. Different methods for applying even a single definition, differences between the individuals doing the delineation, and the natural dynamics of wetland environments create substantial difficulties in defining wetland boundaries on the ground. The only way to provide this type of certainty would be to ignore the natural changes that may occur in wetland boundaries and have the regulatory agency clearly delineate, for regulatory purposes, the wetland limits either on the ground or on a large scale topographic map. Efforts to adopt equivalent definitions and delineation methodologies and to train field personnel might also help to reduce uncertainty and inconsistency in defining wetlands.

ANNOTATED CATALOG OF WETLAND DEFINITIONS

Examples of Federal Definitions

1. Shaw, S. P., and C. G. Fredine, Wetlands of the United States, Their Extent, and Their Value for Waterfowl and Other Wildlife, Circular 39 (Washington, D.C.: U.S. Department of the Interior, Fish and Wildlife Service, 1956).

"The term 'wetlands,' as used in this report and in the wildlife field generally, refers to lowlands covered with shallow and sometimes temporary or intermittent waters. They are referred to by such names as marshes, swamps, bogs, wet meadows, potholes, sloughs, and river-overflow lands. Shallow lakes and ponds, usually with emergent vegetation as a conspicuous feature, are included in the definition, but the permanent waters of streams, reservoirs, and deep lakes are not included. Neither are water areas that are so temporary as to have little or no effect on the development of moist-soil vegetation."

2. 16 U.S.C. 1302 (Water Bank Act).

"...As used in this chapter, the term 'wetlands' means (1) the inland fresh areas described as types 1 through 7 in Circular 39, Wetlands of the United States, published by the United States Department of the Interior (or the inland fresh areas corresponding to such types in any successor wetland classification system developed by the U.S. Department of the Interior), (2) artificially developed inland fresh areas that meet the description of the inland fresh areas described in clause (1) of this sentence, and (3) such other wetland types as the Secretary may designate."

3. From an early introduction to Cowardin, L. M., V. Carter, F. C. Golet, and E. T. LaRoe, Classification of Wetlands and Deepwater Habitats of the United States, Pub. FWS/OBS-79/31 (Washington, D.C.: U.S. Fish and Wildlife Service, 1979).

"...We propose the following preliminary definition designed to overcome some of the problems present in the definition developed at Bay St. Louis.

"Wetlands are areas that, (1) support or are capable of supporting vegetation of any of the families listed by Sculthorpe (1967: 16-20), or (2) have soils that are classified as Histosols except for Folists or in which the suborder contain the elements aqua, pell, or sal, or whose soil moisture regime can be described as perudic, aquic or peraquic and that have not been artificially drained, (3) are irrigated or receive seepage water from a man-made structure such that the soil has water above the surface for one month or more during the year, or (4) are never vegetated but where the water lies from 20" below to 30' above the land surface. Water depths are measured relative to average elevation inland and low water (spring tide) in tidal areas."

4.   Cowardin, et al., 1979.

"Wetland is defined as land where the water table is at, near or above the land surface long enough to promote the formation of hydric soils or to support the growth of hydrophytes."

5.   Federal Executive Order No. 11990: Protection of Wetlands. May, 1977.

Sec. 7 (c).   "The term 'wetlands' means those areas that are inundated by surface or ground water with a frequency sufficient to support and under normal circumstances does or would support a prevalence of vegetative or aquatic life that requires saturated or seasonally saturated soil conditions for growth and reproduction.   Wetlands generally include swamps, marshes, bogs, and similar areas such as sloughs, potholes, wet meadows, river overflows, mud flats, and natural ponds."

6.   Cowardin, et al., 1979.

"Wetlands are lands transitional between terrestrial and aquatic systems where the water table is usually at or near the surface or the land is covered by shallow water.   For purposes of this classification wetlands must have one or more of the following three attributes: (1) at least periodically, the land supports predominantly hydrophytes; (2) the substrate is predominantly undrained hydric soil; and (3) the substrate is nonsoil and is saturated with water or covered by shallow water at some time during the growing season of each year."

7.   33 CFR 323.2.

"The term 'wetlands' means those areas that are inundated or saturated by surface or ground water at a frequency and duration sufficient to support, and that under normal circumstances do support, a prevalence of vegetation typically adapted for life in saturated soil conditions.   Wetlands generally include swamps, marshes, bogs and similar areas."

8.   1985 Food Security Act ("Swampbuster").

Wetland is "land that has a predominance of hydric soils and that is inundated or saturated by surface or groundwater at a frequency and duration sufficient to support and that under normal circumstances does support a prevalence of hydrophytic vegetation typically adapted for life in saturated soil conditions."

<u>Examples of State Definitions</u>

9.   California Coastal Act. Ann. Cal. Pub. Res. Code § 30121.

" 'Wetland' means lands within the coastal zone which may be covered periodically or permanently with shallow water and include saltwater marshes, freshwater marshes, open or closed brackish water marshes, swamps, mudflats, and fens."

10.   Keene-Nejedly California Wetlands Preservation Act. Ann. Cal. Pub. Res. Code § 5812.

" 'Wetlands' means streams, channels, lakes, reservoirs, bays, estuaries, lagoons, marshes, and the lands underlying and adjoining such waters, whether permanently or intermittently submerged, to the extent that such waters and lands support and contain significant fish, wildlife, recreational, aesthetic, or scient ific resources."

11.   Connecticut General Statutes Annual, § 22a-29 (2).

" 'Wetland' means those areas which border on or lie beneath tidal waters, such as, but not limited to banks, bogs, salt marsh, swamps, meadows, flats, or other low lands subject to tidal action, including those areas now or formerly connected to tidal water, and whose surface is at or below an elevation of one foot above local extreme high water; and upon which may grow or be capable of growing some, but not necessarily all, of the following:

Salt meadow grass (*Spartina patens*), spike grass (*Distichlis spicata*), black grass (*Juncus gerardii*), saltmarsh grass (*Spartina alterniflora*), saltworts (*Salicornia europaea*, and *Salicornia bigelovii*), Sea Lavender (*Limonium carolinianum*), saltmarsh bulrushes (*Scirpus robustus* and *Scirpus paludosus var. atlanticus*), sand spurrey (*Spergularia marina*), switch grass (*Panicum virgatum*), tall cordgrass (*Spartina pectinata*), hightide bush (*Iva frutescens var. oraria*), cattails (*Typha angustifolia*, and *Typha latifolia*), spike rush (*Eleocharis rostellata*), chairmaker's rush (*Scirpus americana*), bent grass (*Agrostis palustris*), and sweet grass (*Hierochloe odorata*), royal fern (*Osmunda regalis*), interrupted fern (*Osmunda claytoniana*), cinnamon fern (*Osmunda cinnamomea*), sensitive fern (*Onoclea sensibilis*), marsh fern (*Dryopteris thelypteris*), bur reed family (*Sparganium eurycarpum, Sparganium androcladum, Sparganium americanum, Sparganium chlorocarpum, Sparganium angustifolium, Sparganium fluctuans, Sparganium minimum*), horned pondweed (*Zannichellia palustris*), water-plaintain (*Alisma trivale*), arrowhead (*Sagittaria subulata, Sagittaria graminea, Sagittaria eatoni, Sagittaria engelmanniania*), wild rice (*Zizania aquatica*), tuckahoe (*Peltandra virginica*), water-arum (*Calla palustris*), skunk cabbage (*Symplocarpus foetidus*), sweet flag (*Acorus calamus*), pickerelweed (*Pontederia cordata*), water stargrass (*Heteranthera dubia*), soft rush (*Juncus effusus*), false hellebore (*Veratrum viride*), slender blue flag (*Iris prismatica pursh*), blue flag (*Iris versicolor*), yellow iris (*Iris pseudacorus*), lizard's tail (*Saururus cernuus*), speckled alder (*Alnus rugosa*), common alder

(*Alnus serrulata*), arrow-leaved tearthumb (*Polygonum sagittatum*), halberd-leaved tearthumb (*Polygonum arifolium*), spatter-dock (*Nuphar variegatum, Nuphar advena*), marsh marigold (*Caltha palustris*), swamp rose (*Rosa palustris*), poison ivy (*Rhus radicans*), poison sumac (*Rhus vernix*), red maple (*Acer rubrum*), jewelweed (*Impatiens capensis*), marsh mallow (*Hibiscus palustris*), loosestrife (*Lythrum alatum, Lythrum salicaria*), red osier (*Cornus stolonifera*), red willow (*Cornus amomum*), [narrow- leaf dogwood] (sic) (*Cornus obliqua*), sweet pepper-bush (*Celthra alnifolia*), swamp honeysuckle (*Rhododendron viscosum*), highbush blueberry (*Vaccinium corymbosum*), cranberry (*Vaccinium macrocarpon*), sea lavendar (*Limonium nashii*), climbing hemp-weed (*Mikania scandens*), joe pye weed (*Eupatorium purpureum*), joe pye weed (*Eupatorium maculatum*), thoroughwort (*Eupatorium perfoliatum*)."

12.   Connecticut General Statutes Annual, §22a-38 (15).

" 'Wetlands' means lands, including submerged land, not regulated pursuant to Sections 22a-28 to 35, inclusive, of the 1975 Revision of the General Statutes, as amended, which consists of any of the soil types designated as poorly drained, very poorly drained, alluvial, and flood plain by the National Cooperative Soils Survey, as may be amended from time to time, of the Soil Conservation Service of the United States Department of Agriculture."

13.   Delaware Wetlands Act. 7 D.C.A. §6603 (8).

" 'Wetlands' shall mean those lands above the mean low water elevation including any bank, marsh, swamp, meadow, flat or other low land subject to tidal action in the State along the Delaware Bay and Delaware River, Indian River Bay, Rehobeth Bay, Little and Big Assawoman Bays, the coastal inland waterways, or along any inlet, estuary or tributary waterway or any portion thereof, including those areas which are now or in this century have been connected to tidal waters, whose surface is at or below an elevation of 2 feet above local mean high water, and upon which may grow or is capable of growing any but not necessarily all of the following plants:

"Eelgrass (*Zoxtera marina*), Wedgeon Grass (*Ruppia maritima*), Sago Pondweed (*Potamogeton pectinatus*), Saltmarsh Cordgrass (*Spartina alterniflora*), Saltmarsh Grass (*Spartina cynosuroides*), Saltmarsh Hay (*Spartina patens*), Spike Grass (*Distichlis spicata*), Black Grass (*Juncus gerardii*), Switch Grass (*Panicum virgatum*), Three Square Rush (*Scirpus americanus*), Sea Lavender (*Limomium carolinianum*), Seaside Goldenrod (*Solidago sempervirens*), Sea Blite (*Suaeda maritima*), Sea Blite (*Suaeda linearis*), Perennial Glasswort (*Salicornia virginica*), Dwarf Glasswort (*Salicornia bigelovii*), Samphire [or Slender Glasswort] (*Salicornia europaea*), Marsh Aster (*Aster tenuifolius*), Saltmarsh Fleabane (*Pluchea purpurascens var. succulenta*), Mock Bishop's Weed (*Ptilimnium capillaceum*), Seaside Plantain (*Plantage oliganthos*), Orach (*Atriplex patula var. hastata*), March Elder (*Iva frutescens var. oraria*), Goundsel Bush (*Baccharis halmifolia*), Bladder Wrach (*Fucus vesiculosis*), Swamp Rose Mallow, Seaside Hollyhock or Marsh Mallow (*Hibiscus palustris*), Torrey Rush (*Scirpus torreyi*), Narrow-leaved Cattail (*Typha angustifolia*), and

Broad-leaved Cattail (*T. latifolia*), and those lands not currently used for agricultural purposes containing 400 acres or more of contiguous nontidal swamp, bog, muck, or marsh exclusive of narrow stream valleys where fresh water stands most, if not all, of the time due to high water table, which contribute significantly to ground water recharge, and which would require intensive artificial drainage using equipment such as pumping stations, drain fields or ditches for the production of agricultural crops."

14. Florida--Warren S. Henderson Wetlands Protection Act of 1984. F.S. 403.911 (7).

"For purposes of dredge and fill permitting activities by the department [of Environmental Regulation], 'wetlands' are defined as those areas within the jurisdiction of the department pursuant to Section 403.817."

[Note: §403.817. Legislative intent; determination of the natural landward extent of waters for regulatory purposes. See Florida Rules relating to the method for determining the landward extent of waters.]

15. Georgia Coastal Marshlands Protection Act of 1970. Official Code of Georgia Annotated §12-5-281 (2).

" 'Coastal marshlands' or 'marshlands' means any marshland or salt marsh in the State of Georgia within the estuarine area of the state, whether or not the tide waters reach the littoral areas through natural or artificial water courses. 'Marshlands' shall include those areas upon which grow one, but not necessarily all, of the following: saltmarsh grass (*Spartina alterniflora*), black grass (*Juncus gerardii*), high-tide bush (*Iva frutescens var. oraria*). The occurrence and extent of salt marsh peat at the undisturbed surface shall be deemed to be conclusive evidence of the extent of a salt marsh or a part thereof."

16. Iowa Code Annotated §427.1 (a).

" 'Wetlands' means land preserved in its natural condition which is mostly under water, which produces little economic gain, which has no practical use except for wildlife or water conservation purposes, and the drainage of which would be lawful, feasible and practical and would provide land suitable for the production of livestock, dairy animals, poultry, fruit, vegetables, forage and grains. 'Wetlands' includes adjacent land which is not suitable for agricultural purposes due to the presence of the land which is under water."

17. Maine--Freshwater Wetlands. 38 M.R.S.A. §406 (1).

"Wetland. 'Wetland' means freshwater swamps, marshes, bogs and similar areas of 10 or more contiguous acres that have been designated as freshwater wetlands under section 407." [§407 repealed. See §407-A.]

"Sec. 407-A. Identification of freshwater wetlands.

1. Criteria. For the purposes of this Article, areas identified by the department as freshwater wetlands shall be limited to areas:

A. Which are of 10 or more contiguous acres;

B. Which are characterized predominately by wetland soils and vegetation; and

C. Which are not subject to the jurisdiction of §§ 391 to 396, §§ 471 to 478 or Title 12, §§ 7776 to 7780.

"These areas may contain small inclusions of land that do not conform to the criteria of this subsection."

18. Maine--Coastal Wetlands. 38 M.R.S.A. §472 (2).

"Coastal wetlands. 'Coastal wetlands' are all tidal and subtidal lands including all areas below any identifiable debris line left by tidal action, all areas with vegetation present that is tolerant of salt water and occurs primarily in a salt water habitat, and any swamp, marsh, bog, beach, flat or other contiguous lowland which is subject to tidal action or normal storm flowage at any time excepting periods of maximum storm activity. Coastal wetlands may include portions of coastal sand dunes."

19. Maryland Wetlands and Riparian Rights. §9-101 (j).

"(j) Private wetlands.--'Private wetlands' means any land not considered 'State wetlands' bordering on or lying beneath tidal waters, which is subject to regular or periodic tidal action and supports aquatic growth. This includes wetlands, transferred by the State by a valid grant, lease, patent, or grant confirmed by Article 5 of the Declaration of Rights of the Constitution, to the extent of the interest transferred."

20. Maryland Wetlands and Riparian Rights. §9-101 (m).

"(m) State wetlands.--'State wetlands' means any land under the navigable waters of the State below the mean high tide, affected by the regular rise and fall of the tide. Wetlands of this category which have been transferred by the State by valid grant, lease, patent or grant confirmed by Article 5 of the Declaration of Rights of the Constitution shall be considered 'private wetland' to the extent of the interest transferred."

21. Massachusetts--Protection of Flood Plains, Seacoasts, and Other Wetlands; Definitions. ALM GL C. 131 §40.

"The term 'coastal wetlands', as used in this section, shall mean any bank, marsh, swamp, meadow, flat or other lowland subject to tidal action or coastal storm flowage.

"The term 'freshwater wetlands', as used in this section, shall mean wet meadows, marshes, swamps, bogs, areas where groundwater, flowing or standing surface water or ice provide a significant part of the supporting substrate for a plant community for a[t] (sic) least five months of the year; emergent and submergent plant communities in inland waters; that portion of any bank which touches any inland waters."

22. Massachusetts--Protection of Inland Wetlands. ALM GL C. 131 §40A.

"...In this section, the term 'inland wetlands' shall include the definition of 'freshwater wetlands' as set forth in section forty, and it shall further include that portion of any bank which touches any inland waters or any freshwater wetland, and any freshwater wetland subject to flooding."

23. Michigan--Goemaere-Anderson Wetland Protection Act. M.C.L.A. §281.702.2(g).

"'Wetland' means land characterized by the presence of water at a frequency and duration sufficient to support and that under normal circumstances does support wetland vegetation or aquatic life and is commonly referred to as a bog, swamp, or marsh and which is any of the following:

(i) Contiguous to the Great Lakes or Lake St. Clair, an inland lake or pond, or a river or stream.

(ii) Not contiguous to the Great Lakes, an inland lake or pond, or a river or stream; and more than 5 acres in size; except this subdivision shall not be of effect, except for the purpose of inventorying, in counties of less than 100,000 population until the department certifies to the commission of natural resources it has substantially completed its inventory of wetlands in that county.

(iii) Not contiguous to the Great Lakes, an inland lake or pond, or a river or stream; and 5 acres or less in size if the department determines that protection of the area is essential to the preservation of the natural resources of the state from pollution, impairment, or destruction and the department has so notified the owner; except this subdivision may be utilized regardless of wetland size in a county in which subdivision (ii) is of no effect; except for the purpose of inventorying, at the time."

24. Minnesota Statutes Annotated §105.37.1.

"Subd. 14. 'Public waters' includes and shall be limited to the following waters of the state:

(a)   All water basins assigned a shoreland management classification by the commissioner pursuant to section 105.485, except wetlands less than 80 acres in size which are classified as natural environment lakes;

(b)   All waters of the state which have been finally determined to be public waters or navigable waters by a court of competent jurisdiction;

(c)   All meandered lakes, except for those which have been legally drained;

(d)   All waterbasins previously designated by the commissioner for management for a specific purpose such as trout lakes and game lakes pursuant to applicable laws;

(e)   All waterbasins designated as scientific and natural areas pursuant to Section 84.033;

(f)   All waterbasins located within and totally surrounded by publicly owned lands;

(g)   All waterbasins where the state of Minnesota or the federal government holds title to any of the beds or shores, unless the owner declares that the water is not necessary for the purposes of the public ownership;

(h)   All waterbasins where there is a publicly owned and controlled access which is intended to provide for public access to the water basin; and

(i)   All natural and altered natural watercourses with a total drainage area greater than two square miles, except that trout streams officially designated by the commissioner shall be public waters regardless of the size of their drainage area.

The public character of water shall not be determined exclusively by the proprietorship of the underlying, overlying, or surrounding land or by whether it is a body or stream of water which was navigable in fact or susceptible of being used as a highway for commerce at the time this state was admitted to the union.

For purposes of statutes other than Sections 105.37, 105.38 and 105.391, the term 'public waters' shall include 'wetlands' unless the statute expressly states otherwise.

"Subd. 15.   'Wetlands' includes, and shall be limited to all types 3, 4 and 5 wetlands, as defined in United States Fish and Wildlife Service Circular No. 39 (1971 edition), not included within the definition of public waters, which are ten or more acres in size in unincorporated areas or 2 1/2 or more acres in incorporated areas."

25.   Mississippi Coastal Wetlands Protection Law.   Mississippi Codes Annotated §§49-27-5 (a) and (b).

"(a) 'Coastal wetlands' means all publicly owned lands subject to the ebb and flow of the tide; which are below the watermark of ordinary high tide; all publicly owned accretions above the watermark of ordinary high tide and all publicly owned submerged water-bottoms below the watermark of ordinary high tide.

"(b) The term 'coastal wetlands' shall be interpreted to include the flora and fauna on the wetlands and in the wetlands."

26. New Jersey--Coastal Wetlands. N.J.S.A. 13:9A-2.

"...For the purposes of this act the term 'coastal wetlands' shall mean any bank, marsh, swamp, meadow, flat or other low land subject to tidal action in the State of New Jersey along the Delaware bay and Delaware river, Raritan bay, Barnegat bay, Sandy Hook bay, Shrewsbury river including Navesink river, Shark river, and the coastal inland waterways extending southerly from Manasquan Inlet to Cape May Harbor, or at any inlet, estuary or tributary waterway or any thereof, including those areas now or formerly connected to tidal waters whose surface is at or below an elevation of 1 foot above local extreme high water, and upon which may grow or is capable of growing some, but not necessarily all, of the following:

Salt meadow grass (*Spartina patens*), spike grass (*Distichlis spicata*), black grass (*Juncus gerardii*), saltmarsh grass (*Spartina alterniflora*), saltworts (*Salicornia [e]uropaea* (sic), and *Salicornia bigelovii*), Sea Lavender (*Limonium carolinianum*), saltmarsh bulrushes (*Scirpus robustus* and *Scirpus paludosus var. atlanticus*), sand spurrey (*Spergularia marina*), switch grass (*Panicum virgatum*), tall cordgrass (*Spartina pectinata*), hightide bush (*Iva frutescens var. oraria*), cattails (*Typha angustifolia*, and *Typha latifolia*), spike rush (*Eleocharis rostellata*), chairmaker's rush (*Scirpus americana*), bent grass (*Argrostis palustris*), and sweet grass (*Hierochloe odorata*). The term 'coastal wetlands' shall not include any land or real property subject to the jurisdiction of the Hackensack Meadowlands Development Commission pursuant to the provisions of P.L. 1968, Chapter 404, sections 1 through 84 (C. 13:17-1 through C. 13:17-86)."

26.5. New Jersey Freshwater Wetlands Protection Act. P.L. 1987, c 156; signed 7/1/87.

"Freshwater Wetland means an area that is inundated or saturated by surface water or groundwater at a frequency and duration sufficient to support, and that under normal circumstances does support, a prevalence of vegetation typically adapted for life in saturated soil conditions, commonly known as hydrophytic vegetation; provided, however, that the department, in designating a wetland, shall use the 3-parameter approach (i.e., hydrology, soils and vegetation) enumerated in the April 1, 1987 interim-final draft "Wetland Identification and Delineation Manual" developed by the United States Environmental Protection Agency, and any subsequent amendments thereto.

27. Adirondack Park Agency Act. New York State Executive Law § 802(63).

"'Wetlands' means any land which is annually subject to periodic or continual inundation by water and commonly referred to as a bog, swamp or marsh which are either (a) one acre or more in size or (b) located adjacent to a body of water, including a permanent stream, with which there is free interchange of water at the surface, in which case there is no size limitation."

28. New York Freshwater Wetlands Act. ECL § 24-0107.

"1. 'Freshwater wetlands' means lands and waters of the state as shown on the freshwater wetlands map which contain any or all of the following:

(a) lands and submerged lands commonly called marshes, swamps, sloughs, bogs and flats supporting aquatic or semi-aquatic vegetation of the following types:

(1) wetland trees, which depend upon seasonal or permanent flooding or sufficiently water-logged soils to give them a competitive advantage over other trees; including, among others, red maple (*Acer rubrum*), willows (*Salix spp.*), black spruce (*Picea mariana*), swamp white oak (*Quercus bicolor*), red ash (*Fraxinus pennsylvanica*), black ash (*Fraxinus nigra*), silver maple (*Acer saccharinum*), American elm (*Ulmus americana*), and Larch (*Larix laricina*);

(2) wetland shrubs, which depend upon seasonal or permanent flooding or sufficiently water-logged soils to give them a competitive advantage over other shrubs; including, among others, alder (*Alnus spp.*), buttonbush (*Cephalanthus occidentalis*), bog rosemary (*Andromeda glaucophylla*), dogwoods (*Cornus spp.*), and leatherleaf (*Chamaedaphne calyculata*);

(3) emergent vegetation, including, among others, cattails (*Typha spp.*), pickerelweed (*Pontederia cordata*), bulrushes (*Scirpus spp.*), arrow arum (*Peltandra virginica*), arrowheads (*Sagittaria spp.*), reed (*Phragmites communis*), wildrice (*Zizania aquatica*), bur-reeds (*Sparganium spp.*), purple loosestrife (*Lythrum salicaria*), swamp loosestrife (*Decondon verticillatus*), and water plantain (*Alisma plantagoaquatica*);

(4) rooted, floating-leaved vegetation; including, among others, waterlily (*Nymphaea odorata*), water shield (*Brasenia schreberi*), and spatterdock (*Nuphar spp.*);

(5) free-floating vegetation; including, among others, duckweed (*Lemna spp.*), big duckweed (*Spirodela polyrhiza*), and watermeal (*Wolffia spp.*);

(6) wet meadow vegetation, which depends upon seasonal or permanent flooding or sufficiently water-logged soils to give it a competitive advantage over other open land vegetation; including, among

others, sedges (*Carex spp.*), rushes (*Juncus spp.*), cattails (*Typha spp.*), rice cut-grass (*Leersia oryzoides*), reed canary grass (*Phalaris arundinacea*), swamp loosestrife (*Decodon verticillatus*), and spikerush (*Eleocharis spp.*);

(7) bog mat vegetation; including, among others, sphagnum mosses (*Sphagnum spp.*), bog rosemary (*Andromeda glaucophylla*), leatherleaf (*Chamaedaphne calyculata*), pitcher plant (*Sarracenia purpurea*), and cranberries (*Vaccinium macrocarpon* and *V. oxycoccos*);

(8) submergent vegetation; including, among others, pondweeds (*Potamogeton spp.*), naiads (*Najas spp.*), bladderworts (*Utricularia spp.*), wild celery (*Vallisneria americana*), coontail (*Ceratophyllum demersum*), watermilfoils (*Myriophyllum spp.*), muskgrass (*Chara spp.*), stonewort (*Nitella spp.*), water weeds (*Elodea spp.*), and water smartweed (*Polygonum amphibium*);

(b) lands and submerged lands containing remnants of any vegetation that is not aquatic or semi-aquatic that has died because of wet conditions over a sufficiently long period, provided that such wet conditions do not exceed a maximum seasonal water depth of six feet and provided further that such conditions can be expected to persist indefinitely, barring human intervention;

(c) lands and waters substantially enclosed by aquatic or semi-aquatic vegetation as set forth in paragraph (a) or by dead vegetation as set forth in paragraph (b), the regulation of which is necessary to protect and preserve the aquatic and semi-aquatic vegetation; and

(d) the waters overlying the areas set forth in (a) and (b) and the lands underlying (c)."

29. New York Tidal Wetlands Act. ECL § 25-0103 (1).

"1. 'Tidal wetlands' shall mean and include the following:

(a) those areas which border on or lie beneath tidal waters, such as, but not limited to, banks, bogs, salt marsh, swamps, meadows, flats or other low lands subject to tidal action, including those areas now or formerly connected to tidal waters; and

(b) all banks, bogs, meadows, flats and tidal marsh subject to such tides, and upon which grow or may grow some or any of the following: salt hay (*Spartina patens* and *Distichlis spicata*), black grass (*Juncus gerardii*), saltworts (*Salicornia spp.*), sea lavender (*Limonium carolinianum*), tall cordgrass (*Spartina pectinata* and *Spartina cynosuroides*), hightide bush (*Iva frutescens*), cattails (*Typha angustifolia* and *Typha latifolia*), groundsel (*Baccharis halmilifolia*), marsh mallow (*Hibiscus palustris*) and the intertidal zone including low marsh cordgrass (*Spartina alterniflora*)."

30. New York State ECL §51-0703 (7).

" 'Wetlands.' Land and lands under water which may be permanently, temporarily or intermittently covered with fresh or salt-water and commonly referred to as flood basins or flats, meadows, marshes, shrub swamps, wooded swamps, swamps or bogs."

31. North Carolina--Permits to dredge or fill in or about estuarine waters or state-owned lakes. G.S. §§ 113-229 (n) (2) and (3).

"(2) 'Estuarine waters' means all the waters of the Atlantic Ocean within the boundary of North Carolina and all the waters of the bays, sounds, rivers, and tributaries thereto seaward of the dividing line between coastal fishing waters and inland fishing waters agreed upon by the Department of Natural Resources and Community Development and the Wildlife Resources Commission, within the meaning of G.S. 113-129.

"(3) 'Marshland' means any salt marsh or other marsh subject to regular or occasional flooding by tides, including wind tides (whether or not the tidewaters reach the marshland areas through natural or artificial water-courses), provided this shall not include hurricane or tropical storm tides. Salt marshland or other marsh shall be those areas upon which grow some, but not necessarily all, of the following salt marsh and marsh plant species: Smooth or salt water Cordgrass (*Spartina alterniflora*), Black Needlerush (*Juncus roemerianus*), Glasswort (*Salicornia spp.*), Salt Grass (*Distichlis spicata*), Sea Lavender (*Limonium spp.*), Bulrush (*Scirpus spp.*), Saw Grass (*Cladium jamaicense*), Cattail (*Typha spp.*), Salt-Meadow Grass (*Spartina patens*), and Salt Reed-Grass (*Spartina cynosuroides*)."

32. North Dakota General Property Assessment. N.D. Century Code 57-2-8.4.

"For the purpose of this section 'wetlands' means all types 3, 4, and 5 wetlands, as determined by the commissioner of agriculture and the game and fish commissioner, in accordance with United States Fish and Wildlife Circular No. 39 (1971 edition), drainage of which would be feasible and practical."

33. North Dakota Waterbank Program. N.D. Century Code 61-31-2.

" 'Wetlands' means all types 3, 4 and 5 wetlands, as determined by the commissioner [of agriculture] with the advice of the game and fish commis-sioner, in accordance with the United States Fish and Wildlife Service Circular No. 39 (1971 edition)."

34. Pennsylvania Oil and Gas Act. 58 P.S. §601.103.

" 'Wetland.' Those areas that are inundated or saturated by surface or groundwater at a frequency and duration sufficient to support and that under normal circumstances do support a prevalence of vegetation typically adapted

for life in saturated soil conditions, including swamps, marshes, bogs and
similar areas."

35. Rhode Island General Laws 2-1-14.

"A coastal wetland shall mean any salt marsh bordering on the tidal
waters of this state, whether or not the tide waters reach the littoral area
through natural or artificial water courses, and such uplands contiguous
thereto, but extending no more than fifty (50) yards inland therefrom, as the
director shall deem reasonably necessary to protect such salt marshes for the
purposes set forth in § 2-1-13. Salt marshes shall include those areas upon
which grow some, but not necessarily all of the following:

Salt meadow grass (*Spartina patens*), spike grass (*Distichlis spicata*),
black grass (*Juncus gerardii*), saltmarsh grass (*Spartina alterniflora*), saltworts
(*Salicornia europaea*, and *Salicornia bigelovii*), sea lavender (*Limonium
carolinianum*), saltmarsh bulrushes (*Scirpus robustus*, and *Scirpus paludosus
var. atlanticus*), sand spurrey (*Spergularia marina*), switch grass (*Panicus
virgatum*), tall cordgrass (*Spartina pectinata*), high-tide bush (*Iva frutescens
var. oraria*), cattails (*Typha angustifolia*, and *Typha latifolia*), spike rush
(*Eleocharis rostellata*), chairmaker's rush (*Scirpus americana*), bent grass
(*Argostis palustria*), and sweet grass (*Hierochlee odorats*). The occurrence and
extent of saltmarsh peat at the undisturbed surface shall be construed to be
true evidence of the extent of a salt marsh or a part thereof."

36. Rhode Island General Laws 2-1-20 (d).

"The term 'Fresh water wetlands' as used in this chapter shall include,
but not be limited to marshes; swamps; bogs; ponds; rivers; river and stream
flood plains and banks; areas subject to flooding or storm flowage; emergent
and submergent plant communities in any body of fresh water including rivers
and streams and that area of land within fifty feet (50') of the edge of any
bog, marsh, swamp or pond."

37. South Carolina--Coastal Tidelands and Wetlands. §48-39-10 (G).

"'Tidelands' means all areas which are at or below mean high tide and
coastal wetlands, mudflats, and similar areas that are contiguous or adjacent to
coastal waters and are an integral part of the estuarine systems involved.
Coastal wetlands include marshes, mudflats, and shallows and means those areas
periodically inundated by saline waters whether or not the saline waters reach
the area naturally or through artificial water courses and those areas that are
normally characterized by the prevalence of saline water vegetation capable of
growth and reproduction. Provided, however, nothing in this definition shall
apply to wetland areas that are not an integral part of an estuarine system.
Further, until such time as the exact geographic extent of this definition can
be scientifically determined, the Council shall have the authority to designate
its approximate geographic extent."

38. Tennessee Natural Areas Preservation--Wetlands. T.C.A. 11-14-401 (1) (B).

" 'Wetlands' means lands which have hydric soils and a dominance (fifty percent (50%) or more of stem count based on communities) of obligate hydrophytes. They include the following generic types:

(i)   Fresh water meadows;
(ii)   Shallow fresh water marshes;
(iii)   Shrub swamps with semipermanent water regimes most of the year;
(iv)   Wooded swamps or forested wetlands;
(v)   Open fresh water except farm ponds; and
(vi)   Bogs.

[Note the separate definition for "Bottomland hardwood forests" in §401(1)(A).]

39. Texas--Coastal Wetland Acquisition. Texas Natural Resource Code §33.233(3).

" 'Coastal wetland' means marshes and other areas of high biologic productivity where seawater is present during times other than and in addition to storms or hurricanes as defined by the Beaufort Wind Scale, but does not include any areas seaward of the line of mean annual low spring tide, nor any mainland area where seawater is present only during storms or hurricanes as defined by the Beaufort Wind Scale, and the presence at a given point of vegetation characteristic of marshes containing seawater is prima facie evidence that seawater is present at the point during times other than and in addition to storms or hurricanes as defined by the Beaufort Wind Scale."

40. Vermont--Municipal and Regional Planning and Development. 24 V.S.A. §117-4303(19). Vermont--Water Resources Management. 10 V.S.A. §29-902(5).

" 'Wetlands' means those areas of the state that are inundated by surface or groundwater with a frequency sufficient to support vegetation or aquatic life that depend on saturated or seasonally saturated soil conditions for growth and reproduction. Such areas include but are not limited to marshes, swamps, sloughs, potholes, fens, river and lake overflows, mud flats, bogs and ponds, but excluding such areas as grow food or crops in connection with farming activities."

41. Virginia Code §§ 62.1-13.2 (f), (l), and (m).

"(f) 'Vegetated wetlands' means all that land lying between and contiguous to mean low water and an elevation above mean low water equal to the factor 1.5 times the mean tide range at the site of the proposed project in the county, city or town in question; and upon which is growing on July one, nineteen   hundred seventy-two or grows thereon subsequent thereto, any one or more of the following:

saltmarsh cordgrass (*Spartina alterniflora*), saltmeadow hay (*Spartina patens*), saltgrass (*Distichlis spicata*), black needle-rush (*Juncus roemerianus*), saltwort (*Salicornia spp.*), sea lavender (*Limonium spp.*), marsh elder (*Iva frutescens*), groundsel bush (*Baccharis halimifolia*), wax myrtle (*Myrica sp.*), sea oxeye (*Borrichia frutescens*), arrow arum (*Peltandra virginica*), pickerelweed (*Pontederia cordata*), big cordgrass (*Spartina cynosuroides*), rice cutgrass (*Leersia oryzoides*), wild rice (*Zizania aquatica*), bulrush (*Scirpus validus*), spikerush (*Eleocharis sp.*), sea rocket (*Cakile edentula*), southern wildrice (*Zizaniopsis miliacea*), cattails (*Typha spp.*), three-squares (*Scirpus spp.*), button bush (*Cephalanthus occidentalis*), bald cypress (*Taxodium distichum*), black gum (*Nyssa sylvatica*), tupelo (*Nyssa aquatica*), dock (*Rumex spp.*), yellow pond lily (*Nuphar spp.*), marsh fleabane (*Pluchea purpurascens*), royal fern (*Osmunda regalis*), marsh hibiscus (*Hibiscus moscheutos*), beggar's ticks (*Bidens sp.*), smartweeds (*Polygonum sp.*), arrowhead (*Sagittaria spp.*), sweet flag (*Acorus calamus*), water hemp (*Amaranthus cannabinus*), reed grass (*Phragmites communis*), and switch grass (*Panicum virgatum*).

"The vegetated wetlands of Back Bay and its tributaries and the vegetated wetlands of the North Landing River and its tributaries shall mean all marshes subject to flooding by normal tides, including wind tides, provided this shall not include hurricane or tropical storm tides and upon which one or more of the following vegetation species are growing or grows thereon subsequent to the passage of this amendment:

saltmarsh cordgrass (*Spartina alterniflora*), saltmeadow hay (*Spartina patens*), black needlerush (*Juncus roemerianus*), marsh elder (*Iva frutescens*), groundsel bush (*Baccharis halimifolia*), wax myrtle (*Myrica sp.*) arrow arum (*Peltandra virginica*), pickerelweed (*Pontederia cordata*), big cordgrass (*Spartina cynosuroides*), rice cutgrass (*Leersia oryzoides*), wildrice (*Zizania aquatica*), bulrush (*Scirpus validus*), spikerush (*Eleocharis sp.*), cattails (*Typha sp.*), three-squares (*Scirpus spp.*), dock (*Rumex sp.*), smartweed (*Polygonum sp.*), yellow pond lily (*Nuphar sp.*), royal fern (*Osmunda regalis*), marsh hibiscus (*Hibiscus moscheutos*), beggar's tick (*Bidens sp.*), arrowhead (*Sagittaria sp.*), water hemp (*Amaranthus cannabinus*), reed grass (*Phragmites communis*) and switch grass (*Panicum virgatum*).

"(l) 'Nonvegetated wetlands' means all that land lying contiguous to mean low water and which land is between mean low water and mean high water not otherwise include in the term 'vegetated wetlands' as defined herein and also includes those unvegetated areas of Back Bay and its tributaries and the North Landing River and its tributaries subject to flooding by normal tides including wind tides but not including hurricane or tropical storm tides.

"(m) 'Wetlands' means both vegetated and nonvegetated wetlands."

42. Washington Shoreline Management Act of 1971. R.C.W.A. 90.58.030(2)(f).

" 'Wetlands' or 'wetland areas' means those lands extending landward for two hundred feet in all directions as measured on a horizontal plane from the ordinary high water mark; floodways and contiguous floodplain areas landward two hundred feet from such floodways; and all marshes, bogs, swamps, and

133

river deltas associated with the streams, lakes, and tidal waters which are subject to the provisions of this chapter; the same to be designated as to location by the department of ecology: Provided, That any county or city may determine that portion of a one-hundred-year-flood plain to be included in its master program as long as such portion includes, as a minimum, the floodway and the adjacent land extending landward two hundred feet there from...."

43. Wisconsin Laws of 1977, Chapter 374--REPEALED.

" 'Wetlands' include areas commonly called marshes, swamps, thickets, bogs or wet meadows; areas where water stands at, above or within approximately 18 inches below soil surface for significant portions of years with normal precipitation; areas with soils of the type identified on soils maps as histisols (peat and muck) or as mineral soils that are 'somewhat poorly drained,' 'poorly drained,' or 'very poorly drained,' or as 'wet alluvial lands,' 'marsh,' or 'water'; and areas where aquatic or semiaquatic vegetation is dominant."

44. Wisconsin--Wetlands Mapping. W.S.A. 23.32 (1).

"In this section 'wetland' means an area where water is at, near, or above the land surface long enough to be capable of supporting aquatic or hydrophytic vegetation and which has soils indicative of wet conditions."

45. Wisconsin Department of Natural Resources Policy Statement on Wetland Preservation, Restoration, and Management (N.R. 1.95).

"Wetlands are here defined as those land areas characterized by surface water or saturated soils during at least a part of the growing season such that moist soil vegetation or shallow water plants can thrive. The permanent channels of streams and rivers and the open water of lakes and reservoirs are not included in this definition."

Examples of Miscellaneous Definitions

46. Marinette County, Wisconsin, Shoreland Zoning Ordinance No. 24, §2.29.

Wetlands are "[a]reas where ground water is at or near the surface much of the year or where any segment of the plant cover is deemed an aquatic according to N. C. Fassett's Manual of Aquatic Plants."

47. Western Australia Department of Conservation and Environment, Guidelines to the Conservation and Management of Wetlands in Western Australia, 1977.

"There are many definitions of 'wetlands' some of which are specific to certain geographical areas. In Western Australia wetlands have been defined by the Wetlands Advisory Committee (established by the Department of Conservation and Environment) as:

'Areas of seasonally, intermittently or permanently waterlogged soils or inundated land, whether natural or otherwise, fresh or saline, e.g. waterlogged soils, ponds, billabongs, lakes, swamps, tidal flats, estuaries, rivers and their tributaries.'"

48. Brooks, A., Waterways and Wetlands (London: British Trust for Conservation Volunteers Ltd., 1976).

"By 'wetlands' we mean sites which are waterlogged or water-covered for a significant part of the year: swamps, marshes, bogs, fens and wet grasslands. Such categories often overlap. Ponds may be temporary, marshes may flood. Fens may contain open pools, lake shores may be swamp-fringed. In the same way, wetlands grade into damp scrub, heath or moorland. But in every habitat covered by this Handbook you are likely to get your feet wet. Salt and brackish habitats have, however been excluded."

49. Darnell, R., Impacts of Construction Activities in Wetlands of the United States, EPA-600/3-76-045 (Corvallis, Oreg.: U.S. Environmental Protection Agency, 1976).

Glossary, p. 377. Wetland: "land containing high quantities of soil moisture, i.e., submerged or where the water table is at or near the surface for most of the year."

50. Herdendorf, C.E., S.M. Hartley, and M.D. Barnes, eds. Fish and Wildlife Resources of the Great Lakes Coastal Wetlands Within the United States, Vol. I. Overview (Washington, D.C.: Biological Services Program, U.S. Fish and Wildlife Service, 1980).

Wetlands: "areas which are periodically or permanently inundated and which are characterized, under normal conditions, by vegetation that requires saturated soils for growth and reproduction."

51. Anderson, James R., Ernest E. Hardy, and John T. Roach. A Land Use Classification System for Use with Remote Sensor Data, U.S.G.S. Circular 671 (Washington, D.C.: U.S. Geological Survey, 1972).

"Wetland-non-forested; standing shallow water on herbaceous vegetation."

"Wetland-forested; standing shallow water on woody vegetation."

52.   Larson, J.S., ed., _A Guide to Important Characteristics and Values of Freshwater Wetlands in the Northeast_, Publ. No. 31 (Boston: University of Massachusetts Water Resources Research Center, 1973).

"Freshwater wetlands include, but are not limited to, wet meadows; marshes; swamps; bogs; areas where groundwater, flowing or standing surface water or ice provide a significant part of the supporting substrate for a plant community for a significant part of the year; emergent and submergent plant communities in inland waters; that portion of any bank which touches any inland waters; and land, including submerged land, which consists of any of the soil types designated as but not limited to, very poorly drained by the National Cooperative Soils Survey, as may be amended from time to time, of the Soil Conservation Service of the United States Department of Agriculture."

Appendix 5-B
Wetlands Definitions-Variables

Definition*	Description	Vegetation	Soil	Water level	Any, Both, All, etc.	Size Limitation	Remarks
FEDERAL							
Shaw and Fredine	Coastal/Inland	X	-	X	Both	-	Directed toward wetlands as waterfowl habitat.
16 U.S.C. 1302	Inland/Freshwater	X		X	Both	-	Clause 1 allows for evolving classification schemes.
Early Cowardin	Coastal/Inland	X	X	X	Any	-	
Cowardin et al, 1977	Coastal/Inland	X	X	X	Unclear	-	Water level and one other.
Exec. Order 11990	Coastal/Inland	X	X	X	Both	-	
Cowardin et al, 1979	Coastal/Inland	X	X	X	Any	-	Comprehensive, widely used.
33 CFR 323.2	Coastal/Inland	X	X	X	Both	-	
"Swampbuster"	Coastal/Inland	X	X	X	All	-	
STATE							
California							
30121	Coastal			X		-	"...contain significant... resources."
5812	Coastal/Inland			X		-	
Connecticut							
22a-29	Coastal	X		X	Both	-	Vegetation list.
22a-38	Inland		X			-	Relies upon soil classification.

137

Definition*	Description	Vegetation	Soil	Water Level	Water Any, Both, All, etc.	Size Limitation	Remarks
Delaware 7 D.C.A. 6603	Coastal/Inland	x		x	Both	For fresh-water	Vegetation list. Note freshwater definition immediately following vegetation list.
Florida F.S. 403.911	Coastal/Inland	x	x	x		-	See Florida Rules for determining the landward extent of water.
Georgia 12-5-281	Coastal	x		x	Both	-	Vegetation list; specific to "marshlands".
Iowa 427.1	Inland			x			Makes reference to uselessness of the wetland in its original condition.
Maine 38 M.R.S.A. 406	Freshwater	x	x		Both	10 acres	Provides for nonwetland areas contained within a larger wetland system.
38 M.R.S.A. 472	Coastal	x		x			Tidal "debris line".
Maryland 9-101(j)	Private Coastal			x			
9-101(m)	State Coastal			x			
Massachusetts ALM GL C.131 40	Coastal/Freshwater	x		x	Unclear	-	Syntax confusing.
ALM GL C.181 40A	Inland	x		x	Unclear	-	Provision for banks.
Michigan M.C.L.A. 281.702.1	Inland	x		x	Both	Variable	Special emphasis on contiguity.
Minnesota 105.37	Inland	x		x	Both	Variable	Uses Circular 39.

Definition*	Description	Vegetation	Soil	Water Level	Any, Both, All, etc.	Size Limitation	Remarks
Mississippi 49-27-5	Coastal		x			-	
New Jersey N.J.S.A. 19:9A-2	Coastal	x		x	Both	-	Vegetation list.
New York Exec. Law 802 ECL 24-0107	Coastal/Inland Freshwater	x		x		Variable -	Adirondack Park Agency Act. Vegetation list; area must appear on freshwater wetlands map.
ECL 25-0103	Tidal	x		x	Unclear	-	Vegetation list.
ECL 51-0703	Coastal/Inland			x		-	
North Carolina G.S. 113-229	Coastal	x		x	Both	-	Vegetation list; specific to "Estuarine waters" and "Marshland".
North Dakota N.D.C.C. 57-2-8.4	Inland	x		x	Both	-	Uses Circular 39; specifies that "drainage would be feasible and practical."
N.D.C.C. 61-31-2	Inland	x		x	Both	-	Uses Circular 39.
Pennsylvania 58 P.S. 601.103	Inland	x		x	Both	-	
Rhode Island 2-1-14	Coastal	x		x	Both	-	Vegetation list; provision for adjacent uplands.
2-1-20	Freshwater	x		x	Unclear	-	Syntax confusing.
South Carolina 48-39-10	Coastal	x		x	Both	-	Specifies "Tidelands".
Tennessee T.C.A. 11-14-401	Inland	x	x	x	Both	-	Specified "obligate hydrophytes".

139

Definition*	Description	Vegetation	Soil	Water Level	Any, Both, All, etc.	Size Limitation	Remarks
Texas							
33.233	Coastal	x		x	Unclear	-	Syntax confusing.
Vermont							
24 V.S.A. 117-4303	Inland	x		x	Both	-	
10 V.S.A. 29-902	Inland	x		x	Both	-	
Virginia							
62.1-13.2	Coastal	x		x	Variable	-	Vegetation list; subdivides wetlands into "Vegetated" and "Nonvegetated".
Washington							
R.C.W.A. 90.58.030	Coastal	Unclear		x		-	Vegetated areas designed by the Department of Ecology.
Wisconsin							
Ch. 374	Inland	x	x	x	Any	-	Repealed.
W.S.A. 23.32	Inland	x	x	x	All	-	
N.R. 1.95	Inland	x		x	Both	-	
MISCELLANEOUS:							
Marinette County	Inland	x		x	Either	-	Fassett's Manual of Aquatic Plants used to determine vegetation variable.
Western Australia	Coastal/Inland			x		-	Notes geographic variability of wetland definition.
Brooks, 1976	Freshwater			x		-	
Darnell, 1976	Coastal/Inland			x		-	
Merendorf et al, 1980	Freshwater	x		x	Both	-	Specifically for Great L. Region.
Anderson et al, 1972	Coastal/Inland	x		x	Both	-	Requires standing water.
Larson, 1973	Freshwater	x	x	x	Unclear	-	

OVERVIEW OF EXISTING REGULATORY PROGRAMS[1]

Michele Leslie, Edwin H. Clark II, and Robert B. Reed

INTRODUCTION

Every level of government has regulatory programs that are or could be used to protect wetlands. In these programs the government agency controls, in some manner, either the way in which wetland owners can use their land or activities that may alter wetlands.

Some regulatory programs focus on controlling alterations of the wetland resource itself. Examples include the Section 404 program of the Clean Water Act at the federal level, various wetlands protection laws adopted by some state governments, and some zoning provisions at the local level.

Other regulatory programs focus not on the wetland resource, but on the activity that may cause the alteration. Protecting wetlands may be only a small part of these regulatory programs. Examples include permitting requirements for dams and water diversions, controls over waste water discharges, and regulations controlling the disposal of hazardous wastes.

Still other programs may regulate the use and alteration of wetlands in order to protect other resources (particularly wildlife) that depend upon the proper functioning of these areas. For example, the Endangered Species Act has been used to prevent several different types of wetlands alterations when such changes would be detrimental to wildlife species officially listed as endangered.

In many cases, several different regulatory programs at different levels of government may pertain. And in some cases the most well-known regulations are not those pertaining directly to the activity, but those that come into effect when the application for a permit under the direct regulatory program

The authors are former associate, former vice president, and former research fellow, respectively, The Conservation Foundation, Washington, D.C.

triggers additional laws requiring review, coordination, and environmental impact assessments.

Questions about legislative language and intent as well as such basic issues as how a wetland should be defined often make the precise scope of regulatory programs difficult to define. Questions continually arise about the reach of regulatory programs and the processes used to implement them.

The answers to these questions are rarely clear, may be different in different regions, and are often modified by the most recent legislative amendment, administrative determination, or court decision. Thus, attempts to define the scope of existing regulatory programs and identify inadequacies in these programs must be interpreted cautiously. This is particularly true of the "Section 404 program" implemented by the U.S. Army Corps of Engineers (Corps) and the U.S. Environmental Protection Agency (EPA). Because of the importance of this program and the controversies surrounding its implementation, it is the primary focus of this paper.

FEDERAL REGULATORY PROGRAMS

Section 404 of the federal Clean Water Act[2] is the most extensive and controversial federal wetlands regulatory program, and is the only federal program that directly and specifically regulates the alteration of wetland resources. Section 404 requires a permit to be obtained from the Corps before dredged or fill material can be discharged into any waters of the United States. Its protection of wetlands therefore, is limited to those physical alterations (and associated chemical and biological impacts) associated with the disposal of such dredged or fill materials in a wetland area.

The §404 program is administered by both the Corps and EPA, while the U.S. Fish and Wildlife Service (FWS) and the National Marine Fisheries Service (NMFS) have important advisory roles. The Corps has the primary responsibility for the permit program and is authorized, after notice and opportunity for a public hearing, to issue permits for the discharge of dredged or fill material. The Corps receives about 11,000 to 12,000 permit applications per year. Tens of thousands of other discharges are covered by general permits issued on a regional or nationwide basis; these usually do not require individual permits as long as the discharger complies with standard conditions issued by the Corps.

EPA has a responsibility to review and comment on permit applications being evaluated by the Corps. In addition, the agency's responsibilities include: preparing, in conjunction with the Corps, guidelines for the specification of disposal sites (404(b)(1)); denying or restricting the use of any defined area as a disposal site if such use would have certain unacceptable adverse effects (404(c)); administering provisions for state assumption of the permit programs (404(h)); determining the applicability of exemptions specified in section 404(f) to the permitting requirements; and general enforcement responsibilities (309).

The primary role of the FWS in the §404 permit program is one of consultation and assistance under the Fish and Wildlife Coordination Act (FWCA).[3] The specifics of this role have changed over the years as reflected in a series of revisions of the interagency Memoranda of Agreement (MOA) between the U.S. Department of the Interior (DOI) and the Corps that detail procedures for review of permit applications, provision of recommendations to the Corps, and elevation of decisions to higher levels of authority within the two agencies under certain conditions. The DOI has designated FWS to represent them in §404 permit reviews and negotiations.

The NMFS has review responsibilities similar to the FWS for certain Section 404 permit actions when they relate to marine resources. NMFS has a range of resource protection responsibilities under the FWCA, the Magnuson Fishery Conservation and Management Act,[4] the Marine Protection Research and Sanctuaries Act of 1972,[5] the Marine Mammal Protection Act, and the Endangered Species Act. Its §404 review procedures are set forth in a Memorandum of Understanding (MOU) with the Corps which is similar to that signed with the DOI.

The environmental guidelines used to evaluate §404 permit applications are those issued by EPA in conjunction with the Corps pursuant to §404(b)(1) of the Act. These guidelines generally prohibit discharge of dredged or fill material into waters of the U.S. unless there is no available, practicable alternative having less impact on the aquatic ecosystem; the dischargers will neither violate other applicable laws (such as state water quality standards, toxic effluent standards, Endangered Species Act) nor significantly degrade the waters they are discharged into; and all appropriate and practicable steps must be taken to minimize and otherwise mitigate impacts on the ecosystem.

Under the authority of §404(c), EPA may prohibit, withdraw, or restrict disposal of dredged or fill material into waters of the United States if the discharge would have unacceptable adverse effects on municipal water supplies, shellfish beds and fishery areas (including spawning and breeding areas), wildlife, or recreational areas.

EPA works with the Corps during the permit decision process whenever possible to ensure unacceptable adverse impacts are avoided. EPA generally raises significant environmental issues on about one sixth of proposed permits. Most of these are addressed by the Corps in its permitting decision process. The Corps and EPA have developed a process[6] which addresses permit review issues such as the interpretation of the §404(b)(1) guidelines.

In many instances, the requirements of the §404 program overlap the requirements of Section 10 of the Rivers and Harbors Act of 1899.[7] This statute requires the Corps to regulate "all work or structures" that are placed in or could affect the navigable waters of the United States. The Corps is responsible for implementing the Section 10 permit program, although the evaluation process includes review by other agencies and notification of the public as well. The agency estimates that approximately two-thirds of §404 permit applications must also be reviewed under these provisions.

Program Coverage and Exemptions

Substantial controversy exists about what areas, what types of alterations, and what types of activities fall under the requirements of §404.

The geographic scope of regulatory authority under §404 has been subject to extensive litigation. In 1975, the courts confirmed that Congress had intended that the §404 program be broadly applied to waters of the U.S., not just to traditionally navigable waters.[8] Vigorous congressional efforts to restrict the jurisdiction of §404 in response to this decision through legislative amendment were unsuccessful.[9] Some recent court cases have extended the applicability of §404 to inland wetlands that are groundwater-dependent or infrequently flooded by surface water.[10] In 1985, EPA issued a legal memorandum[11] which concluded that the §404 requirements do apply to the millions of acres of "isolated waters" which are or could be used as habitat by migratory birds or endangered species. However, this issue remains legally and publicly contentious.[12]

The extent to which §404 regulates different types of alterations is also a subject of controversy. Section 404 relates only to the discharge of dredged or fill material. Wetlands, however, are also subject to a number of other different types of physical alteration such as drainage, excavation, and the diversion or removal of their water supply (see Table 6-1). Such activities are not regulated under this section unless they also involve the discharge of dredged or fill material.

If, however, an activity that results in these and other types of alterations also results in the discharge of dredged or fill material into the wetlands, it will in many cases be subject to the §404 permitting requirements unless it is exempted by the statute. The definition of terms such as discharge and fill material, however, can be very controversial, and thus the extent to which §404 applies to activities that alter wetlands without directly filling them remains unclear. The displacement of surface material into wetlands during land clearing operations, for instance, may fall under the Act.

Table 6-1

TYPES OF WETLAND ALTERATION

Physical

1. Filling: adding any material to change the bottom level of a wetland or to replace the wetland with dry land;

2. Draining: removing the water from a wetland by ditching, tiling, pumping, etc.;

3. Excavating: dredging and removing soil and vegetation from a wetland;

4. Diverting Water Away: preventing the flow of water into a wetland by removing water upstream, lowering lake levels, or lowering groundwater tables;

5. Clearing: removing vegetation by burning, digging, application of herbicide, scraping, discing, mowing or otherwise cutting;

6. Flooding: raising water levels, either behind dams or by pumping or otherwise channeling water into a wetland;

7. Diverting or Withholding Sediment: trapping sediment, through construction of dams, channelization or other types of projects; thereby inhibiting the regeneration of wetlands in natural areas of deposition, such as deltas;

8. Shading: placing pile-supported platforms or bridges over wetlands, causing vegetation to die;

9. Conducting Activities in Adjacent Areas: disrupting the interactions between wetlands and adjacent land areas, or incidentally impacting wetlands through activities at adjoining sites;

Chemical

1. Changing Nutrient Levels: increasing or decreasing levels of nutrients within the local water and/or soil system, forcing changes in wetland plant community;

2. Introducing Toxics: adding toxic compounds to a wetland either intentionally (e.g. herbicide treatment to reduce vegetation) or unintentionally, adversely affecting wetland plants and animals;

Biological

1. Grazing: consumption and compaction of vegetation by either domestic or wild animals;

2. Disrupting Natural Populations: reducing populations of existing species, introducing exotic species or otherwise disturbing resident organisms.

Coverage for other activities with less obvious or less significant impacts, such as the placement of pilings for platform or bridge supports, is less firmly established. The regulation of these activities often depends upon the specific facts of the case, and the regulatory decisions are likely to rely on case-by-case determinations. Many of these questions are being fought out in the courts.

The courts have tended to take an expansive view of the range of activities subject to regulation under the §404 program. In the landmark "Lake Ophelia case,"[13] the term "discharge of dredged or fill material" was broadly interpreted to cover land clearing activities that involve a redeposit of soil or vegetation into the waters of the United States.[14]

Other kinds of activities, such as channelization and excavation, are regulated as §404 discharges if they involve more than what the Corps considers to be *de minimus* discharge of dredged or fill materials into the waters of the United States.

However, some activities which can adversely affect and even destroy wetlands, such as drainage and groundwater pumping, are often conducted without discharging dredged or fill material. If there is no such discharge, §404 does not apply.

Some consulting firms are reported to be taking advantage of the uncertainty about the range of §404 applicability by intentionally modifying wetland areas in such a manner as to escape the §404 permitting requirements. For instance, if they can destroy and keep the site free of native wetlands vegetation for five years without exceeding the Corps definition of what is a *de minimus* discharge of dredged or fill material, the Corps may determine that the site is no longer under its jurisdiction.

In addition to these uncertainties, a number of activities that are directly related to the physical loss and alteration of wetlands are specifically exempt from regulation under §404(f). The most important of these are:

147

1. normal farming, silviculture, and ranching practices (as part of established operations);

2. maintenance, including emergency reconstruction of recently damaged parts of currently serviceable structures such as dikes, dams, levees, and similar specified structures;

3. construction or maintenance of farm or stock ponds or irrigation ditches or the maintenance (but not construction) of drainage ditches;

4. construction of temporary sedimentation basins on a construction site which does not include placement of fill material into waters of the United States; and

5. construction or maintenance of farm or forest roads or temporary roads for moving mining equipment if best management practices are followed.

These exemptions do not apply if the discharge is part of an activity whose purpose is to convert an area of the waters of the United States into a use to which it was not previously subject, where the flow or circulation of waters of the United States may be impaired, or the reach of such waters reduced. This limitation on the §404(f) exemptions would, for example, require a farmer to obtain a permit for a discharge to convert a wetland area to upland cropping.

The Corps has also issued a series of nationwide and general permits which allow certain activities to occur without specific permit approval (see Appendix 6-A). Probably the most controversial of these is Nationwide Permit 26 which, subject to the requirements of the §404(b)(1) guidelines, allows fills affecting up to ten acres in headwaters and isolated waters. For fills affecting one to ten acres, the Corps has to be notified before the fill occurs to allow the agency to determine whether the proposed fill can appropriately take place under the general permit. For fills affecting less than one acre, no notification is required, but the proposed activity must still satisfy the conditions governing activities under the general permit.

The Corps also issues regional general permits (covering a limited geographic area) for activities similar in nature to those covered under the nationwide or general permits if these activities will have minimal individual and cumulative environmental impacts.

In addition to formal permits, the Corps has procedures (involving opportunities for public and interagency reviews) for issuing letters of permission where, in the opinion of the district engineer, the proposed work would be minor, not have significant individual or cumulative impact on environmental values, should encounter no appreciable opposition, and meets other requirements governing the implementation of §404.

Program Implementation

Substantial controversy also surrounds the way in which the government is implementing the §404 program. Some observers argue that existing laws may be sufficient in principle, but because of incomplete implementation or inconsistent enforcement, they do not adequately protect wetlands. Other observers argue that EPA and the Corps have unreasonably expanded the coverage of the program.

In evaluating individual §404 permit applications, the Corps evaluates their compliance with the §404(b)(1) guidelines and carries out a public interest review at the district level. This review involves balancing such public interest factors as: conservation interests, economics, aesthetics, wetlands protection, cultural values, navigation, fish and wildlife values, water supply, and water quality. Individual permits applications are judged according to the following criteria:

1. whether they satisfy the §404(b)(1) guidelines;

2. whether they are consistent with Coastal Zone Management Plans in areas having approved plans;

3. whether the state in which the activity is to occur has determined that it would result in a violation of the state's water quality standards;

4. the relevant extent of public and private needs;

5. where unresolved conflicts of resource use exist, the practicability of using reasonable alternative locations and methods to accomplish project purposes; and

6. the extent and permanence of the beneficial and/or detrimental effects the proposed project may have on public and private uses to which the area is suited.

Determining the appropriate balance among these different criteria is extremely difficult and can be very complex and contentious. As a result the relative weight given to different factors may vary from one case to another. All discharges, however, must satisfy the first three criteria.

The §404 program involves substantial shared authorities, competing interests, and overlapping responsibilities among the agencies involved. Since the working relationships among various participating agencies often are established through MOAs and internal agency procedures, they can be modified at the discretion of senior agency officials. Thus, the balance of influence in the §404 permitting process can shift without formal congressional direction or approval. In recent years, for example, the influence of the FWS in the permitting process declined as a result of a 1982 MOA revision, and then was strengthened by a subsequent revision.

Most of the actual implementation of the program takes place at the regional level. Unfortunately, this may complicate matters further because the different agencies may have different regional structures. As a result, states often must deal with cross-cutting jurisdictional boundaries and even multiple offices of the same agencies. Although the Corps has attempted to modify its district boundaries so they are more consistent with political boundaries, seventeen states have more than one district office. The extreme case is Missouri which has five.

The General Accounting Office (GAO) recently conducted a review of many aspects of the implementation of the §404 program.[15] This study found that the Corps districts did take the comments of the reviewing agencies into account in making permit decisions, and often modified the permit conditions, or even denied the permit entirely, in response to these comments. The study found, however, that if the agencies could not agree at the district level, the commenting agencies rarely appealed cases for higher level review because they believe that the appeal process is cumbersome and often ineffective.

A very small percentage of permit applications are formally denied, but many more are modified or withdrawn by the applicant during the review process. In fiscal year 1986, the Corps denied an estimated 500 out of perhaps 14,000 applications--a denial rate of approximately three and a half percent.[16] The agency issued about 10,500 permits and some 3,000 applications were cancelled or withdrawn by the applicant. In fiscal year 1981, 291 out of 10,718 applications were denied.[17] This suggests that the rate of permit denial has increased somewhat in recent years.[18]

The 1986 GAO survey also showed that the Corps issued permits over the denial recommendations of resource agencies in about one-third (with a range of one-fifth to almost two-thirds) of cases where there were major permit decision disagreements.[19] In relatively few of these cases, however, did the resource agency request that the disagreement be raised for resolution by senior agency personnel.

The Corps estimated that for approximately 50 percent of the individual §404 permits it does issue, it requires some mitigation (including project redesign to avoid or reduce effects on wetlands).[20]

Enforcement authority is shared between the Corps and EPA, with at least potential overlapping of roles. The Corps, as the permitting agency, has primary responsibility for monitoring and enforcing compliance with §404 permit conditions and also pursues many actions against unpermitted (un-authorized) discharges. Although the law does not prevent EPA from taking enforcement actions against noncompliance with permit conditions, EPA generally targets its limited enforcement efforts towards discovery of and enforcement against unpermitted discharges. Anyone in violation of the §404 program, either by conducting an unauthorized activity or by violating permit conditions, is subject to civil or criminal action, or both. As of 1987, violators may be assessed administrative penalties in lieu of a civil judicial referral action.

The GAO reported that about 5,000 alleged violations are processed in Corps district offices each year, of which about 40 percent relate to §404 permits and 30 percent relate to combined §10 and §404 permits.[21] Corps district officials estimated that about 80 percent of reported alleged violations involve unpermitted discharges and the others are for noncompliance with permit conditions.

Because of limited funding for enforcement, a large proportion of violations are not discovered by government officials, rather they are brought to the attention of Corps or EPA personnel by interested members of the public.[22]

The GAO concluded that Corps districts do not systematically seek out violators of §404 permit requirements, nor do they always conduct follow-up investigations of suspected violations brought to their attention. Also, EPA was found to exercise only limited involvement in the program's enforcement. In response, the GAO has recommend·l that the Corps work with EPA to develop a coordinated enforcement program utilizing the resources of both agencies to provide for surveillance, inspection and penalty assessment when violations occur.

Concerns About Program Effectiveness and Efficiency

Only limited information exists about the effectiveness of the §404 program. For instance, no definitive data are available to measure program impacts in terms of wetlands saved or lost.[23] Further, permit documents do not always include the information necessary to begin compiling such data.

Nevertheless, several studies have concluded that the §404 program has reduced wetlands losses, although the level of reduction is uncertain. The Office of Technology Assessment (OTA) cited Corps estimates that permit applicants in 1980-1981 proposed the alteration of a total of 100,000 acres in all Corps districts excluding Alaska. The OTA study found that reviews conducted pursuant to both federal and state requirements resulted in the final permits authorizing alterations in only half this acreage. In addition, the final permit conditions called for 5,000 acres of wetlands to be restored or enhanced in partial compensation for those acres that would be converted.[24]

In a more recent study, the GAO[25] polled several Corps district offices and found that estimates of program effects varied widely. For example, the Vicksburg District reported that it permitted the conversion of 839 acres, or about 60 percent of total acreage proposed for alteration by applicants in fiscal year 1986, and required 10 acres of mitigation in that year. In contrast, the Jacksonville District authorized the conversion of 1,187 acres or 76 percent of that applied for, but also required that permittees create a total of 168 acres of wetlands and enhance 3,998 acres as mitigation.

Some groups, primarily resource agencies and environmental interests believe that the Corps has not been rigorous enough in protecting wetlands. As summarized by the GAO, resource agencies such as the FWS believe that the Corps is not: (1) delineating wetland boundaries broadly enough; (2) considering cumulative impacts of permit decisions; and (3) requiring permit applicants to consider practicable alternatives to development activities in wetlands.[26]

The problem of cumulative impacts is particularly difficult to address under the current regulatory system which uses a permit by permit approach. In addition, many small losses are allowed without any permitting, and many other losses occur outside of the §404 regulatory process. Even where permits are required, the impact of several conversions in an area may be much more significant when they are considered as a whole, rather than as the individual losses considered separately.

But concern about the program is not limited only to people who wish to preserve wetlands. The complex §404 permit program, as well as a number of recently developed aggressive state programs, have been the source of major frustration among developers and private landholders as well.

One complaint is inconsistency. The institutional complexity of the §404 permit program has led to inconsistent policies and practices which contribute both to frustration within the regulated community and to uneven protection of wetlands. Areas noted for inconsistency include: wetland delineation procedures; EPA and Corps regulatory guidance; regulatory implementation among the various Corps districts (some district offices tend to be more restrictive in granting permits or requiring mitigation than others); and the uneven degree of involvement of various federal and state agencies in different regions and in different cases within the same region.

Some members of the regulated community believe too much time is required to process §404 permit applications, and that delays are unreasonably burdensome. Permit processing periods can be particularly long when state and local agencies are involved in approving the permit, or when the proposed alteration is particularly controversial.

The problem of delays was eased at one point in recent years. The Corps calculated that regulatory reforms instituted in 1982 sharply reduced the length of time to obtain individual §404 permits from an average of about 130 days in 1981 to about 77 days in 1986.[27] Applications requiring an Environmental Impact Statement (EIS), which account for less than one percent of all applications, were taking about three years to process.

But the permit processing workload has continued to increase in the past few years, while funding and personnel resources have remained at about the same level. Consequently, some districts are again having difficulties processing applications promptly.

Some members of the regulated community also believe that existing regulatory programs fail to adequately account for special circumstances. Costly wetlands protection measures often are required in cases where applicants believed that potentially affected wetlands had limited value. Oil and gas development companies have asserted that the failure to account for low wetland values in many Alaskan areas constitutes an unreasonable limitation on economic development.[28]

Program Costs

Fiscal year 1987 expenditures for the Corps regulatory program (including responsibilities under §404, §§9 and 10 of the Rivers and Harbors Act, and §103 of the Marine Protection Research and Sanctuaries Act) were about $56 million, of which an estimated $38 to $40 million was for permit processing activities, and $12 to $13 million was for enforcement related activities.[29] The remainder was for miscellaneous studies and other regulatory authorities.

The President's budget for fiscal year 1989 would increase funding for the Corps regulatory program to $60.4 million. Requested funding for EPA activities related to §404 is about $7.7 million, which would continue a trend of $1 million annual increases for this program since fiscal year 1987.

In addition to these agency costs, the applicants may experience significant costs to process permits and modify projects. Permit fees have been held to relatively low levels,[30] but they may represent only a small part of the costs of processing permits for the applicants. Another potentially major cost item can be delays in construction and lost opportunities. The

American Petroleum Institute put the costs of 55 permit delays in southern Louisiana at $19 million in lost or deferred production.

Other Federal Programs

Although §404 is the most important federal wetlands regulatory program, a number of other programs have been enacted over the past 20 years which may also control alterations of wetland areas (see Table 6-2). These programs, however, were established for other purposes, and may offer only limited protection to wetlands.

These other programs may be able to control types of alteration not directly addressed by §404. §404, for instance, does not directly regulate nonphysical wetland alterations, such as chemical contamination or the release of excess nutrients into wetlands. Nor does it address such biological impacts as invasions or introductions of exotic plant and animal species. Such chemical and biological alterations can, as demonstrated by the example of California's Kesterson Reservoir, severely degrade many of the wetlands' functions. But they are extremely unlikely to trigger any §404 permit requirement (except, possibly, if they involve the discharge of dredged or fill material into a wetland).

Some types of alterations can, however, be controlled under other federal statutes. For instance, the Clean Water Act requires National Pollutant Discharge Elimination System (NPDES) permits for any discharges of pollutants into the waters of the United States including wetlands. Nonpoint-source pollution may be controlled under the 1987 Water Quality Act. The Resource Conservation and Recovery Act (RCRA) controls the disposal of hazardous wastes and the Comprehensive Environmental Response, Compensation and Liability Act (CERCLA, better known as Superfund) provides for the clean up of abandoned hazardous waste disposal sites. Both should benefit wetlands because these have in the past been common sites for the disposal of such wastes.

TABLE 6-2

FEDERAL REGULATION OF PRIVATE
ACTIVITIES AFFECTING WETLANDS*

Statutory Authority	Implementing Measures	Explanation
Section 404 of the Clean Water Act (33 USC 1344)	a) Section 404 Dredge and Fill Permit Program Regulations (51 FR 219, at 41220 et seq.) (November 13, 1986); 33 CFR 320 et seq.	Secretary of the Army, acting through the Corps, issues permits for the discharge of dredged or fill material into the waters of the US. Mainly governs new development and construction activities in wetlands. Discharges of material in wetlands less than 1 acre, located above stream headwater or in isolated waters, are generally or authorized under nationwide permit provisions. Corps guidelines describe the agency's policies, and provides guidance on permit processing procedures.
	b) Section 404(b)(1) Guidelines (40 CFR 230)	EPA, in conjunction with the Corps, developed these substantive criteria for evaluating permit applications. They outline impact analysis considerations, procedures for material analysis and testing, and actions to minimize adverse effects. Also generally describe advance identification procedures, to be used when EPA or permitting authority identifies possible future disposal sites or areas generally unsuitable for disposal.
	c) Rule on Activities Exempt from 404 Permit Program Requirements (40 CFR 232 et seq.)	EPA regulation provides detailed guidance on activities exempt from 404 permit requirements, such as those associated with "normal" farming and forestry practices that do not change or restrict the flow or circulation of US waters.
	d) Section 404(c) Procedures (40 CFR 231 et seq.)	EPA rules for exercising its "veto" authority for 404 permit decisions.
	e) Section 404 State Program Transfer Regulations (40 CFR 233 et seq.)	EPA procedures for state assumption of 404 program administration. Details requirements for program approval, operation and enforcement, and provisions for federal oversight.

....

* This table does not include federal support and development programs and policies which may affect private activities through economic incentives.

157

Statutory Authority	Implementing Measures	Explanation
Section 10 of the Rivers and Harbors Act of 1988 (33 USC 403)	Section 10 Permit Regulations for Structures or Work Affecting Navigable Waters (51 FR 41220; 33 CFR 322)	The Corps issues 10 permits for dredge or fill activities, and building of structures (e.g., piers or docks) to ensure that these actions do not adversely affect navigability.
Water Act (33 USC 1341)	Section 401 of the Clean Water Agreements made on a state-by-state basis.	Section 404 permit applicants must obtain state certification that proposed discharges would comply with water quality standards. Some states generally waive exercise of this author.
Fish and Wildlife Coordination Act (16 USC 661 et seq.)	Administrative agreements between agencies.	Federal permit actions related to water projects (e.g., 404 Federal Energy Regulatory Commission (FERC) hydropower (facility licensing) are subject to requirements of the Coordination Act. The USFWS and the NMFS have agreed with regulatory agencies on procedures for exercising review responsibilities to ensure that "equal consideration" be given to fish and wildlife.
Section 402 of the Clean Water Act (33 USC 1342)	National Pollutant Discharge Elimination System (NPDES) Regulations (40 CFR 125; 40 CFR 122)	Water quality criteria and EPA regulations for issuing permits for the discharge of "any pollutant or combination of pollutants" into US waters; discharges regulated under 404 are excepted.
Section 307 of the Coastal Zone Management Act (16 USC 1456)	Regulations on Federal Consistency with Approved Coastal Management Programs (15 CFR 930.1 et seq.)	Requires applicants for federal licenses or permits to conduct an activity in the coastal zone of a state with an approved CZM plan obtain state certification of consistency with the plan.
Executive Order 11990 on Protection of Wetlands (42 FR 26961 (1977))	Incorporated within organizational policies and procedures on an agency-by-agency basis.	Strong directive to federal agencies, including federal and licensing agencies, to minimize the destruction, loss or degradation of wetlands and to preserve and enhance their beneficial values.

Table 2 (continued)

Statutory Authority	Implementing Measures	Explanation
Executive Order 11988 on Floodplain Management (45 FR 26951 (1977))	Incorporated within organizational policies and procedures on an agency-by-agency basis.	Strong directive to federal agencies, including regulatory and licensing agencies, to reduce flood risks and preserve the natural and beneficial values of floodplains.
Endangered Species Act (16 USC 1531 et seq.)	Endangered Species Committee Regulations (50 CFR 402 et seq.)	The FWS and the NMFS issued joint guidelines on review procedures for ensuring that federal actions (including permitting) would not jeopardize listed species.
Wild and Scenic Rivers Act (16 USC 1278 et seq.)	Wild and Scenic Rivers Designated as Components of Water Resources Projects Protection (36 CFR 297.1 et seq.) Areas Designated by Congress as Unsuitable for Mining (30 CFR 761).	FERC and other federal agencies shall not license or support water projects that would have direct adverse effects on the values for which a scenic river was designated. Also restricts mining activities.
Resource Conservation and Recovery Act of 1976 (42 USC 6901 et seq.)	Standards for Owners and Operators of Hazardous Waste Disposal Facilities (40 CFR 264 et seq.)	Holds owners and operators of hazardous waste facilities accountable for meeting performance standards, including prevention of adverse effects on wildlife, vegetation and hydrologic characteristics surrounding the site.
Comprehensive Environmental Response, Compensation, and Liability Act of 1980 (42 USC 9601 et seq.)	Comprehensive Environmental Response, Compensation and Liability Act (CERCLA) Natural Resource Claims Procedures (40 CFR 306).	Outlines procedures to be used by government agencies in obtaining compensation from private interests responsible for release of hazardous substances that cause injury to natural resources.

Possible alterations resulting from the construction of hydroelectric power facilities may also be controlled by the requirement that such facilities be licensed by the Federal Energy Regulatory Commission (FERC), and those resulting from the construction of interstate pipelines are similarly controlled by the fact that they must be licensed by the Interstate Commerce Commission. Provisions of the Lacey Act restrict the importation of exotic plants and animals that potentially could affect wetlands as well as other habitats.

Finally, some federal programs can prevent any type of alteration of wetlands in order to protect certain wildlife resources that depend on the wetlands for their survival. The Endangered Species Act prohibits the taking of endangered or threatened species by any individual, and requires a review of any federally sponsored or permitted project that might impact critical habitats, such as wetlands, for such species. And the Migratory Bird Treaty prohibits the killing of migratory birds unless allowed by law. It was the Migratory Bird Treaty that caused the federal government to stop supplying irrigation water to the Westlands District in California when its return flow was found to be the cause of waterfowl deaths in the Kesterson Reservoir.

Other types of activities which could alter wetlands may also be controlled by federal regulations, particularly if they require a federal permit or federal financial support. In such cases, although the federal action may be unrelated to wetlands protection, it can trigger the requirements of the National Environmental Policy Act (NEPA), which requires the permitting or funding agency to consider the impact of their action on the environment.

The extent to which all of these other federal laws have been used to prevent the alteration of wetlands is not clear. Most have been used for this purpose infrequently, if at all. For others, such as the Endangered Species Act or RCRA, wetlands impacts are more commonly considered.

160

STATE REGULATORY PROGRAMS

States can assume significant regulatory authority under many federal laws. Under §401 of the Clean Water Act, states have the authority to review any federal permit of license which may result in a discharge to waters of the United States, including §404 permit applications, to ensure that actions would be consistent with the state's water quality standards. Although several states exercise this authority, some state program managers believe that the §401 certification provision is not an effective wetlands protection tool because most states have not developed specific water quality criteria for wetlands.[31] Some states, including Minnesota and Ohio, have promulgated antidegradation water quality policies or standards to increase the effectiveness of the certification process. However, many other states essentially waive exercise of their authority under §401, or rarely if ever deny certification.

The Clean Water Act also allows EPA to delegate substantial authority for administration of the §404 permit program to the states, but Michigan was the only state to have assumed such authority by the end of 1988. Major impediments to state delegation include:

o   The Clean Water Act does not provide sufficient funds for the federal government to assist the states to assume wetlands permitting.

o   The Act currently does not allow the state to assume permitting responsibility in waters: (1) which are subject to the ebb and flow of the tide, plus adjacent wetlands; and (2) waters which are presently used or may be susceptible to use (through reasonable improvement) to transport interstate or foreign commerce, plus adjacent wetlands. Jurisdiction over these areas is retained by the Corps.

This limitation means that the §404 permitting requirements could become even more confused if there is state delegation because either of two different agencies, which often have not established close working relationships, will have permitting authority depending upon where the particular fill is being proposed.

o   Aside from that restriction, the act does not provide for partial delegation.   In some cases a sharing of authority may be more attractive to a state than assuming total responsibility.

o   Because EPA is responsible for delegation, that agency also oversees the delegated programs.   Some states may be concerned about the agency being too tight in its oversight, particularly since many issues between EPA and the Corps remain unresolved.   This could accentuate the problem of permittees facing different permit requirements and stringency in nonnavigable reaches than they do in navigable reaches.

o   Even if all §404 authorities could be delegated, the Corps would still retain §10 permitting responsibilities in and adjacent to navigable reaches.   These authorities cannot now be delegated. Thus, under current circumstances, a permittee in navigable reaches would have to obtain two separate permits, one from the state and one from the Corps.   The Corps estimates that two-thirds of its §404 permits also require review under §10.

Thus, several legislative changes would be needed to encourage delegation of §404 permitting responsibilities to the states.   Where such delegation does occur, the state agency, EPA, and the Corps will carefully need to agree on operating procedures and modes of cooperation in order to ensure that the delegated program is implemented effectively and efficiently.

A number of states have adopted their own wetlands regulatory programs (see Table 6-3).   Like federal programs, these may be designed to control certain types of wetlands alterations, to control the activities that result in such alterations, or to protect particular resources that rely on wetlands.

Table 6-3

MATRIX OF STATE WETLAND PROGRAMS

(Number of Programs)

State	401	SEPA	Taxa-tion	Acqui-sition	Research	Coastal Specific	Coastal Other	Inland Specific	Inland Other	Exec. Orders
Alabama	1	-	1	1	2	1	1	-	-	1
Alaska	1	-	-	-	-	1	1	-	1	-
Arizona	1	-	1	-	-	-	-	-	1	-
Arkansas	1	-	-	1	1	-	-	-	1	1
California	1	1	2	6	-	-	-	-	-	-
Colorado	1	-	-	1	1	-	-	-	-	-
Connecticut	1	1	1	3	1	1	2	1	-	-
Delaware	1	-	2	2	1	1	1	-	-	-
Florida	1	-	2	4	1	1	3	1	2	-
Georgia	1	-	1	3	1	1	3	1	1	-
Hawaii	1	-	-	-	-	-	-	-	1	-
Idaho	1	-	1	2	2	1	-	-	-	-
Illinois	1	-	1	2	-	-	-	-	2	-
Indiana	1	1	-	1	-	1	1	-	-	-
Iowa	1	-	2	1	-	-	-	-	-	-
Kansas	1	-	-	-	2	-	-	-	-	2
Kentucky	1	-	2	2	1	1	4	2	-	-
Louisiana	1	-	1	1	-	1	2	1	-	-
Maine	1	1	4	2	-	1	2	-	3	-
Maryland	1	1	2	3	1	1	4	2	-	-
Massachusetts	1	1	1	5	-	2	2	2	1	-
Michigan	1	-	1	3	1	3	1	2	-	-
Minnesota	1	2	1	2	-	1	1	1	-	-
Mississippi	1	-	2	3	1	1	1	-	-	-
Missouri	1	-	2	1	1	-	-	-	-	-
Montana	1	-	-	-	-	-	-	-	-	1

163

State	401	SEPA	Taxa-tion	Acqui-sition	Research	Coastal Specific	Coastal Other	Inland Specific	Inland Other	Exec. Orders
Nebraska	1	1		1	1				1	1
Nevada	1								2	
New Hampshire	1		1	1		1	2	1	1	
New Jersey	1		2	4	1	1	3			
New Mexico	1	1	1	2	1					
New York	1	1	2	3	3	2	2	1		
North Carolina	1	1	2	3		2	2			
North Dakota	1				2				1	
Ohio	1		2	2	3	2	3			
Oklahoma	1		2	1	1	2	3	1		
Oregon	1		1	4				1		
Pennsylvania	1	1	2	1		1	1		1	1
Rhode Island	1	1				1	1		1	
South Carolina	1		2	2						
South Dakota	1		2	2						
Tennessee	1		2	1	1					
Texas	1		1	2	2	2	2	2	2	
Utah	1		1	2						
Vermont	1	1	3	4	2	1	2	1		
Virginia	1	1	1	1	1	2	5	2	5	
Washington	1		1						1	
Wisconsin	1			1						
Wyoming	1									
West Virginia	1		1	2		2	2		2	

Some, as written, appear more explicit and more comprehensive than federal regulations. Incomplete information together with uncertainty about how many of these programs are actually being interpreted and implemented, however, make a precise assessment of the extent of state regulatory protection difficult.

It does appear as if the degree of wetlands regulation by states varies widely, with coastal wetlands generally receiving greater protection than inland wetlands. All coastal states (including those bordering the Great Lakes) except Georgia, Illinois, Indiana, Minnesota, Ohio, and Texas have coastal zone management programs that regulate wetlands as part of the federal Coastal Zone Management Program. Georgia and Minnesota have state coastal regulatory programs that affect wetlands, but they are independent of the federal program.

Although more attention has been given coastal wetlands, 14 states now administer specific wetlands protection laws that include freshwater wetlands: Connecticut, Florida, Maine, Massachusetts, Michigan, Minnesota, New Hampshire, New Jersey, New York, Oregon, Pennsylvania, Rhode Island, Vermont, and Wisconsin. Several states also use other state programs, such as floodplain management and shoreland protection, to restrict some activities affecting inland wetlands.

One area which is substantially ignored by most existing regulatory programs, and where the states clearly have the lead, is in regulating the water suppliers that wetlands need for their survival. Many wetlands alterations are caused by upstream water withdrawals or other hydrological changes. Many states, particularly in the West, have adopted extensive regulatory programs to control such withdrawals. Often, however, nourishing wetlands is not considered to be a beneficial water use under state water laws. In these cases, the state water allocation system apparently cannot be used to ensure that wetlands receive water.

LOCAL REGULATORY PROGRAMS

Local governments have substantial regulatory authority over wetlands through their zoning and other land use and development controls. Local governments can implement wetlands zoning regulations as part of a comprehensive zoning program or adopt them through a separate wetlands ordinance. Local officials may also tighten control over wetlands uses through implementation of local floodplain regulations, subdivision regulations which may require maintenance of open space in wet areas, performance standards, building codes, and other techniques.[32] These types of regulations can apply to activities and methods of alterations, as well as to the wetlands resource itself.

In addition to these standard land use authorities, several states with wetlands regulatory laws delegate implementation of these programs to local governments. Cowles et al.[33] identified Connecticut, Florida, and New York as states which permit such local administration of state programs. Vermont's program is implemented through district environmental commissions, and the administration of a program in Massachusetts involves a system of 2,500 local conservation commissioners that comment on or directly regulate wetlands uses.

States that retain implementation authority at the state level may nevertheless encourage or require local officials to participate in wetlands decisionmaking. Even states without specific wetlands regulation programs afford local governments some capacity to protect wetlands through implementation of other programs, such as state floodplain management and shoreland protection.

CONCLUSIONS

Although many different programs at the federal, state, and local level could be used to protect wetlands, there is little information available to indicate how extensively these programs are used, or how much protection they actually provide.

Some observers believe that the existing programs do, for the most part, provide adequate authority. The weakness, they argue, is in their faulty implementation and weak monitoring and enforcement.

Others argue that the nation's wetlands cannot effectively be protected without extensive legislative changes. At the least, the patchwork of existing programs causes confusion about who is responsible for what. This confusion is exacerbated by such factors as different programs using different wetland definitions, a lack of adequate coordination among the different agencies responsible for the various programs, and a lack of coordination between the regulatory and nonregulatory programs.

The responsible agencies at both the federal and state level have steadily been trying to improve their programs, responding both to the demands of the regulated community and the environmentalists. The responsible agencies are undertaking continuing efforts to make the programs more efficient and equitable. But the best of efforts are unlikely to resolve all the problems. Some are created by the statutory language establishing the programs. And some may be inherent in any program which attempts to control what individuals can do with the property they own.

REFERENCES

1. This paper is, in part, based on and incorporates information provided by representatives of federal agencies participating in the National Wetlands Policy Forum. However, the paper does not necessarily represent agency positions.

2. Section 404 of the Clean Water Act (33 U.S.C. §1344).

3. 16 U.S.C., §661, et seq.

4. 16 U.S.C. §1431, et seq.

5. Ibid.

6. Memorandum of Agreement between EPA and the Corps under §404(q) of the Clean Water Act.

7. 33 U.S.C. §§401, 403, 404, 406, 407 (Rivers and Harbors Act of 1899).

8. Natural Resources Defense Council, Inc. v. Callaway, 392 F. Supp. 685, (D.D.C. 1975).

9. Blumm, M.C., "The Clean Water Act's Section 404 Permit Program Enters its Adolescence: An Institutional and Programmatic Perspective," Ecology Law Quarterly 8:410-472, 1980.

10. Tripp, J.T.B., "The Status of Wetlands Regulations," Environment 28(2):44-45, 1986.

11. U.S. Environmental Protection Agency, Office of General Counsel, Memorandum dated September 12, 1985, p. 4.

12. Jackson, J.K. and W.A. Nitze, "Wetlands Protection Under Section 404 of the Clean Water Act - The Riverside Bayview Decision, its Past and Future," University of Montana Public Land Law Review 7:21-43, 1986.

13. Avoyelles Sportsmen's League, Inc., et al. v. Alexander, et al., 473 F. Supp. 525 (W.D. LA. 1979).

14. Parenteau, P.A. and J.T.B. Tripp, "Federal Regulations Handles, Effectiveness and Remedies," Transactions of the Forty-Fifth North American Wildlife and Natural Resources Conference (Washington, D.C.: Wildlife Management Institute, 1980), pp. 392-401.

15. General Accounting Office, Wetlands: The Corps of Engineers Administration of the Section 404 Program, GAO-RCED-88-110 (Washington, D.C.: U.S. Congress, General Accounting Office, 1988).

16. Ibid.

17. Office of Technology Assessment, Wetlands: Their Use and Regulation, OTA-0-206 (Washington, D.C.: U.S. Congress, Office of Technology Assessment, 1984).

18. The 1981 and 1986 estimates are not strictly comparable, because in 1982 the Corps initiated regulatory reforms which shifted many dredge and fill activities from the "individual" permit classification to the "nationwide" or "regional" permit classifications; Frank Torbett, U.S. Army Corps of Engineers, personal communication, 1987.

19. General Accounting Office, Wetlands: The Corps of Engineers Administration of the Section 404 Program.

20. Torbett, U.S. Army Corps of Engineers, personal communication.

21. General Accounting Office, <u>Wetlands: The Corps of Engineers Administration of the Section 404 Program</u>.

22. Office of Technology Assessment, <u>Wetlands: Their Use and Regulation</u>.

23. General Accounting Office, <u>Wetlands: The Corps of Engineers Administration of the Section 404 Program</u>.

24. Office of Technology Assessment, <u>Wetlands: Their Use and Regulation</u>.

25. General Accounting Office, <u>Wetlands: The Corps of Engineers Administration of the Section 404 Program</u>.

26. Ibid.

27. Torbett, U.S. Army Corps of Engineers, personal communication.

28. Hoffman, R.W., W.P. Metz, and K.C. Myers, "The Cost of Petroleum Development in the Arctic." Unpublished manuscript provided by ARCO Alaska, Anchorage, Alaska, 1987; and Robertson, S.B., "The Alaska Arctic Coast: Wetland or Desert?" Unpublished manuscript provided by ARCO Alaska, Anchorage, Alaska, 1987.

29. General Accounting Office, <u>Wetlands: The Corps of Engineers Administration of the Section 404 Program</u>.

30. Office of Technology Assessment, <u>Wetlands: Their Use and Regulation</u>.

31. Cowles, C.D., L.B. Haas, G.J. Akins, W. Britt, T. Huffman, and A. Wing, <u>State Wetland Protection Programs: Status and Recommendations</u>. Draft (Washington, D.C.: Office of Wetland Protection, U.S. Environmental Protection Agency, 1986).

32. Kusler, J.A., <u>Our National Wetland Heritage: A Protection Guidebook</u> (Washington, D.C.: Environmental Law Institute, 1983).

33. Cowles, et al., <u>State Wetland Protection Programs</u>.

For more information on regulatory programs, see also:

Baldwin, M.F., "Wetlands: Fortifying Federal and Regional Cooperation," <u>Environment</u> 29(7):16-20; 39-42, 1987.

Bean, M.J., <u>The Evolution of National Wildlife Law</u> (New York: Praeger Publishers, 1983), pp. 211-213.

Eichenberg, T. and J. Archer, "The Federal Consistency Doctrine: Coastal Zone Management and 'New Federalism'," <u>Ecology Law Quarterly</u> 14(1):9-68, 1987.

Kusler, J.A., "Strengthening State Wetland Regulations," U.S. Fish and Wildlife Service FWS/OBS-78/98 (Washington, DC: U.S. Fish and Wildlife Service, 1978).

Rapoport, S., "The Taking of Wetlands Under Section 404 of the Clean Water Act," Environmental Law 17(1):111-124, 1986.

Rosenbaum, N., "The State Role in Wetlands Protection. Environmental Comment" (Washington, D.C.: Urban Land Institute, July 1978), pp. 9-15.

Activities Allowed by the U.S. Army Corps of Engineers
Under Nationwide or General Permits

The Corps of Engineers is authorized to issue general permits--regional, if issued by a division or district engineer, and nationwide, for activities permitted throughout the nation--for activities of similar nature with minimal individual and cumulative adverse effects. General permits may be granted under Section 10 (§10) of the Rivers and Harbors Act or Section 404 (§404) of the Clean Water Act. Such permits allow certain activities to occur with little delay or paperwork, although several categories require applicants to notify the district engineer before commencing activity. Briefly, such activities and the programs to which they pertain, include:

1. the placement of aids to navigation and regulatory markers (§10);

2. structures constructed in artificial canals (§10);

3. the repair, rehabilitation, or replacement of any previously authorized, currently serviceable structure or fill (§10 and §404);

4. fish and wildlife harvesting devices and activities (§10);

5. tide gages and scientific structures, such as water quality testing devices (§10);

6. survey activities, including core sampling, and seismic exploratory operations (§10 and §404);

7. outfall structures and associated intake structures where the effluent from that outfall has been permitted under the National Pollutant Discharge Elimination System program (§10 and §404);

8. structures for the exploration, production, and transportation of oil, gas, and minerals on the outer continental shelf (§10);

9. structures placed in anchorage areas to facilitate mooring of vessels (§10);

10. noncommercial, single boat mooring buoys (§10);

11. temporary buoys and markers placed for recreational use (§10);

12. discharge of material for backfill or bedding for utility lines (§404);

13. bank stabilization activities of limited scale, designed to reduce erosion, that do not fill or impair flow into or out of a wetland (§10 and §404);

14. minor road crossing fills that do not restrict flows and involve the discharge of less than 200 cubic yards of fill material (§10 and §404);

15. discharges of dredged or fill material incidental to the construction of bridges across navigable waters, not including causeways or approach fills (§404);

16. return water from an upland, contained dredged material disposal area (§404);

17. fills associated with small hydropower projects at existing reservoirs licensed by the Federal Energy Regulatory Commission (§404);

18. discharges of dredged or fill material into non-wetland waters of the U.S. of less than 10 cubic yards, not placed for stream diversion (§10 and §404);

19. dredging of no more than 10 cubic yards from navigable waters without connecting them to artificial waterways (§10);

20. structures, work, and discharges for the containment and cleanup of oil and hazardous substances (§10 and §404);

21. structures, work, and discharges associated with authorized surface coal mining activities (§10 and §404);

22. minor work, fills, or temporary structures required for the removal of wrecked, abandoned, or disabled vessels (§10 and §404);

23. activities conducted by other agencies under the provisions of the National Environmental Policy Act (§10 and §404);

24. activities covered under §10, permitted by states that administer their own §404 permit programs, when a §404 permit is also required (§10);

25. discharge of concrete for structural use into tightly sealed cells (§404); and

26. discharges of dredged or fill material into waters or wetlands which cause the loss or substantial adverse modification of less than 10 acres of water or wetland (§404).

CHAPTER 7

MITIGATION POLICY

Michele Leslie

In common usage, mitigation means alleviating or reducing severity or harm. As the term relates to government policies, it embodies concepts which are complex and continually evolving. The Council on Environmental Quality (CEQ) broadly defined mitigation options for all federal activities affecting the environment as follows in its 1978 National Environmental Policy Act (NEPA) guidelines:[1]

o   avoiding the impact altogether by not taking a certain action or parts of an action;

o   minimizing impacts by limiting the degree or magnitude of the action and its implementation;

o   rectifying the impact by repairing, rehabilitating or restoring the impacted environment;

o   reducing or eliminating the impact over time by preservation and maintenance operations during the life of the action; and

o   compensating for the impact by replacing or providing substitute resources or environments.

A number of federal and state agencies have developed mitigation policies and practices related to wetland protection, which reflect the CEQ policy in terms of the agencies' specific missions and mandates. But these policies and their implementation remain highly controversial. Some of the major policy issues remaining unresolved include: the methodology used to determine appropriate mitigation; the timing of mitigation efforts; what types of mitigation are acceptable and should these be given an order of priority; what amount of mitigation should be required and how to measure wetlands values being mitigated; who should undertake and pay for mitigation; how compliance with mitigation requirements should be ensured; and how the process of deciding on what mitigation is required can be accelerated.

Ms. Leslie is former associate, The Conservation Foundation, Washington, D.C.

This paper provides background information and a brief discussion of key issues. It is organized in three major sections:

o   Extent of Mitigation: Scope of the Problem

o   Current Mitigation Policies

o   Major Mitigation Policy Issues

EXTENT OF MITIGATION: SCOPE OF THE PROBLEM

Requirements that wetland losses be mitigated are currently imposed on the private sector through the federal Section 404 permitting process and similar state and local wetlands regulatory programs. The CEQ regulations and guidelines implementing the National Environmental Policy Act and the Wetlands Executive Order[2] also impose mitigation requirements upon federal actions that alter wetlands. These requirements may indirectly require mitigation by the private sector if the federal activity involves issuing a permit for private action.

The U.S. Army Corps of Engineers (Corps) currently estimates that it requires some mitigation (including project redesign to avoid or reduce effects on wetlands) for more than 50 percent of the individual Section 404 permits it issues. These totalled about 8,800 in 1986.[3]

In its review of wetlands use and regulation, the Office of Technology Assessment (OTA) studied permits issued during 1980 and 1981, and found that 66 percent of all individual permits had been modified substantially to reduce project impacts.[4]

During the study period, the Corps' permits allowed 50,000 acres of wetlands to be lost, but resulted in the avoidance of another 50,000 acres of losses, and the creation or restoration of 5,000 acres of wetlands as compensatory mitigation. Thus, 45 percent of proposed losses, in terms of acreage, were unmitigated, and 90 percent of permitted losses were uncompensated. (These estimates are based upon permit records, and are not field verified.)

No information exists on the extent to which mitigation occurs for wetlands alterations not subject to individual Section 404 permits.

CURRENT MITIGATION POLICIES

U.S. Army Corps of Engineers

The Corps' mitigation policy is stated in its regulations implementing the Section 404 program described in 33 CFR 320.4(r). This policy statement includes the following:

> Mitigation is an important aspect of the review and balancing process [economic need for a project along with other factors of the public interest] on many Department of the Army permit applications. Consideration of mitigation will occur throughout the permit application review process and includes avoiding, minimizing, rectifying, reducing, or compensating for resource losses. Losses will be avoided to the extent practicable. Compensation may occur on-site or at an off-site location.[5]

The Corps policy statement defines mitigation as "practically any permit condition or best management practice designed to avoid or reduce adverse effects,"[6] and allows for "off-site" compensatory mitigation which replaces or provides substitute resources or environments.

In addition, the Corps' policy includes consideration of the positive public interest aspects of proposed projects when determining whether mitigation will be required.[7]

175

Environmental Protection Agency

The U.S. Environmental Protection Agency's (EPA) §404(b)(i) guidelines, which are the environmental criteria for the Corps' evaluation of discharges of dredged or fill material, address mitigation in several sections. The specific requirement for mitigation is found in 40 CFR 230.10(d). The agency believes that policy guidance on mitigation is needed, but has postponed issuing an agency statement until an interagency mitigation working group has completed its deliberations. Some regional offices have developed their own working policies. EPA believes that the guidelines generally provide for a sequence for mitigation that starts with examining practicable alternatives for avoiding adverse effects, and allows for compensation only as a last resort.[8]

U.S. Fish and Wildlife Service

The U.S. Fish and Wildlife Service (FWS) has developed a comprehensive mitigation policy that it applies in meeting its review and comment responsibilities under the §404 program, as well as its other review responsibilities under the Fish and Wildlife Coordination Act, NEPA (42 U.S.C. 4321, 4363), the Endangered Species Act of 1973 (16 U.S.C. 1531 et seq.), and Federal Energy Regulatory Commission (FERC) licensing procedures. The FWS policy focuses on habitat value, and incorporates the following guiding principles: 1) that avoidance be recommended for the most valued resources; and 2) that the degree of mitigation requested correspond to the value and scarcity of the habitat at risk.[9] The FWS has established a set of four wetlands resource categories, linked to general mitigation planning goals (Table 7-1), and uses a methodology called Habitat Evaluation Procedures (HEP) for evaluating the importance of the wetlands for wildlife habitat.

National Marine Fisheries Service

The National Marine Fisheries Service (NMFS) has as its general policy a commitment to participate with government agencies and private developers during pre-application or early planning stages to "anticipate problems, identify alternatives for achieving objectives, reduce possibility of conflict, and minimize adverse effects on living marine resources and their habitats." In the case of essential public interest projects where practical alternatives are un-available, NMFS will recommend measures to mitigate habitat losses. Also, when appropriate, NMFS will recommend habitat enhancement measures including rehabilitation.[10]

Table 7-1
U.S. Fish and Wildlife Service Resource
Categories and Mitigation Planning Goals

Resource category	Designation criteria	Mitigation planning goal
1	High value for evaluation species and unique and irreplaceable.	No loss of existing habitat value.
2	High value for evaluation species and scarce or becoming scarce.	No-net-loss of in-kind habitat value.
3	High-to-medium value for evaluation species and abundant.	No-net-loss of habitat value while minimizing loss of in-kind habitat value.
4	Medium-to-low value for evaluation species.	Minimize loss of habitat value.

Source: 46 Federal Register 7646, November 13, 1986.

State Mitigation Policies

The State of Florida's Department of Environmental Regulation has developed a detailed "Mitigation Rule" for the evaluation of permit appli-cations.[11] This rule defines mitigation as:

177

an action or series of actions that will offset the adverse impacts of a project on the waters of the state altered by the project. Mitigation does not mean: (a) avoidance of environmental impacts by restricting, modifying or eliminating the proposed dredging and filling; (b) cash payments; (c) conveyance of interests in land unless the conveyance will offset potential adverse impacts of the proposed dredging and filling, such as cumulative impacts. The state will consider marsh creation as a mitigation option if the permit applicant wishes.

Specific provisions include in-kind mitigation, a 2:1 replacement ratio, and 25-year monitoring.

In 1986, New Jersey's Division of Coastal Resources adopted a mitigation policy intended to "assure no-net-loss of aquatic habitat productivity, including flora and fauna."[12] New Jersey's Freshwater Wetlands Protection Act (L. 1987, c. 167), enacted in July 1987, allows for mitigation and establishes a preference for on-site creation or restoration of wetlands whose ecological value equals that of the wetlands to be disturbed.[13] If on-site mitigation is not feasible, off-site mitigation and deed restriction of private property or an equivalent monetary donation to the Wetlands Mitigation Bank created by the statute is permitted. Land donations to the Wetlands Mitigation Bank are allowed only as a last alternative.

California's mitigation policies focus on avoidance of losses, but the state will also consider a range of options for protecting and enhancing wetland values. The California Coastal Conservancy, established by the state legislature in 1976, was empowered to implement restoration and enhancement programs within the coastal zone. This agency has worked to develop innovative mitigation approaches, including pilot mitigation bank programs in San Francisco Bay and Humboldt Bay, as options for permit applicants.

State wetlands protection programs also typically include mitigation requirements, some of which are much clearer than those required under the federal program.

MAJOR MITIGATION POLICY ISSUES

There has been a long history of bureaucratic wrangling among the federal agencies involved in the Section 404 permit program, with mitigation policy and mitigation requirements for specific permits being key areas of disagreement. Additional state and local requirements may contribute to an already contentious and complicated permit application and review process. Many members of the regulated community have noted that the complexity of federal and state agency relationships in this area has added to the confusion, frustration and delays which they have experienced, while the environmental community has been concerned about what it sees as the lax way in which mitigation requirements have been imposed and entered.

In 1986, some disagreements between the Corps and EPA on mitigation policy were aired during an oversight hearing of the Environmental Pollution Subcommittee of the Senate Environment and Public Works Committee.[14] EPA expressed concern that the Corps' proposed rule for implementing the Section 404 permit program may be inconsistent with the intent and requirements of the general guidelines for §404 permits.[15] Specifically, EPA was concerned that the Corps did not identify avoidance of adverse impact on wetlands as the preferred regulatory option and that references to compensatory mitigation raised major questions. In response to these concerns, the Corps did place emphasis on avoidance in its final rule.[16] In addition, an interagency working group, consisting of representatives of EPA, the Corps, FWS, and NMFS, was formed to develop guidance on implementing mitigation requirements of the guidelines. A joint policy document was originally scheduled to be completed by June 30, 1987.[17] However, by the end of 1988, the interagency group was still working to reach agreement on a number of issues, including: whether the guidelines specify a sequence for considering mitigation options (such as avoidance, then minimization, then compensation), whether the guidelines include a "no-net-loss" provision, and details of interagency coordination.

When Should Mitigation be Required?

Currently, mitigation is required only under the following circumstances:

o   as a condition of most §404 permits;

o   for most federal projects subject to NEPA or the Executive Order on Wetlands Protection;

o   for some FERC licensing actions; and

o   for some private activities subject only to state regulation.

Major types of alterations that generally seem to avoid formal mitigation requirements include: most inland wetland conversions for agricultural uses (historically, about 85 percent of realized total losses); many silvicultural activities; most small-acreage losses in the upper reaches of streams and in wetlands that are not part of a tributary system (for example, discharges of fill material in wetlands less than one acre, located above the headwaters point on streams and in isolated waters, are generally authorized and excluded from mitigation requirements under §404); losses that represent the continuing effects of past actions or natural processes; some types of chemical contamination or biological alteration; and any other wetlands altering activities that are outside the §404 permit process.

Attempts to tighten mitigation requirements or expand them to other types of activities or indirect losses, or other types of conversions that they do not now cover would obviously raise significant political and economic issues, and may require legislation.

A significant mitigation question is also being raised by the FERC's need to relicense hydroelectric facilities.   Many of these were originally licensed before wetlands protection was an official government concern.   The older licenses are coming up for renewal, and a question has arisen over whether the facilities should have to compensate for past wetlands conversion as a condition of being relicensed. (FERC currently does require wetlands mitigation or enhancement in some license renewal cases, but does not require mitigation for past conversions in all instances.) The same issue can be expected to arise in other federal license renewal requirements subject to NEPA.

Finally, under a no-net-loss policy, there is the question of who should be responsible for compensating for the continuing naturally-caused losses, losses representing the continuing effects of past actions (such as losses related to general hydrologic changes caused by water resources projects), and other losses that are not associated with current regulated activities. It seems unreasonable to require the regulated activities to compensate for such losses when they are completely unrelated to the regulated activity. Many of these losses are caused by natural processes (for example, sea-level rise), result from past government actions (such as flood protection levees), or for other reasons are not attributable to any individual or party. These types of effects, which often are cumulative, probably could only be offset by publicly-sponsored mitigation efforts.

What Types and Locations of Mitigation Are Acceptable?

This issue is at the heart of several general policy debates as well as being a part of most controversial permit decisions.

One general policy question is the extent to which "sequencing" should be required. Sequencing implies that some types of mitigation--avoiding and minimizing impacts--are preferable to others--compensating for lost areas--and every effort should be made to avoid impacts before compensation is even considered. The CEQ definition of mitigation (see page 173) leaves the question of sequencing open to interpretation. Those favoring sequencing note that the ultimate success of the two most common forms of compensation, which are restoration and creation, is highly uncertain (see Chapter 9, "Views on Scientific Issues Relating to the Restoration and Creation of Wetlands"). The uncertainty of success, and potentially high risk of failure, is the basis for the conservative view that such compensatory actions are less desirable from the standpoint of resource protection. Opponents of sequencing argue for a more flexible approach which allows maximum flexibility in tailoring mitigation requirements, allowing compensation to be considered before exhausting all avoidance options. The Corps currently leans towards the more flexible approach. EPA favors more rigorous sequencing, arguing that avoiding the impact is the most desirable mitigation alternative.

A second general policy issue is what types of compensation are allowable. A wide range of compensation measures have been proposed or implemented. One study summarizes the different types as follows:[18]

o   increasing public access to an area;

o   acquisition of other wetland areas to provide enhanced protection, or acquisition with a management commitment;

o   restoration or creation, either as general compensation or as replacement for a specific habitat type;

o   indemnification or monetary payment for lost natural resource benefits; and

o   mitigation banking, which involves compensatory off-site wetlands enhancement or creation.

Most federal and state regulatory agencies now generally consider the first two of these compensatory approaches to be unacceptable unless: 1) the expressed goal of increasing public access is to compensate for losses of public recreational opportunities; or 2) the acquisition includes enhancement or assurance of appropriate management measures to compensate for lost values. Most regulatory agencies also prefer on-site mitigation to off-site compensation, and if off-site compensation is necessary, compensation within an adjacent area to compensation in a remote area.[19]

A related question is the acceptability and desirability of mitigation banking. This is a relatively new and promising, though still controversial concept for off-site compensation. One of the earliest and best known banks was created by the Tenneco LaTerre Corporation on 7,000 acres of marsh in coastal Louisiana. Tenneco has implemented a marsh management strategy to enhance fish and wildlife habitat and retard or reverse conversion of the marsh to open water. Over the twenty-five year term of the banking agreement, the bank may provide mitigation for up to 61 typical oil and gas canals.[20]

Other mitigation banking projects have involved government acquisition of degraded or former wetland areas, which are then restored using funds obtained by selling credits to developers who need to mitigate for wetland alterations resulting from their projects. Such banking programs can be preferable to individual restoration or creation projects, which often yield little habitat value, especially when the acreage is small or when permit applicants have no experience in wetland restoration.[21]

However, mitigation banks do not necessarily avoid many of the technical and policy concerns associated with off-site compensation. Mitigation banks may be no better managed than other restoration efforts, and the wetlands they contain may provide fewer functions than the original converted area. Some fear that banks may be abused, encouraging avoidable wetlands losses by providing an easy compensation option. Administrative and budgetary resources also would be needed to support government involvement in the banks, which could range from general oversight to complete management. If the banks remain in private ownership, their wetlands may be subject to conversion in the future. Thus banks also raise a number of complex administrative, legal and technical issues which complicate their use.

What Amount of Mitigation Should be Required?

The question of how much mitigation should be required raises very difficult policy issues. How much cost can be imposed upon the developer?

Should this be related to the value of the wetlands under consideration, to the economic value of the development being proposed, to the financial capacity of the developer, to some other factor, or to a combination of these factors? What factors should be considered in valuing a wetland?

In cases where mitigation involves some compensation for lost wetland values, the issue of compensation ratio is usually raised. In other words, if one acre of wetland would be lost as a consequence of some permitted action, how does one calculate the number of acres that should be enhanced or created to achieve full compensation of the lost wetland functions and values? It is important to reiterate that many members of the scientific community caution that the ultimate success of many types of compensatory actions, particularly wetland creation, is uncertain (see Chapter 9, "Views on Scientific Issues Relating to the Restoration and Creation of Wetlands").

A no-net-loss policy may be based on the physical area lost or the wetland functions and values lost. A no-net-loss policy may, therefore, imply either a 1:1 replacement of acres lost or a 1:1 replacement of values lost. A goal of increasing the nation's wetlands inventory implies that more than a one for one replacement would occur. But in many cases, neither the alteration nor the compensation may be total. Alterations may result in only partial loss of wetland functions. And compensation may involve enhancing existing wetlands rather than creating new wetlands.

Some states such as Florida have adopted a two-for-one rule--two acres must be restored or created for every acre lost. Current New Jersey policy requires different levels of mitigation (1:1, 2:1, etc.) depending upon whether the proposed mitigation is on- or off-site, and if off-site, whether it is in the same drainage basin as the land converted. Federal agencies are evaluating the use of more sophisticated wetland function and value evaluation techniques for estimating the appropriate compensation ratio for individual permit applications. These tools attempt to measure the value of the functions provided by both the wetlands being altered and the compensatory wetlands, and base the compensation requirements on the comparison of these functional values.

Although there are dozens of wetland evaluation techniques including professional judgment, the most widely used approaches are the FWS's HEP, which was developed as an impact assessment tool; and the Federal Highway Administration's (FHwA) technique developed by Adamus and Stockwell, which was developed as a planning tool.[22] The Adamus technique is more comprehensive and suitable for regulatory determinations because it accounts for more wetland functions than HEP.[23] However, many observers believe that substantially more research and development is needed before such techniques can be used with confidence. The Corps is leading an interagency effort to improve the predictability of the Adamus method, renamed the Wetland Evaluation Technique (WET), and adapt it for use on a personal computer. EPA researchers are focusing their efforts on compiling existing scientific information on how well compensatory wetlands are functioning and the processes that must be considered in developing compensatory wetlands (such as succession). EPA is also concentrating on field evaluation of the functions of created/restored wetlands compared to natural wetlands.

How Should the Timing of Compensation Relate to Alteration?

The fact that compensatory wetlands may not be fully functioning for many years after the restoration or creation activities begin raises the issue of whether the existing wetlands should be converted before the compensation is provided. Allowing the alteration to precede compensation results in a temporary loss of wetland functions. Where these functions are particularly valuable, this loss could be costly. Where wetlands are plentiful or the functions already degraded, the temporary loss is likely to be less serious. The temporary loss issue is complicated by the fact that the ultimate success of restoration and creation efforts is uncertain. If such efforts prove unsuccessful over the long term, the temporary loss becomes permanent.

Who Should Undertake and Who Should Pay for Mitigation?

Current policies generally dictate that the permit applicant should undertake and pay for the private costs of mitigation. This general policy, however, leaves several issues unclear.

One is the competence of the permittee to carry out the mitigation properly. Particularly in the case of restoration and creation, substantial biological and hydrological expertise is needed to implement the projects effectively. The permittee could be required to retain a firm that has certified expertise in this area, although such an approach would involve establishing a new government certification and licensing program. A qualified government agency might be responsible for undertaking or overseeing the compensatory activities, but this can confuse the question of who is ultimately responsible for the success and cost of the activities.

Ultimate liability for the success of the mitigation project is another issue that remains unclear. Should the permittee be responsible for assuring that the mitigation efforts are successful? If the permittee is not responsible, who is? The regulatory agency? And how long should this liability last--one year, five years, twenty years, or in perpetuity? The longer the liability lasts, the more difficult it will be to impose it on private developers, for they may go out of business, move out of the area, or otherwise undergo changes that make it difficult for government to ensure that they carry out their responsibilities. In other programs involving such long term liability issues, bonding or insurance requirements have been imposed on the responsible party. The Corps has, in some regulatory actions, required bonding of permit conditions pursuant to 33 C.F.R. 325.4.

Other questions of who should pay are implicit in other mitigation issues. For instance, the question of how much mitigation should be required can be recast as how much should be paid for and by whom. The issue of ensuring that mitigation efforts are successful, addressed below, also raises these questions.

Who Should Ensure Compliance with Mitigation Requirements?

The effectiveness of current Section 404 program mitigation policies is uncertain. The Corps' current policy is that district engineers carry out inspection and surveillance with all means that are at the district engineer's disposal.[24] But, in reality, very few resources are available leaving weaknesses in: verifying that §404 permit conditions are met; monitoring the success of mitigation efforts; and taking effective enforcement action when permits conditions are not adhered to.

The lack of adequate monitoring of permit conditions, particularly in the area of verifying the success of restoration and creation projects, has been frequently cited as a serious problem. One of the reasons that so little is known about the feasibility of wetlands restoration and creation is that past efforts have not been vigorously inspected or monitored. A more effective enforcement program would, therefore, not only make the nation's overall wetlands management efforts more effective, but could provide information that might impose scientific understanding of the viability of compensation projects.

Such a program, however, could be expensive, raising the question of who should be responsible for and pay for this monitoring: the federal government, state governments, local governments, or the permittee? The federal government may have the expertise to carry out these activities, but may not be able to do so efficiently if its field offices are located at substantial distances from the project site. Federal agencies are also facing serious budget constraints. State or local governments might be better able to carry out the monitoring responsibilities because their offices are likely to be located closer to the permitted and mitigation sites than the federal government. However they may lack the technical as well as the financial resources to carry out these activities.

The permittee could be required to monitor the success of the mitigation efforts in the same way that waste water dischargers are required to monitor their effluent. A variation on requiring the permittee to do the monitoring would be to require the permittee to hire an independent firm to do the monitoring, much as CPAs are hired to audit financial records.

How Can the Process be Accelerated?

In addition to all of the policy issues related to mitigation, permittees can experience substantial costs because of the uncertainty and delay involved in getting agreement on mitigation requirements. This is particularly a problem in terms of intergovernmental coordination. The applicant typically starts by discussing mitigation proposals with the Corps. These proposals, however, are subject to review and comments by EPA and the FWS. Once these hurdles are passed, a state agency may demand some changes which then have to be renegotiated with the various federal agencies. And in some cases, local agencies may also have to give their approval.

Each level of government and each agency may well have its own special interests that are very hard to reconcile. The permittee has the strongest incentive to bring about this reconciliation, but this can be a frustrating, drawn out process.

Two ways of dealing with this problem would be: 1) to clearly assign the decision responsibility on mitigation requirements to one agency at the federal or state level; or 2) to establish a "one stop" mitigation approval process. The former would be politically difficult under the current diffused wetland regulatory programs. The second may hold more promise (and has been used by some Corps districts), but has not always been successful when attempted in other programs.

REFERENCES

1.   43 Federal Register 55975-56907.

2.   Protection of Wetlands, Executive Order 11990, May 24, 1977.

3.   Frank Torbett, U.S. Army Corps of Engineers, personal communication, 1987.

4.   U.S. Congress, Office of Technology Assessment, 1984.   The 1981 and current statistics are not strictly comparable, because, in 1982, the Corps initiated regulatory reforms which shifted many dredge and fill activities from the "individual" permit classification to the "nationwide" or "regional" classifications (Frank Torbett, U.S. Army Corps of Engineers, personal communication, 1987).   No information exists on the extent to which mitigation is undertaken in   activities covered by these general permits.   Presumably, because no mitigation review is conducted, less would occur.

In addition, neither statistic accounts for the amount of mitigation that the permittee may have voluntarily incorporated in the original application.   As people become more familiar with the regulatory requirements, they may well be more likely to incorporate mitigation into their project plans before they submit their permit applications.

5.   51 Federal Register 41227, November 13, 1986.

6.   51 Federal Register 41208, November 13, 1986.

7.   In a footnote to its permit regulations, the U.S. Army Corps of Engineers acknowledges that its policy is not a substitute for the mitigation requirements necessary to ensure that a permit action complies with the Section 404(b)(1) Guidelines.   An interagency working group has been working to develop further guidance. See 51 Federal Register 41227, November 13, 1986.

8.   45 Federal Register 85336-85357, November 13, 1986.

9.   46 Federal Register 7644-7633, November 13, 1986.

10.   48 Federal Register 53147, November 13, 1986.

11.   Smallwood, M., "Mitigation Rule Success Criteria,"   State of Florida Interoffice Memorandum (Tallahassee, FL: Department of Environmental Regulation, 1986).

12.   Kantor, R.A. and D.J. Charette, "Wetlands Mitigation in New Jersey's Coastal Management Program," National Wetlands Newsletter 8(5):14-15, 1986.

13.   Tubman, L., "New Jersey Adopts a Tough Wetlands Protection Act that Offers a Model for Country," The Water Reporter 11(13):93-95, 1987.

14.   Kusler, J. and H. Groman, "Mitigation: An Introduction,"   National Wetlands Newsletter 8(5): 2-3, 1986.

15.   Wilson, J.J.   Letter to the Honorable Robert K. Dawson, Assistant Secretary of the Army (Civil Works), from Jennifer Joy Wilson, Assistant Administrator for External Affairs, U.S. Environmental Protection Agency, Washington, D.C., April 23, 1986.

16.   51 Federal Register 41206-41260, November 13, 1986.

17. Jensen, L.J. and R.K. Dawson. Letter to the Honorable John H. Chafee, U.S. Senate, from Lawrence J. Jensen, Assistant Administrator - Office of Water, U.S. Environmental Protection Agency and Robert K. Dawson, Assistant Secretary of the Army (Civil Works), Washington, D.C., December 3, 1986.

18. Dial, R.S. and D.R. Deis, <u>Mitigation Options for Fish and Wildlife Resources Affected by Port and Other Water-Dependent Developments in Tampa Bay, Florida</u>, Biological Report 86(6) (Slidell, La.: National Coastal Ecosystems Team, U.S. Fish and Wildlife Service, 1986).

19. Grenell, P., "The Coastal Conservancy's Emerging Role in Shaping Wetland Mitigation Approaches: Standards and Criteria" (Oakland: California Coastal Conservancy, 1987).

20. Kerr, R., <u>Wetlands Mitigation Banking: A Study of the Development and Implementation of the Tenneco LaTerre Bank</u> (Washington, D.C.: Regulatory Innovations Staff, U.S. Environmental Protection Agency, 1987); and Soileau, D.M., <u>Final Report on the Tenneco LaTerre Corporation Mitigation Banking Proposal Terrebonne Parish, Louisiana</u> (Lafayette, La.: U.S. Fish and Wildlife Service, 1984).

21. Riddle, E.P., "Mitigation Banks: Unmitigated Disaster or Sound Investment?", <u>California Waterfront Age</u> 3(1):37-40, 1987.

22. Adamus, P.R. and L.T. Stockwell, <u>A Method for Wetland Functional Assessment</u>, Report FHWA-1P-82-83 (Washington, D.C.: U.S. Department of Transportation, 1983).

23. Zedler, J.B. and M.E. Kentula, <u>Wetlands Research Plan</u> (Corvallis, Oreg.: Environmental Research Laboratory, U.S. Environmental Protection Agency, 1985).

24. Personal communication, U.S. Army Corps of Engineers, 1986.

See Also:

Blomberg, G., "Development and Mitigation in the Pacific Northwest," <u>Northwest Environmental Journal</u> 3(1):63-91, 1987.

Postles, B. and J.M. Dean, "The Wetlands Mitigation Issue in South Carolina," Baruch Institute Technical Report USC-B1-87-1 (Columbia: University of South Carolina, 1987).

Race, M.S. and D.R. Christie, "Coastal Zone Development: Mitigation, Marsh Creation and Decision-Making," <u>Environmental Management</u> 6(4):317-328, 1982.

U.S. Congress, Office of Technology Assessment, <u>Wetlands: Their Use and Regulation</u> (Washington, D.C.: U.S. Government Printing Office, 1984).

GOVERNMENT PROGRAMS INDUCING WETLANDS ALTERATIONS

Malcolm F. Baldwin, Michele Leslie, and Edwin H. Clark, II

INTRODUCTION

In the course of meeting other public objectives, government construction, funding, technical assistance, economic assistance, and tax programs can affect wetlands. These effects can occur directly, as an inseparable part of a government action. They also can occur indirectly, where government activities create conditions that encourage wetlands alteration by others.

In a few cases, wetlands alteration has been a conscious purpose of government action. For example, the oldest federal wetlands laws, the Swamp Lands Acts of 1849, 1850, and 1860, were enacted to encourage the drainage of wetlands, which were considered a threat to public health or a public nuisance. At various times, government agencies at all levels have built drainage projects for the purpose of converting wetlands for agricultural, recreational, and other uses.

Some government programs indirectly benefit or result in the creation of wetlands. For example, government-assisted construction of farm ponds can incidentally result in the development of new wetlands. Similarly, government supported irrigation, highway, and other types of projects can create localized wetlands. The development of sewage treatment facilities may involve the preservation or creation of wetlands for the purpose of treating municipal wastewater.

In most cases, the alteration of wetlands by government action is not purposeful. Typically, government projects are developed to provide some

The authors are president, Baldwin Associates, Great Falls, VA; former associate and former vice-president, respectively, The Conservation Foundation, Washington, D.C.

social good--for example, safer transportation, better housing, cleaner water, or higher incomes--and any damages or benefits to wetlands are not an intended central or primary consequence. In many cases, the public good provided as a result of the government action is substantial.

Direct Impacts

A common cause of direct impacts is infrastructure investment such as the construction of roads and dams. In some of these programs, the government agency implementing the program is the only party involved. For instance, the U.S. Army Corps of Engineers (Corps) may construct a dam that floods a wetland area, or build a flood control project that drains one.

In some instances, the government agency may only provide funding to an intermediary--often a different level of government--which actually undertakes the activity. For instance, the Federal Highway Administration (FHwA) provides funds to state governments for the construction of highways, and the U.S. Environmental Protection Agency (EPA) provides funds to local governments for the construction of sewage treatment plants.

Not all direct impacts result from such construction activities, however. Some impacts can occur as government agencies such as the Bureau of Land Management (BLM) or the Department of Defense (DOD) manage and use their extensive land holdings. Activities such as grazing cattle on public forest or rangeland can, for instance, alter wetlands which exist there if insufficient regard is given to protecting wetlands or riparian areas.

Indirect Impacts

Indirect impacts can occur when the government creates economic incentives which encourage private individuals to take actions that alter wetlands. For instance, high agricultural price supports provide an incentive for farmers to cultivate additional acreage, possibly altering wetlands in the process; or special tax breaks encourage increased development, some of which occurs in wetland areas.

Indirect impacts can be difficult to anticipate. At times there is a major question as to whether a government agency initiating an action can reasonably be expected to know that the action would alter identifiable wetland areas. In the case of a highway project, it is possible to identify specific wetland areas that would be transected and thus altered by a given route. However, in the case of agricultural price supports, such *ex ante* identification is difficult.

The matter is complicated by the fact that an action may have both direct and indirect impacts. Thus a highway built through a wetland has an obvious direct impact. But, even if the highway does not itself traverse the wetland, it may stimulate an indirect effect such as the associated private residential and commercial development which does occur in wetlands.

TYPES OF GOVERNMENT PROGRAMS THAT AFFECT WETLANDS

Federal Programs

The federal government undertakes a wide variety of programs that can result in wetlands alteration, either directly or indirectly. An appendix to this paper contains an extensive (though not exhaustive) listing of programs likely to have effects on wetlands. Some of the most significant are those relating to water resources development, agricultural subsidies (although these are intended to be offset by the Swampbuster provisions of the Food Security Act of 1985), the construction of other types of infrastructure, and the management of federal lands.

Water Resource Development Programs

Dam construction, navigation projects, irrigation projects, harbor dredging, stream channelization, impoundments for flood control, and coastal erosion control projects all can result in wetlands alteration directly or indirectly. Wetland losses caused by the development of levees, navigation projects, and other federal water resource management projects have been significant in the lower Mississippi Valley's bottomland hardwood forests, and in Louisiana coastal areas. Western irrigation, drainage, and water supply projects have significantly affected western wetland and riparian areas. Small watershed impoundments have reduced wetlands in the south and east. The construction of sewage treatment facilities and attendant indirect effects of community growth also have adversely affected wetlands. The major agencies involved in these programs are the Bureau of Reclamation (BuRec), the Corps, and the Soil Conservation Service (SCS), which together spend $4.3 billion annually on water projects; EPA, at $2.4 billion per year; and the Tennessee Valley Authority (TVA), which operates 35 dams located on a 650-mile reach of the Tennessee River.[1] The Federal Energy Regulatory Commission (FERC) licenses private hydroelectric development in U.S. navigable waters, including small hydro projects that may have cumulatively important wetland impacts.

Other Public Works Programs

The federal aid program for highway construction, now funded at about $15 billion annually, has had substantial impacts on wetlands. These include the direct effects of construction and hydrological modifications, as well as operational impacts of salt and pollutant runoff. Airport construction and expansion projects, and electrical transmission line projects have caused similar effects related to the clearing or filling of wetlands within project areas. Small public works assistance programs and Community Development Block Grants also probably have resulted in some wetland losses and modifications. Superfund clean-up and disposal operations may also have affected wetlands, positively with regard to the reduction of contaminant availability, and negatively in cases where waste management facilities were located within wetland areas. The Strategic Petroleum Reserve program for oil pipelines and storage facilities in Louisiana is an example of an energy construction program that had some adverse effects on wetlands. Major federal agencies involved in these programs are FERC, the Department of the Interior (DOI), the Department of Transportation, the Department of Housing and Urban Development, the Department of Commerce, the Department of Energy, and EPA.

Public Land Management

About one-third of U.S. lands are owned and managed by the federal government. Within these public lands, which are concentrated in the western U.S. and Alaska, management policies and practices have important implications for wetlands. Western riparian wetlands have been altered by grants of transmission line rights-of-way, timber operations, public land grazing permits, and projects relating to recreational, and energy and mineral resource development on public lands. Management decisions affecting national parks, wildlife refuges and national forests have positively affected some wetlands and negatively affected others. The major federal land management agencies are DOI, the U.S. Forest Service (USFS), and the Defense Department (Army, Navy, Air Force).

Economic Benefit Programs

The federal government undertakes a wide range of programs that provide economic benefits to the public or segments of the public. The economic benefits of some of these programs create conditions that act as incentives, inducing the beneficiaries of the programs to alter wetlands. Although the impact of these programs on wetlands may be indirect, the extent of resulting wetlands alteration can be substantial.

As discussed later in this paper, recent studies indicate that the most important of the economic benefit programs, in terms of effects on wetlands, are agricultural efficiency payment programs, involving either price support or income support. Similar types of benefits may be provided to other segments of society. Examples include low interest loans for the construction of new industrial facilities or low cost housing. The subsidized federal flood insurance program may also have inadvertently stimulated the conversion of wetlands.

In some cases the subsidy may take the form of a tax break, or tax breaks may reinforce the direct subsidy. For instance, until recently, farmers could receive both a low cost loan and a tax break for draining lands which would be used for the production of crops whose price was supported by the federal government.

State Programs

Most states carry out a wide range of programs which can stimulate wetlands alterations in much the same way as the federal programs described above. States build water resource projects, highways, and all other forms of infrastructure. They manage large areas of land. And they provide some economic benefit programs, although these are likely to be much less extensive than those provided by the federal government.

Some programs affecting wetlands exist uniquely at the state level. For instance, states control the allocation of water supplies, and in allowing an applicant to divert water from a stream or withdraw it from the ground, they may deplete the supply of water to a downstream wetland. They may also permit other types of facilities that may alter wetlands.

Local Government Programs

Local governments typically undertake a narrower range of activities than either the federal or state governments, but they too may substantially alter wetlands. They construct a large amount of infrastructure--roads, sewage treatment plants, water supply systems, solid waste disposal facilities, and municipal buildings--that can directly or indirectly alter wetlands. They also may own or manage land that contains wetlands, which may be drained to put the land to recreational or other uses.

Local governments typically are responsible for land use controls. These authorities can be used to protect wetlands, but they can also help stimulate their alteration. For instance, local land use plans and implementing zoning ordinances may call for industrial or commercial developments in wetland areas. Large-lot zoning for residential areas may result in development sprawling over a larger area than would otherwise occur, with resulting adverse impacts on wetlands. And rising property tax obligations can create an incentive to develop land that would otherwise be kept as open space.

IMPACTS OF PRESENT FEDERAL PROGRAMS ON WETLANDS

A recent study by the Environmental Law Institute[2] concluded that the water resources projects carried out by the Corps, BuRec, and SCS, and those licensed by FERC, may be among the most important federal activities directly affecting wetlands. The federal highway program ranked highest among the other public works programs, while among public land programs, the BLM's livestock grazing program was most significant.

Some federal activities, like the construction of the Interstate Highway System and other roadways, have had broadly distributed effects on wetlands. Another example is the Small Watershed Program of the SCS, which is intended to reduce farm erosion and control floods, and has caused wetland drainage or inundation in many watersheds smaller than 250,000 acres across the U.S.

A total of 662 projects, most involving some structural work (such as construction of channels, diversions or dams) have been completed since the small watershed program's inception.[3] Another 574 projects are in construction or pre-construction phases. Recent projects tend to focus on on-the-farm land treatment or conservation measures rather than structural alternatives.

The National Flood Insurance Program, which influences development within many coastal and riverine areas that include wetlands, is a third national program with widely distributed effects on wetlands.

However, the effects of many federal programs on wetlands are more regional in character. This results, in part, from the fact that many programs are targeted to deal with regional problems or needs, which may be of national significance (such as ensuring the navigability of major waterways or the availability of adequate water supplies for agricultural areas). It also reflects the regional distribution patterns of wetlands themselves. Consequently, a major study on the effects of federal programs on wetlands currently being carried out by the DOI addresses this issue in a geographic context. The study, required under §402(a) of the Emergency Wetlands Resources Act (P.L. 99-645), will be presented to the Congress in two reports: one addressing the Lower Mississippi Alluvial Plain and the Prairie Pothole Region; and the second addressing other key wetland areas of the United States. The following regional summaries are based on background studies prepared for the DOI effort, as well as other independent sources.

Forested Wetlands of the Mississippi Delta

The lower Mississippi alluvial plain contains substantial areas of valuable wetlands which are experiencing a continuing rapid rate of alteration. At the time of European colonization, this area is thought to have included nearly 24 million acres of bottomland hardwood forested wetlands.[4] By 1937, only 11.8 million acres remained. Since that time, another 6.5 million acres of hardwood forests have been cleared, mainly for agricultural development, leaving less than 5.2 million acres of wetlands today--about 20 percent of the original acreage.

Consultants to the DOI prepared two background reports on this region. One of these uses a complex econometric model to estimate the impact of federal flood control and drainage projects and other potential causes of regional wetlands loss during the period between 1935 and 1984.[5] This study concluded that: (1) at least 25 percent of total forested wetland depletion in the region since 1935 was due to construction losses and induced clearing associated with Corps and SCS flood control and drainage projects; (2) the federal role was more important to wetland conversion than any other single factor; and (3) real increases in agricultural prices since 1935 were also important, but induced only about half as much clearing as the federal projects.

The second background study uses a model which simulates the farmers' decision to convert wetlands into farmland, and the impact of a range of public policy conditions on this decision. The conversion decision is represented as an investment decision reflecting efforts to maximize long-term financial return and minimize financial risk. This study focuses on the potential impact of federal agriculture programs, conservation programs and tax code provisions.[6]

The model includes information on farm and timberland prices, land clearing and development costs, agricultural production data (crop yields, commodity prices, and production costs), federal program benefits and tax code provisions, and estimates of timbering and hunting lease revenues. It simulates representative model farms in four Delta counties.

The results of the simulations indicated that basic economic conditions are no longer as favorable to bottomland development as they have been in the past. Production costs have risen sharply over the past decade, and commodity prices have not kept pace. Under current market conditions, opportunities for profitable conversion and development of wetlands in the Delta are limited, even with agricultural subsidies in place.

The authors of this paper found, however, that federal agricultural and price support subsidies did significantly increase the profitability of conversion and agricultural development in the Delta. Former special tax code provisions also would have favored the conversion of wetlands, but not to the degree of agricultural programs.

Because of the importance of these subsidies, the effects of the new tax provisions in the Tax Reform Act of 1986, and the Swampbuster provisions of the 1985 Food Security Act are likely to be substantial under current farming conditions. However, under improved economic conditions for agriculture (for example, higher commodity prices), conversion of additional wetlands could become profitable even without federal inducements. Kramer and Shabman are currently updating their analyses to examine the potential effects of recent modifications in agricultural programs and the tax code.[7]

The Prairie Pothole Region

The Prairie Pothole Region comprises a 227,000 square mile area, located mainly in Canada, but taking in about 60,000 square miles within Montana, North Dakota, South Dakota, Iowa, and Minnesota. The region gets its name from its numerous small, shallow, scattered depressions of freshwater wetlands, and is a prime waterfowl production area in the central flyway.[8] Only seven million acres of the estimated original area of approximately 20 million acres of prairie wetlands in the U.S. remain, with losses continuing at an estimated rate of 20,000 to 33,000 acres annually.

The Department of the Interior has examined the effects of federal highway, water resource development, agriculture, and tax programs on the wetlands of the Prairie Pothole Region. Two supporting studies examine the effects of federal agriculture and tax provisions and incentives on farmers' decisions to convert prairie potholes for agricultural uses. One study was a farm level simulation model, used to estimate the effects of various programs on the net present values of six representative farm types.[9]

This model involved a series of stochastic analyses, using 1975-1984 data on production costs, crop prices, taxes, and other key variables. Scenarios were developed to test the effect on conversion of such federal programs as U.S. Fish and Wildlife (FWS) easements, the U.S. Department of Agriculture's (USDA) Water Bank program, cost sharing for drainage, price and income supports, disaster assistance/crop insurance, interest rate subsidies, and favorable treatment of drainage costs for income tax purposes.

Results of these analyses indicated that for all farms, under all scenarios (including the absence of all federal programs), net present values were higher when wetlands were drained. Thus, drainage improved a farm's income, whether or not a particular federal program was in place. Federal agriculture and tax programs had a significant effect on farm profitability. Of the factors examined, price and income supports had the greatest effect on the incentive to convert wetlands.

The second study reviewed past research on the effects of government programs on regional wetlands losses, supplemented by selected case studies and interviews.[10] This study also suggests that price and income supports are key incentives. Since the cost of drainage increases over time as the cheapest opportunities are exhausted, the importance of these incentives for profitability (and thus the effectiveness of Swampbuster) may increase. However, a scheduled decline in price and income supports could work to diminish the effectiveness of Swampbuster over time.

Highways and highway construction, many of which are supported under the Federal Aid Highway Program (FAHP), were identified as significant factors affecting wetland conversions in the Prairie Pothole Region. Road ditches along highways are often used to drain pothole wetlands located on farmlands. Although such use of the drainage ditches is illegal, effective enforcement has been lacking.

The second study also suggests that government programs, such as the Water Bank program, which pay farmers for wetlands protection, are effective disincentives to conversion for some farmers, but not for others. Interest rate subsidies and tax provisions seem to have only modest effects on farmers' decisions to convert wetlands.

Coastal Louisiana

Coastal Louisiana includes about 2.5 million acres of fresh to saline marshes, and 637,400 acres of forested wetlands dominated by bald cypress-tupelo swamps.[11] This area accounts for about 40 percent of the total acreage of coastal wetlands within the lower 48 states.[12] Although there are no published estimates of the original extent of Louisiana coastal wetlands, regional mapping studies suggest that as much as 900,000 acres have been lost since 1900.[13] The rate of loss has accelerated in recent years, and is now estimated to be about 40 to 60 square miles per year, or nearly 100 acres per day.[14]   At this rate, Louisiana's coastal wetlands could disappear within the next 100 years.

Although the loss of Louisiana's coastal wetlands is in part due to natural processes (for example, sea-level rise and subsidence), the construction of an extensive system of federally-funded flood control, navigation, and hurricane protection projects, as well as the private construction of canals (particularly for oil and gas exploration), have been key sources of the problem.[15]   Major water projects have included:

The Mississippi River and Tributaries (MR&T) Project evolved from the federal government's first authorized flood control effort (initiated in 1879). Of particular relevance to coastal Louisiana was the construction of about 449 miles of levees and river control structures within the Atchafalaya Basin Floodway.   These modifications have interfered with natural overbank flooding that once transported freshwater and sediments into adjacent wetlands.   The regulation of Atchafalaya River discharge to prevent the Mississippi River from changing its course has interfered with the large-scale "switching" process associated with delta building.   Land building is now limited to a few deltaic areas, with much of the sediment that reaches the mouth of the river being channeled to deep water areas.

Major Navigation Channels have included the Gulf Intracoastal Waterway, an east-west, 302-mile channel initially constructed in 1938 and then enlarged in 1942; the Houma Navigation Canal; the Mississippi River-Gulf Outlet; Barataria Bay Waterway and Bayou Segnette Waterway; and the Atchafalaya River Channel.   These projects involved the loss of thousands of acres of wetlands through excavation and deposition of spoil materials.   The federally supported efforts also provided greater access to coastal Louisiana's oil and gas resources, inducing private development of vast networks of drainage and navigation canals.   These canals have altered inland wetlands by changing flow and salinity patterns.   They also are considered a major direct cause of Louisiana's current land loss problems.[16]

Hurricane Protection Projects, which were initiated during the 1960s, include the Lake Pontchartrain and Vicinity Hurricane Protection Project; the New Orleans to Venice Hurricane Protection Project; and the Larose to Golden Meadow Hurricane Protection Project. These projects, which are levee systems, have caused the loss of wetlands due to construction, excavation and drainage. Those wetlands included within the protected areas are subject to increased development pressures. Some of the wetlands losses incurred during project development have been partially mitigated.[17]

California

The Central Valley of California extends 400 miles from Redding in the north to the mountain ridges below Bakersfield. In total, it encompasses about 16,000 square miles. At the time of European colonization, the Valley contained about four million acres of permanent, seasonal, and tidal wetlands including freshwater and brackish marshes and riparian wetlands, representing about 96 percent of the total wetland acreage thought to have existed originally in California.[18] It is estimated that only 10 percent--some 373,584 acres--of this original resource remains in the Central Valley, of which 81,184 acres are publicly owned and 292,400 acres are held privately.

The Central Valley also is one of the nation's premier agricultural areas, accounting for billions of dollars in production. Agricultural development has been and continues to be the major direct cause of wetlands losses in the area. However, much of this development would have been impossible without federal and state supported irrigation, drainage and other water supply projects.[19]

As in the case of coastal Louisiana, the history of government water projects in the Central Valley is long and intricate. In 1850, just after California became a state, Congress initiated its first program affecting wetlands in the Valley, offering incentives for the construction of drains and levees. Both federal and state involvement in flood control and irrigation

203

increased through the 1900s, with government making a major commitment to the Central Valley Project (CVP) during the Great Depression.

Both the CVP and the state water projects represent major hydrological modifications of an area ranging from north of San Francisco down to Los Angeles. They transport freshwater from the northern areas around San Francisco Bay, southward into the San Joaquin Valley. Today, the CVP consists of 20 dams and reservoirs, eight electric generating facilities, 1,437 miles of canals, and many miles of associated pipelines, aqueducts and drains,[20] and plans exist for more additions.

These projects have caused the direct loss of many acres of wetlands, through construction activities, diversion of water, and interruption of seasonal flooding patterns. In addition, the availability of subsidized water most certainly stimulated increased agricultural development in the Valley, much of which occurred through the extensive conversion of privately-owned wetland areas.

In the early 1980s, irrigation return flow from a federal irrigation district was found to be seriously contaminating the wetlands contained in the Valley's Kesterson Wildlife Refuge. This water picked up high levels of selenium, boron, and other contaminates from the land it was used to irrigate. The contamination has caused serious reproductive problems for waterfowl using the refuge. As a result, the refuge has been closed and the Bureau of Reclamation is being required to remove and bury all of the contaminated soil and vegetation.

Ongoing studies are identifying similar problems in other areas in the San Joaquin Valley as well as other western refuges and wetland areas.

Other Wetland Systems

Florida's freshwater wetlands have been substantially modified over the past century. Much of this alteration has resulted from extensive drainage projects and other development activities that have changed regional hydrology. Rapid urbanization continues to pose a major challenge to these systems, although state managers have been aggressive in their efforts to stem wetlands losses.

In general, the fragile Arctic tundra wetlands in Alaska have been subjected to few perturbations. One exception is recent oil and gas development activities on the North Slope, which have resulted in localized losses and modifications of wetlands. However, there is no consensus regarding the ultimate or cumulative environmental effects of such activities within the region.

CONTROLS OVER THE IMPACTS OF THESE PROGRAMS

In recent years the federal government has adopted, through legislation, executive orders, and agency guidance, a number of mechanisms for reducing inadvertent wetland impacts. Some state governments have adopted similar protective measures although these are usually less aggressive and fewer in number. Local governments may incorporate more sensitivity to wetlands in their land use planning and control processes, and are likely to be influenced by guidance and requirements issued by the state or federal government with respect to actions funded by inter-governmental transfers. The following analysis, however, focuses primarily on actions at the federal level.

Swampbuster

The "Swampbuster" provision of the Food Security Act of 1985[21] specifies that persons cultivating crops on wetlands converted (drained, filled) after December 23, 1985 are ineligible to receive any federal farm program benefits. The Swampbuster provision does not include sanctions for alteration of wetlands, except where planting is involved. Case-specific determinations of Swampbuster applicability are to be made on an annual basis, with withholding of benefits to apply only during the year(s) when planting occurs. Swampbuster applies only to the planting of annual crops, and does not apply to the planting of perennials (such as pasture and orchards). U.S. Department of Agriculture regulations, issued in September 1987, provide guidance on the implementation of Swampbuster.

The Tax Reform Act

The Tax Reform Act of 1986[22] removed several tax inducements to wetland conversions. The act eliminated the reduced (capital gains) tax rate for the sale of land that had been "improved" by drainage, disallowed deductions for the costs of land clearing or water diversion resulting in wetlands conversion, and eliminated the 10 percent investment tax credit which could be used to offset costs of drainage tile or similar wetlands drainage engineering. The Act also eliminated other tax provisions, such as rapid building depreciation, a provision that favored investment in real estate development over other investments.

Water Resource Legislation

Several recent Congressional actions have sought to mitigate adverse impacts of water resources projects on wetlands and other environmental resources. The Water Resources Development Act of 1986 authorized over 270 waterway projects with an ultimate federal cost of $9.5 billion, and a nonfederal cost, through new cost-sharing features, of $7 billion.[23] In addition to the anticipated effects of local cash cost sharing in restraining the number and size of projects, the Act requires fish and wildlife mitigation to occur before, or concurrently with, project construction. However, the degree to which mitigation will be undertaken depends upon the level of funding that the Congress appropriates for this purpose. In addition to mitigation activities, the Act addresses environmental problems related to a number of specific projects. It deauthorized numerous previously authorized but unbuilt projects.

A compromise measure on the Garrison Diversion Unit, a major multi-pur-pose dam and irrigation project located in the prairie region, was signed by

President Reagan in 1986. This irrigation project was for years criticized for its impacts on prairie wetlands of North Dakota. Congress reduced the construction acreage from 250,000 to 100,000 acres and, among other things, established a federal/state-funded Wetlands Trust to protect, enhance, restore, and manage prairie pothole wetlands.[24]

National Environmental Policy Act (NEPA)

NEPA and its environmental impact statement (EIS) requirement apply to most of the federal programs described above. If a proposed action is likely to cause significant environmental impacts, the resulting EIS offers a means to assess and mitigate wetland impacts. Federal agencies with jurisdiction and expertise--such as EPA and FWS for wetlands--must review and comment on EISs. EPA has an additional special review function under Section 309 of the Clean Air Act, under which it has raised wetland concerns about federal projects to the Council on Environmental Quality.

A majority of states have also adopted EIS requirements or their functional equivalent.

Fish and Wildlife Coordination Act

This Act requires federal agencies to consider the impacts of their water resource projects on fish and wildlife and the views of the FWS. The FWS regularly reviews and comments on wetland impacts of such projects, but its views are advisory only.

Executive Orders

An Executive Order on wetlands was issued in 1977 by President Carter[25] along with a related Executive Order on floodplains.[26]

These executive orders were intended to reduce the costs of unnecessary wetland and floodplain development. However, no monitoring of federal agency compliance with these orders has occurred to measure their effects. References to the orders are frequently included in environmental impact statements on federal projects affecting wetlands or floodplains. A regional wetland study for the OTA in North Carolina concluded that "the Soil Conservation Service dramatically changed their (sic) policies and procedures in wetland areas as a result of this directive and others such as the National Environmental Policy Act."[27]

Permit Programs

Many types of facilities require one or more permits from federal or state agencies before they can be built or begin operation. These include hydro-electric facilities, other types of electrical generating facilities, electric transmission lines, oil and gas pipelines, mines, bridges, and discharge and emission permits for new industrial facilities. As a result of the various initiatives listed above, the responsible federal and state agencies usually can and often must consider the impacts of these facilities on wetlands when evaluating the permit application.

REFERENCES

1. U.S. Government Manual: 1987/1988 (Washington, D.C.: National Archives and Records Administration, 1987), p. 686.

2. Environmental Law Institute, Federal Policies which May Adversely Affect the Quantity and Quality of Wetlands. Working Paper (Washington, D.C.: U.S. Environmental Protection Agency, 1985).

3. Carl Bouchard, U.S. Soil Conservation Service, personal communication, 1987.

4. Stavins, Robert, Conversion of Forested Wetlands to Agricultural Uses: An Econometric Analysis of the Impact of Federal Programs on Wetland Depletion in the Lower Mississippi Alluvial Plain, 1935-1984 (New York: Environmental Defense Fund, 1987), p. 42.

5. Ibid.

6. Kramer, R. and L. Shabman, "Incentives for Agricultural Development of U.S. Wetlands: A Case Study of Bottomland Hardwoods of the Lower Missis-sippi River," in, Agriculture and the Environment. Annual Policy Review of

the National Center for Food and Agricultural Policy (Washington, D.C.: Resources for the Future, 1986), pp. 175-201.

7.   Gagliano, S.M., K.J. Meyer-Arendt, and K.M. Wicker, "Land Loss in the Mississippi River Deltaic Plain," Transactions 31(1981):295-300; and Gosselink, J.G., C.C. Cordes, and J.W. Parsons, An Ecological Characterization Study of the Chenier Plain Coastal Ecosystem of Louisiana and Texas, FWS/OBS-78/9-78/11 (3 vols.) (Slidell, La.:   Office of Biological Service, U.S. Fish and Wildlife Service, 1979).

8.   Tiner, R.W., Wetlands of the United States: Current Status and Recent Trends (Newton Corner, Mass.: U.S. Fish and Wildlife Service, 1984).

9.   McColloch, P.R., D.J. Wissman, and J. Richardson, "An Assessment of the Impact of Federal Programs on Prairie Pothole Drainage," National Wetlands Newsletter 9(4):3-6, 1987.

10. Leitch, J.A. and W.C. Nelson, Review of the Effect of Selected Federal Programs on Wetlands in the Prairie Pothole Region (Minneapolis, Minn.: Barton-Aschman Associates, Inc., 1986).

11. Michot, T.C., Louisiana Coastal Area Study, Interim Report on Land Loss and Marsh Creation: Planning Aid Report (New Orleans, La.:   U.S. Army Corps of Engineers, 1984).

12. Alexander, C.E., M.A. Broutman, and D.W. Field, An Inventory of Coastal Wetlands of the USA (Washington, D.C.:   National Oceanic and Atmospheric Administration, U.S. Department of Commerce, 1986).

13. Gagliano, Meyer-Arendt, and Wicker, "Land Loss in the Mississippi River Deltaic Plain," Transactions; and Gosselink, Cordes, and Parsons, An Ecological Characterization Study of the Chenier Plain Coastal Ecosystem of Louisiana and Texas.

14. Louisiana Wetland Protection Panel, Saving Louisiana's Coastal Wetlands: The Need for a Long-Term Plan of Action, EPA-230-02-87-026 (Washington, D.C.:   Louisiana Geological Survey and the U.S. Environmental Protection Agency, 1987).

15. Ibid.

16. Turner, R.E., R. Costanza, and W. Scaife, "Canals and Wetland Erosion Rates in Coastal Louisiana," Boesch, D.F., ed. Proceedings of the Conference on Coastal Erosion and Wetland Modification in Louisiana: Causes, Consequences, and Options, FWS/OBS-82/69 (Washington, D.C.:   U.S. Fish and Wildlife Service, 1982), pp. 73-84.

17. Hankla, D.L., New Orleans to Venice, Louisiana, Hurricane Protection Project, Fish and Wildlife Coordination Report (Lafayette, La.: U.S. Fish and Wildlife Service, 1984).

18. Dennis, N.B., M.L. Marcus, and H. Hill, <u>Status and Trends of California Wetlands</u>. Report to the Assembly Committee on Natural Resources (Sacramento, Calif.: State Capitol, 1984).

19. Government subsidies through the Bureau of Reclamation include interest-free repayment, basing irrigators' repayment on "ability to repay," and allowing repayment of costs beyond ability to pay with revenues from federal hydro-power. (SEE Wahl, R., <u>Bureau of Reclamation Subsidies for Irrigation. Draft</u> (Washington, D.C.: Office of Policy Analysis, U.S. Department of the Interior, 1987)).

The federal share of costs of water resources projects have ranged up to 93 percent of total costs. U.S. Water Resources Council, <u>Options for Cost-Sharing, Part 5a: Implementation and OM&R Cost-Sharing for Federal and Federally Assisted Water and Related Land Programs</u> (Washington, D.C.: U.S. Water Resources Council, 1975), p. 41.

In recent years, the irrigation return flow from these projects has also been found to be seriously contaminating some of the wetland areas which remain.

20. U.S. Fish and Wildlife Service, "Federal Involvement in the Water Resources of the Central Valley," draft discussion paper by Felix Smith, Sacramento, Calif., 1987.

21. Title XII, P.L. 99-198.

22. P.L. 99-514.

23. Roe, R.A., "A New Direction in Water Resources Development," <u>Environmental Law Reporter</u> May 1987:10144.

24. National Audubon Society, <u>Audubon Wildlife Report</u> (San Diego, Calif.: Academic Press, Inc., 1987), p. 217.

25. Protection of Wetlands, Executive Order 11990, May 24, 1977.

26. Floodplain Management, Executive Order 11988, May 24, 1977.

27. Duke School of Forestry and Environmental Studies, <u>Wetland Trends and Policies in North Carolina and South Carolina</u> (Washington, D.C.: U.S. Congress, Office of Technology Assessment, 1982), p. 73.

Federal Programs with Potential Direct Effects on Wetlands
(* denotes NEPA applicability)

DEPARTMENT OF AGRICULTURE

Soil Conservation Service

Small Watershed (PL-566) Program.* Technical assistance and cost sharing to states and localities for planning, designing, installing watershed improvements, flood prevention, irrigation, drainage, sediment control, and water-based recreation. P.L. 83566 as amended; 43 USC 422a-422h.

Rural Electrification Administration

Rural Electrification Loans.* Long-term loans to rural electric cooperatives, public utility districts, municipalities, and other qualified applicants for supply of electricity to rural areas (includes development of transmission corridors). 7 USC 901-916, 930-940.

Forest Service

National Forest Planning.* Requires comprehensive plans for national forests to meet multiple uses. National Forest Management Act of 1976. 16 U.S.C. 1600-1614.

DEPARTMENT OF COMMERCE

Economic Development Administration

Economic development.* Grants for public works, business development, technical assistance, public works impact projects, and state and local economic development planning. Public Works and Economic Development Act of 1965 (42 USC 3131 et seq.).

DEPARTMENT OF DEFENSE

Army Corps of Engineers

Regulatory Program.* The Corps must issue permits for activities affecting discharge in or obstruction to U.S. waters or for activities affecting navigable waters of the U.S. 33 USC 1344 (§404 Clean Water Act of 1972, as amended), 33 USC 401, 403, 404, 406, 407 (Rivers and Harbors Act of 1899).

Small Flood Control Projects and Small Navigation Projects.* The Corps designs and constructs projects for which nonfederal sponsoring agencies assume responsibilities for project costs, maintenance, and public access. 33 USC 701s, and 33 USC 577.

Beach Erosion Control Projects.* To control beach and shore erosion of public shores the Corps designs and constructs projects not specifically authorized by Congress if nonfederal sponsoring agencies assume responsibilities for project costs, maintenance, public access, and water pollution control. 33 USC 426g.

Congressionally Authorized Water Resource Development.* Specific project design and construction in accordance with specific Congressional legislation. Congress authorized and funded forty-one new Corps and BuRec projects under new cost sharing arrangements with non-federal entities. P.L. 99-88.

DEPARTMENT OF ENERGY

Strategic Oil Reserve Program.* Program to establish and maintain underground oil storage for use in oil emergencies requiring construction of pipelines and facilities in Louisiana. 42 U.S.C. 6231-6234.

Fossil Energy - Coal Loan Guarantees.* Guaranteed loans to medium sized operators to finance development of new underground coal mines, expansion of existing mines, and construction of coal preparation plants that will reduce sulfur content. Energy Policy and Conservation Act, P.L. 94-163; Energy Conservation and Production Act, P.L. 94-395; Power Plant and Industrial Fuel Use Act of 1978, P.L. 95-620.

Bonneville Power Administration.* Planning, operation, and management of the Bonneville Power Administration, including long-range planning for electric power generation, transmission, marketing, use and conservation in the Northwest.* 16 USC 832-839.

ENVIRONMENTAL PROTECTION AGENCY

Office of Water

Sewage Treatment.* Construction grant program for sewage treatment facilities. Clean Water Act, as amended.

National Pollution Discharge Elimination System Permits.* EPA (or states that have assumed NPDES permits) must approve pollution discharge permits for new sources. Clean Water Act, as amended.

Office of Solid Waste and Emergency Response--Superfund. Program for cleaning up and relocating hazardous wastes under the Comprehensive Environmental Response, Compensation, and Liability Act (CERCLA). 42 USC 9601-9675.

FEDERAL EMERGENCY MANAGEMENT ADMINISTRATION

National Flood Insurance Program.* Provides federally-subsidized flood insurance against loss of real or personal property from floods, according to community land use regulations meeting federal standards. National Flood Insurance Act of 1968 and Food Disaster Protection Act of 1973, 42 USC 4001-4128.

FEDERAL ENERGY REGULATORY COMMISSION

Hydroelectric Power Licensing.* Licenses must be approved by the FERC for private hydroelectric projects on U.S. navigable waters. Existing projects must be approved for relicensing. Federal Power Act of 1920, as amended. 16 USC 791 et seq.

Small hydro program.* Licenses must be approved by FERC for small hydroelectric projects. The Public Utilities Regulatory Policies Act of 1978 requires electric utilities to buy electricity from small hydroelectric generators of 30 megawatts or less. 16 USC 2701-2708.

Natural Gas Pipeline Certification.* The FERC must approve certification of interstate natural gas transportation systems. 15 USC 717, 3301-3432.

DEPARTMENT OF HOUSING AND URBAN DEVELOPMENT

Community Development Block Grant Program.* Grants to small cities for housing, urban development, and recreation projects. 42 USC 5301-5317, as amended.

Mortgage Insurance.* Multiple programs for insuring lenders against loss on mortgage loans for single homes, condominiums, and row houses. National Housing Act, as amended, 12 USC 1709 et seq.

DEPARTMENT OF THE INTERIOR

Office of Surface Mining

Surface Coal Mining* Establishment of standards for federal coal surface mining and reclamation and for state coal surface mining under the federal program. 30 USC 1232 et seq.

Bureau of Land Management

BLM Land Use Planning Program.* Land use planning programs for BLM units, and Habitat Management Plans for wildlife habitats on public lands. 43 USC 1701 et seq.

Minerals Management Service

Federal Coal Leasing Program.* Management of federal coal leasing under criteria established by the Mineral Leasing Act of 1920 as amended. BLM actions include establishment of leasing schedules, development of criteria for determining commercial quantities required for production, criteria for relinquishing leases, diligence requirements, and royalty requirements. 30 USC 201 et seq.

Outer Continental Shelf Leasing Program.* Leasing of oil and gas and other mineral in U.S. waters over continental shelf. A five year leasing plan is required. Outer Continental Shelf Leasing Act, as amended. 43 USC 1331-1356, 1812-1824.

Bureau of Reclamation

Reclamation Act Program.* Construction and operation of irrigation, flood control and power projects in 17 western states. 43 USC 411 et seq.

Bureau of Outdoor Recreation

Outdoor Recreation Program.* BOR reviews and approves State Outdoor Recreation Land and Water Recreation Programs. 16 USC 4601-4 to 4601-11.

TENNESSEE VALLEY AUTHORITY*

Programs for electric power generation, flood control, recreation, fertilizer development, economic development, natural resources development, and valley agricultural development. Tennessee Valley Authority Act of 1933, as amended. 16 USC 831 et seq.

DEPARTMENT OF TRANSPORTATION

Federal Aviation Administration

Airport Improvement Program.* Grants to states, counties, municipalities, and other public agencies for planning, constructing, improving or repairing a public use airport. Federal cost sharing varies for various parts of an airport project, including noise controls. Airport and Airway Improvement Act of 1982, as amended, P.L. 97-248, and P.L. 96-193.

Federal Highway Administration

Highway Planning and Construction Program.* Grants in aid to states for construction and rehabilitation of interstate and other highways. Title 23 USC, "Highways" as amended P.L. 97-424 and 98-229.

Coast Guard

<u>Bridge Permit Program</u>.* Requires permits for all bridge projects over navigable waters. 33 USC 3525.

Federal Railroad Administration

<u>Railroad Rehabilitation and Improvement</u>.* Financial assistance for acquiring or rehabilitating and improving railroad facilities, or for developing new railroad facilities. 45 USC 831.

<u>Urban Mass Transportation Administration</u>.* Programs for capital improvement grants, research and training, and managerial training grants for urban mass transportation. Urban Mass Transportation Act of 1964, as amended, 49 USC 1601 et seq.

NUCLEAR REGULATORY COMMISSION

<u>Nuclear plant licensing</u>.* Licensing of nuclear power plants and monitoring of safety and other requirements. Atomic Energy Act of 1954, as amended, 42 USC 2021.

VIEWS ON SCIENTIFIC ISSUES RELATING TO THE RESTORATION AND CREATION OF WETLANDS

J.A. Kusler

This paper is an effort to summarize scientific opinions on common questions regarding the restoration and creation of wetland areas. It does not address related policy issues.

Much of the material is taken from papers presented at the October, 1986 National Wetland Symposium: Mitigation of Impacts and Losses, held by the Association of State Wetland Managers.[1] The report also draws upon a preliminary review of papers prepared by a team of experts assisting the EPA Wetlands Research Program.

Throughout, this report uses the term "restoration" to mean returning a damaged or destroyed wetland to a former, normal, or unimpaired state or condition. "Creation" refers to bringing a wetland into existence where it did not formerly exist, which may require filling, dredging, or water level manipulation. The term "enhancement" occasionally appears in literature, and is used here to mean the alteration of a degraded wetland or a naturally occurring wetland to improve one or several functions (installation of water control structures to increase open water in marshes and benefit waterfowl, for example).

The term "success" of wetland restoration and creation is evaluated in terms of the extent to which a project accomplishes specific goals. A project intended only to reproduce vegetation would, therefore, be judged successful if it met that goal. A restoration or creation project intended to replicate a natural system, however, would need to replace the full range of natural functions in order to be considered successful.

Mr. Kusler is chairman of the Association of State Wetland Managers, and a science and policy advisor to the National Wetlands Policy Forum.

<u>Can wetlands be successfully restored or re-created in terms of the functions</u> <u>of naturally occurring wetlands?</u>

A simple answer to this question is not possible, and any answer must be based upon limited information. The long term "success" of most wetland restoration/creation efforts or wetland enhancement efforts in meeting specific goals is simply not known.

Often no specific goals are articulated prior to restoration/creation efforts. Similarly, the characteristics of the original wetlands are rarely inventoried or studied in depth prior to the damage or destruction, so it is impossible to determine whether they have been re-created.

Perhaps most important, there have been very few follow-up studies and very little post-project monitoring of vegetation, hydrology, fauna or other characteristics for public or private projects and most of the monitoring to date has been short-term (six months, one year, two years, at most five years). Such short-term evaluation provides only a modest indication of long-term success.

Most intentional efforts to restore or create wetlands have been in two principle types: 1) impoundment of streams to create waterfowl habitat, and 2) various "mitigation" projects by private and public developers, including efforts to restore dredge spoil. Unintentional efforts include reservoir construction, road construction, and highways and other fills which block drainage.

Based upon the limited studies of both intentional and unintentional creation projects to date, wetlands scientists seem to agree that no wetland can be duplicated or replicated exactly. Most natural systems are far too complex, and represent thousands of years of geologic and hydrologic processes with resulting accumulations of soil profiles and ecologic niches of plant and animal species. Most natural wetland systems are persistent features in the landscape. Persistence requires a more or less continuous water supply, sediment balance (erosion and deposition are in more or less balance), and periodic flooding, fires or droughts to interrupt successional sequences. Without these, the wetlands disappear.

Although it is impossible to duplicate natural systems, wetlands with some characteristics approximating natural systems can be restored or created in some circumstances to substitute for damaged or destroyed wetlands. For example, the U.S. Fish and Wildlife Service (FWS), state conservation agencies and many local "duck clubs" have created certain types of wetlands (mostly marshes) using dikes or dams. The U.S. Army Corps of Engineers (Corps) has successfully revegetated dredge spoil at many sites and has been studying restoration and creation in such areas for a number of years. However, the new wetlands invariably have some different characteristics than the original wetlands, at least for the early years of succession so far studied. Neither all wetland types nor all functions may be able to be created. As in the case of waterfowl wetlands, creation efforts also often require long term, quite intensive hydrological management.

What are the major problems affecting restoration and creation projects?

Follow-up studies of wetland restoration/creation projects indicate that about half of the projects failed in one or more respects. This does not mean that some type of vegetation did not grow at the restored or re-created site or that some functions were not re-created. Rather, it means one or more goals were not met. Common problems include:

A. **Inadequate design resulting in total failure.** In a few cases the design of the project is altogether inadequate and the project fails totally in achieving its stated goals (e.g., no vegetation grows at the site). This is most likely to occur when the hydrology is insufficient to sustain hydrophytic vegetation.

B. **Inadequate design resulting in partial failure.** Many sites demonstrate partial failure. Often revegetation of a restored or re-created area occurs, but the new plant species are different from those of the original system. Often little is known about the requirements of particular

219

species and the variations that subtle differences in hydrology, soils, salinity, and other factors may produce. However, in some cases, the prairie pothole region for instance, vegetation similar to that originally present may gradually become established.

C. **Failure to implement the design.** Some sites fail, either partially or totally, because the design is never implemented due to lack of resources, impossibility (such as a flood destroyed the site), lack of trained staff, or outright violation of permit conditions. Such implementation failures are fairly common, although the extent of the failure varies widely.

D. **Wetland lacked persistence.** In many cases, the site is quickly overrun by exotic species such as purple loostrife or *Phragmites* (reed grass). Exotic species are a particular problem in disturbed soils. Other types of deterioration are caused by sedimentation, wave action, water pollution, drying, or other factors. Such problems are particularly common in urban situations. Restored or created wetlands are often subject to severe sedimentation (due to human activities in the watershed or high gradient slopes adjacent to the wetland), lack of vegetation on the slopes, or the location of the wetlands on naturally sediment-rich streams. Also, many natural wetlands remain wet because an impermeable or semi-impermeable soil layer exists that prevents water from draining out. Where it has been disturbed, attempts to re-create such a layer may not always succeed.

<u>What are the reasons for the partial or total failures?</u>

Several major reasons for lack of success to date include:

A. From a scientific perspective much is still unknown about how natural wetlands function. Even less is known about how to restore or re-create certain wetland types and functions. Wetland evolution, change, and persistence respond to chance events. Some uncertainty will always remain.

B. Until recently, there has been little effort to monitor wetland restoration/creation projects. Careful monitoring is still rare. Thus, no cause and effect relationships have been established between creation techniques and success for many types of wetlands.

C. It is very difficult to restore or re-create hydrology and soils in some instances, due to site limitations, lack of available soils, etc.

D. Few guidebooks or guidance materials exist that summarize what is known. Consequently, those designing wetlands and agencies evaluating plans are operating with very limited technical guidance.

E. Many of the individuals attempting to design wetland restoration projects have little expertise or practical experience in the subject matter. Hydrologists and soil scientists are apparently often not involved in wetland restoration and creation projects, despite the overwhelming importance of wetland hydrology in sustaining systems.

F. Most projects do not include baseline studies of the natural wetlands before destruction. The lack of such studies complicates efforts to restore these wetlands or their functions.

G. Quite often, those responsible for the actual grading, seeding, replanting and other activities have no concept of the intent of the project or lack sufficient expertise. Wetland restoration and creation cannot be approached solely as an engineering task.

H. In some instances developers and agencies intentionally refuse to carry out plans or are unable to do so due to lack of funding or other problems.

Are some wetlands easier to restore or create than others?

As one might expect, the cost and probability of success in meeting particular goals is much greater in some instances than others. The type of

221

wetland is important, but the specific characteristics of the site are even more important. In general it appears to be easier to restore certain types of coastal and estuarine wetlands (tidal marshes) than inland wetlands because the hydrology is more easily determined and replicated (tide ranges), and far fewer plant species live in these areas. However, one researcher has concluded that restoration or re-creation of high marsh, dominated by *Spartina patens* (salt meadow grass), is very difficult because of the sensitive elevation requirements of this species and the difficulty contractors typically have in meeting these requirements. Others who have attempted sea grass restoration also report a very low success rate for planting sea grasses where they did not formerly grow, but have had some success in replanting at formerly occupied sites.

At inland locations it is easier to create marshes than bogs and forested wetlands. Water depths and elevations may be less critical and replanting unnecessary. Cattails colonize easily but provide only some of the functions of more complex wetlands vegetation types. Restoration of forested wetlands is, of course, a long term process. Inland wetlands along major water bodies (lakes, streams) are easier to replicate than groundwater wetlands due to available water supply and observable hydrology.

<u>Are some wetland functions easier to evaluate than others</u>?

Some functions are more successfully evaluated than others. When it is difficult to evaluate these functions in natural or restored wetlands, it is obviously very difficult to compare the success of restored or created wetlands in replacing the natural functions. Functions that should be evaluated include:

A. **Flood storage and conveyance.** It is possible to quantitatively evaluate flood storage and flood conveyance functions and values (benefits to particular individuals, lands, etc.) of both naturally occurring and restored or created wetlands. However, detailed investigations to date have been rare. Such functions can also be restored or created through proper contouring of the land. However, the functions and benefits may be quickly lost or reduced in restored or created systems subject to high rates of sedimentation. Still, given adequate funds and studies there is a high probability of success for restoration/creation.

B. **Groundwater recharge and discharge.** Evaluation of groundwater recharge and discharge functions and potential benefits of a naturally occurring wetland is technically possible but often expensive and rarely undertaken. Detailed studies can also <u>suggest</u> possible recharge or discharge benefits of a restored or re-created wetland, but there are wide margins of possible error. Actual functions are very difficult to predict since organic materials often quickly collect on the bottom of created wetlands, reducing recharge even where underlying soils are ideal. Such unintentional seals are common in stormwater detention facilities designed for infiltration. For these reasons, recharge has a low probability of success for restoration or creation projects, but may also not have been an important function of the original wetland.

C. **Game birds.** There has been substantial experience in enhancing, restoring, and creating game bird habitat. Given adequate funds, there is a relatively high probability of success, although continued management (e.g., water level manipulation) and maintenance of the systems may be necessary.

D. **Fisheries.** Evaluation of the utilization of natural wetlands by fish and shellfish for food sources or nursery habitat is, to some extent, possible, although quantified estimates of function and value are difficult and expensive. Projections of fishery potential for restored or created wetlands is even more difficult since circulation patterns in restored wetlands are often problematic, particularly where sediment loadings are high. The probability of success for restoration/ creation is not known.

E. **Endangered species habitat.** It is extremely difficult to determine all of the critical parameters in endangered species habitat and, therefore, to re-create such habitat. There is a low probability of success for restoration/creation.

F. **Other wildlife.** It is often possible to estimate the potential for a specific naturally occurring wetland to be used by a particular species. In some cases, projection techniques are already developed. However, it is more difficult to project whether and how much a particular species will use a restored or created system, because the actual vegetation and other characteristics of such a system are difficult to predict. The probability of success for restoration or creation may be low, medium, or high, depending upon the species.

G. **Pollution control potential.** It is difficult to estimate the pollution control potential (sediment, nutrients, heavy metals, etc.) of a natural wetland, although some progress is being made in gathering quantitative data concerning the filtering capability of particular wetland types under specific circumstances. The major uncertainties concern the ultimate fate of the nutrients and pollutants in the system (for example, will they ultimately be released? If so, when, and in what form?). The roles natural versus restored or re-created wetland soils may play in nutrient and pollutant removal, the impacts of pollutants after they are released to the receiving waters, and effects of the nutrients, sediment, and pollutants on the wetlands themselves remain largely unknown. It is even more difficult to estimate the pollution control potential of a proposed restored or re-created wetland since ultimate plant species are uncertain. Ironically, wetlands which filter pollutants efficiently may become pollution problems themselves. The probability of success for restoration or creation is unclear but probably moderate.

H. **Scientific study and educational potential.** The potential usefulness of a natural wetland for scientific study or education depends not only on its characteristics, but also on its proximity to users and their will to use it. It is even more difficult to evaluate the potential value of a disturbed and restored or created system, although such systems may in themselves serve as study areas. The probability of success depends upon the above factors.

I. **Heritage or archeological value.** It is possible to describe the "historical"

224

or other heritage significance of a marsh (e.g., the Concord, Massachusetts marshes near Longfellow's home) but impossible to provide a quantitative evaluation of their value. It may be possible to restore or re-create such marshes, but not their heritage or archaelogical values.

What are the most critical parameters in wetland restoration and creation?

Scientists agree that without adequate long-term hydrologic and hydraulic design, restorating or creating persistent wetlands is not possible. "Wetlands" must continue to be periodically "wet" at proper depths, for proper lengths of times, with adequate salinity and water quality, and with periodic cycles such as floods. Such a hydrologic regime is necessary but not totally sufficient. Wetland soil type, slope, revegetation and other factors may be equally important in particular instances.

Is "in-kind" restoration or creation necessary from a scientific point of view?

As indicated above, it is impossible ever to provide entirely "in-kind" restoration or creation. The importance of approximating the natural system depends upon the role the specific wetland plays in the entire watershed, including all the functions of that wetland in relationship to uplands and other water areas.

In-kind replacement often best fits into the prior system and has the greatest chance of duplicating the functions of the original wetland. The technical feasibility and probability of success of in-kind replacement may also be greater than out-of-kind (in many instances) because the original wetland can serve to guide the restoration or replacement effort. But out-of-kind replacement may, in some cases, be technically easier to carry out and serve particular goals more fully. For example, out-of-kind replacement of shrub/scrub or forested wetlands with open marshes may increase waterfowl potential, though it reduces habitat for other species.

<u>How long will it take for a restored or re-created system to approximate the original system and its functions?   What happens to the wildlife in the interim?</u>

The answers depend upon the type of wetland. It may be possible to restore or re-create a lush stand of marsh vegetation in a few years. Restoration of a red maple swamp will take decades. Although these re-created or restored systems may visually resemble the originals, the long term hydrology (floods, sedimentation, etc.) and soils may be quite different. A build-up of organic soils approximating the original system may take thousands of years.

Restoration or creation of particular functions and values also varies. Flood storage and flood conveyance capability may be quickly re-created since these functions do not depend upon soils or vegetation. Waterfowl habitat may be created in a few years. Habitat for endangered species, however, may never return.

If a wetland is not totally destroyed, wildlife (e.g., waterfowl, frogs, salamanders, fish) may continue to use the undamaged portion, but in reduced numbers, and some species will disappear. Even where there is broad-scale disturbance or destruction, some species can temporarily migrate to other areas.   However, some rare or endangered species, species unable to migrate, or species with critical habitat needs not met elsewhere may perish.

<u>Do "restoration" projects have a higher probability of success than "creation"?</u>

In general, yes. Efforts to restore a damaged wetland at the same site often benefit from the original hydrology and from nearby seed stocks which may make replanting unnecessary. Wetland creation involving the establishment of short and long term hydrology similar to the original system is more difficult and costly. Continued maintenance of such systems is also often needed.

How essential are "mid-course corrections" for restoration or creation projects and the continued maintenance (over time) of these systems?

Given the limited state of scientific knowledge concerning restoration and creation, projects must generally be approached as experiments with the need for possible modifications in six months, a year, or several years, if what was originally proposed does not work. Examples of self-maintaining restored/created wetlands of 10-20 years do exist, but modifications needed for many wetlands include: regrading, replanting, fertilization, control of exotics, and water level manipulation (if a control structure exists).

From a long-term management perspective, it is best for wetland restoration and creation projects to be designed as self-sustaining systems. However, this may not be possible where sedimentation rates or nutrient levels are high or changes in the natural hydrology have taken place. In such circumstances, the project should provide for continued management and maintenance over a period of many years if wetlands are to continue functioning. This may include periodic dredging of a portion of the system, water level manipulation, replanting, etc. Such continued management currently is provided for wetlands on wildlife refuges. However, it has been rare for other types of wetlands.

Can off-site wetland restoration/creation serve the same functions as on-site restoration/creation?

Off-site wetland restoration/creation cannot serve the same functions *to the immediate area, hydrologic regime, habitat, or people* as the original wetland. As noted previously, wetlands have evolved as part of a broader hydrological and ecological landscape. Removal of a wetland at a particular site and substitution elsewhere can rarely serve the same sort of functions to the entire system or even particular parts of the system. This may be critical if the original wetland reduced pollution to a specific lake, provided bird-watching opportunities for a particular neighborhood, acted as a science study area for a particular school, reduced flood flows for a specific sub-division, or met other site-specific needs.

On the other hand, creation or enhancement of a wetland at another site may, in a particular instance, provide greater regional flood control, waterfowl habitat, water pollution control, or other benefits.

Can wetland "enhancement" improve the functions of naturally occurring or degraded systems?

The FWS has used dikes, dams and other techniques to increase and manipulate water levels for many years for the purpose of enhancing waterfowl habitat. Other types of management such as deepening portions of a wetland, controlling exotic plant species, controlling nuisance animals (e.g., muskrats), and planting of particular species can, in some instances, increase specific wetland functions. Remedial measures such as destruction of dikes or closure of drainage systems can also be used to restore functions in degraded wetlands.

Modification of natural wetlands to increase particular functions may mean, however, that other functions are decreased. For example, diking of a wetland for waterfowl may limit the access of the area to juvenile shrimp seeking a nursery area. In addition, most modifications will require continued maintenance if they are to persist over a long period of time.

How might the uncertainties and possibilities of failure in restoration/creation efforts be reduced?

A certain amount of uncertainty is inherent in all restoration/creation projects. But a variety of measures that could reduce failures and improve success rates over time, include:

A. Those restoring or creating wetlands should gather good baseline topographic, hydrologic, vegetation, and wildlife information on any wetlands they intend to alter. The best guidance for restoring or re-creating a wetland is often detailed information on the original wetland.

B. Those restoring or creating wetlands should not (in most instances) attempt to create wetland types with very narrow tolerances in water depth, salinity, etc., because these may be very difficult to duplicate. For example, *Spartina patens* (salt meadow grass) in the Northeast grows in a very narrow tidal range difficult to duplicate even with careful grading of a site.

C. Where there is a possibility that all or a portion of a restoration project will not "succeed," additional acreage could be provided to insure at least an equal ratio between destroyed and restored wetlands. For example, a 2:1 or 3:1 ratio might be appropriate for efforts to restore *Spartina patens* because there has been such a low success ratio to date.

D. The restoration and creation plans could be carefully reviewed by people with expertise and experience in mitigation. This would be especially useful in the case of large-scale mitigation proposals, particularly those involving experimental or high risk elements.

What are other major opportunities for improving wetland restoration/creation?

The general success of future wetland restoration and creation projects could be improved through a variety of additional measures, including:

A. Systematic scientific monitoring of restoration and creation projects is needed to determine in what situations restoration and creation can best meet stated goals, and the criteria and procedures needed for such successful studies (for example, hydrology, soils, nutrients, maintenance needs, and costs). Baseline studies of natural systems prior to alteration as well as follow-up studies at 1-, 2-, 5-, 10-, and 20-year intervals are needed.

B. Demonstration projects could be undertaken to test particular restoration and creation approaches.

229

C. Existing scientific knowledge concerning restoration and creation should be translated into guidebooks and "how to" information to assist both those designing restoration and creation projects and those evaluating such projects. However, because of a variety of local conditions and inherent natural uncertainties, flexible guidelines, rather than a rigid "cookbook", are needed. Workshops and other training sessions should also be held by agencies, universities, and private organizations to facilitate dissemination of existing information.

D. Additional research could be conducted to develop and test increasingly precise and accurate wetland evaluation techniques to help measure natural wetland functions, the impact of various types of activities on those functions, and the functions of various restored, re-created, or enhanced systems.

E. A certification program, or at least strengthened requirements for establishment of credentials, could be adopted to insure that those planning and implementing restoration and creation projects have the necessary expertise.

REFERENCE

1. October, 1986 National Wetland Symposium: "Mitigation of Impacts and Losses," held by the Association of State Wetland Managers, Berne, New York.

For a brief overview of wetland restoration and creation issues, see articles in the <u>National Wetlands Newsletter</u> 8(5) 1986, Environmental Law Institute, Washington, D.C.

For many general references concerning wetland restoration/creation, see Rebecca B. Wolf, Lyndon C. Lee and Rebecca R. Sharitz, <u>Wetland Creation and Restoration in the United States from 1970 to 1985</u>, (Berne, NY: Society of Wetland Scientists, 1986).